Advances in
Mixed Methods Research

Advances in
Mixed Methods Research
Theories and Applications

Edited by
Manfred Max Bergman

Los Angeles • London • New Delhi • Singapore

First published 2008

SAGE Publications Ltd
1 Oliver's Yard
55 City Road
London EC1Y 1SP

SAGE Publications Inc.
2455 Teller Road
Thousand Oaks, California 91320

SAGE Publications India Pvt Ltd
B 1/I 1 Mohan Cooperative Industrial Area
Mathura Road, Post Bag 7
New Delhi 110 044

SAGE Publications Asia-Pacific Pte Ltd
33 Pekin Street #02-01
Far East Square
Singapore 048763

Library of Congress Control Number 2007937357

British Library Cataloguing in Publication data
A catalogue record for this book is available from the British Library

ISBN 978-1-4129-4808-1
ISBN 978-1-4129-4809-8 (pbk)

Typeset by Cepha Imaging Pvt Ltd, Bangalore, India
Printed in Great Britain by The Cromwell Press Ltd, Trowbridge, Wiltshire
Printed on paper from sustainable resources

Contents

Introduction: Whither Mixed Methods?

Manfred Max Bergman

Mixed methods research, i.e. the combination of at least one qualitative and at least one quantitative component[1] in a single research project or program, has experienced a tremendous increase in popularity in the social, behavioral, and related sciences in recent years. Such popularity can be gauged in many ways: claims by mixed methods researchers themselves, an increase in the number of publications on this topic, the inclusion of mixed methods designs in textbooks focusing primarily on mono method designs, the founding of the *Journal of Mixed Methods Research* by Sage Publications in 2007, increased numbers of research projects employing this design and method, a mushrooming of conferences and workshops dealing with this topic, etc. While there are costs and benefits associated with such rapid growth, the field is also marked by the peculiarity that many writers predict a new era of mixed methods, despite the fact that mixed methods design, if not by name then certainly by practice, has probably enjoyed a greater popularity over the lifetime of the social and related sciences than mono method studies. Before introducing the chapters in this book, I would like to briefly delineate the context from which the idea for this book arose.

The costs and benefits of the popularity of mixed methods research

As with all popular topics, rapid growth in attention is associated with costs and benefits. Some critics have argued that mixed methods designs are a fashion or fad, currently forcing many researchers interested primarily in mono method research to integrate some kind of mixed methods component into their research in order to improve the marketability of their project proposal or publication. Such popularity may indeed lead to simplistic applications of this design. For example, it is not uncommon to find a lone ethnographer with a short, part-time work contract, attached to a large-scale, quantitatively oriented research project, working quietly at a corner desk, and hardly having contact with the other researchers of the project. Another quite unobtrusive way to play the mixed methods card without being too constrained by design modifications may consist of a vague inclusion of a few, unconnected 'expert interviews' within a quantitative survey design. Indeed, many research projects running under the banner of mixed methods design seem to consist of a qualitative and a (usually dominant) quantitative component, which hardly connect in their conceptualization or execution (see the chapters by Alan Bryman and Ray Pawson) – a phenomenon that gave rise to the label 'quasi-mixed studies' (Tashakkori and Creswell, 2007). While some benefits may indeed arise from such superficial designs, they usually do not take sufficient advantage of the 'other' method and, thus, of a more integrated mixed methods design. In addition, such simplistic approaches to mixed methods research may ultimately lead to disappointment as, contrary to some of the more optimistic expectations and claims, a mixed methods design may not automatically achieve some of the most coveted and elusive goals, such as providing the final judgment on whether or how a constructivist perspective is either superior or inferior to a more positivist perspective (or how to maintain concurrently a constructivist and positivist framework within one project), establishing an uncontestable construct validity of an instrument or research result, or being able to identify universal, causal laws via mixing methods. Yet failing to reach these goals is rarely the fault of mixed methods design. Misunderstandings about specific methodological approaches and an occasionally misguided optimism in mixed methods research are due in part to a pervasive methods specialization in teaching and applying research methods, lack of significant contact and interest in 'the other' methodological approaches, failure to either ask or answer mixed methods-related research questions, as well as some fundamental ways in which theorists and practitioners have prematurely carved out methods-related territories, especially in relation to the still-prevalent qualitative-quantitative divide. Granted, few theorists and researchers conduct overt battles along these lines nowadays, but this does not mean that the 'paradigm wars' (Guba and Lincoln, 1994; House, 1994) are over. Instead, it appears that both sides have agreed to a détente, which, in my opinion, is currently hindering social science research because the lines of demarcation between the fiefdoms, upon rigorous inspection, do not sufficiently reflect the boundaries of the paradigms. It appears to me that these lines are drawn mostly for political and strategic, and less for substantive reasons.

Contemporary theorists interested in mixing methods have inherited a legacy that makes it difficult to integrate qualitative and quantitative approaches on a more profound level. They usually have to take refuge in a rather freely interpreted form of philosophical pragmatism (e.g. Maxcy, 2003; Morgan, 2007). Interestingly, practitioners employing mixed methods design rarely have that problem. For nearly a century, researchers have successfully combined different kinds of data and analyses without hitting the barrier, which theoreticians have predicted – apparently, mixed methods research works far better in practice than in theory.

Just as mere contact between different ethnic groups does not automatically reduce prejudices between them, as proposed by the Contact Hypothesis (Allport, 1954), so does contact between qualitatively and quantitatively oriented researchers not necessarily decrease the deeply engrained prejudices against 'the other' methods. Contact between qualitative and quantitative proponents due to a mixed-methods project may even increase prejudices against 'the other' method as, under certain circumstances, both may claim that their worst suspicions about the other methods are confirmed by the narrow-mindedness and incapacity of the others.

Yet, the increase in popularity of mixed methods design has many positive consequences too. Not only does it obviously benefit those who have specialized in this form of method and design, but it also forces researchers and theorists to return to more fundamental questions in relation to research design and how it connects to research questions, data collection, data analysis, and interpretation of findings. While most textbooks on research methods do indeed cover many of these topics in greater or lesser detail, a kind of shift in focus can be observed in more recent publications: nowadays, many textbooks on specific methods tend to either concentrate on highly particular analytic techniques or merely summarize, often quite superficially, a small selection of secondary literature on the more general research topics.

Mixed methods research undermines many taken-for-granted assumptions across a wide range of research methods topics as it explicitly brings together different sets of assumptions. Indeed, practitioners tend to conduct mixed methods research, which should actually not be possible, if some of the demarcations between qualitative and quantitative research methods were taken seriously. As more theorists and practitioners are drawn to this challenging design, its contours, content, and boundaries become fuzzy. Rather than considering this fuzziness as a disadvantage, I regard it as an opportunity to revisit coagulated but insufficiently or incorrectly specified assumptions about particular methods and designs. As different authors disseminate their version of mixed methods research, they bring to light not only their own and others' limitations, but also new ways of thinking about conducting research more generally. The heterogeneity of researchers from different fields and backgrounds, as well as their different sets of assumptions and aims indeed widens the scope of what is useful and possible with regard to this exciting research approach.

Surreptitiously, the popularity of mixed methods research will have an important impact also on how to conduct mono method research because revisiting, reframing, and resolving some well-established points of contention between qualitative and quantitative research – still quite prevalent in textbooks on research methods today – will filter though to non-mixed methods research. Indeed, advancements in mixed methods research will have a positive and liberating effect on all types of analyses, particularly with regard to how research can be conducted beyond the current technical and theoretical limits. As such, mono method research will not be replaced by mixed methods research but will, on the one hand, make more powerful and more specific contributions to research in general, and, on the other hand, mono method research will be more fruitfully and more clearly integrateable within a mixed methods research design. Indeed, while mono method research may well exist without mixed methods research, mixed methods research cannot exist without mono method research.[2] It is therefore in the interest of mixed methods researchers to learn from and to work closely with mono method researchers.

A new era of mixed methods?

In line with the arguments above, any development in mixed methods will not necessarily come from developments in mono method research but such developments will have important implications for many mono method designs. So is this what the 'new era' of mixed methods is about, as proclaimed by Tashakkori and Teddlie in 1998 and again by Tashakkori and Creswell in 2007? Tashakkori and Teddlie (1998) divide the 'evolution' from mono method research to mixed methods research into two stages. The first stage lasted from 1960s to the 1980s, and it ostensibly involved the acceptance of mixed methods in order to overcome mostly the epistemological, ontological, and axiological weaknesses of qualitative and quantitative paradigms.[3] The second stage, from the 1990s onward, includes a more integrated approach in which the distinctions between qualitative and quantitative research blur, giving rise to mixed model research.[4] Based on, among others, House (1994) and Guba and Lincoln (1994), they argue that a mixed methods paradigm can bridge epistemological, ontological, and axiological differences between qualitative and quantitative methods, thus providing a royal road to true knowledge as derived from empirical research (see also Brewer and Hunter, 2006).

Upon closer inspection, most books on mixed methods published in the past 20 years seem to want to return to some form of positivism or at least post-positivism. Tashakkori and Teddlie, for example, do not make that claim explicitly, even in their later publications (e.g. 2003), nor do Creswell and his colleagues (e.g. 2003; 2007). Nevertheless, a careful reading of the reasons behind mixed methods research design is often (but not exclusively) discussed in relation to eliminating all kinds of biases, explaining the true nature of a phenomenon under investigation, or improving various forms of validity or quality criteria via mixed methods design. Brewer and Hunter (2006) argue also in this vein, but make this argument more forcefully. They postulate that 'the purpose of triangulation (as this multimethod approach is often called) is to ease validation which ... involves comparing various readings of the same or nearly identical social situations. From these comparisons we infer the level of measurement validity that the measures have attained.' This is principally achieved by combining, refreshingly, *four* research styles (instead of only two kinds of methods or 'paradigms,' also known as 'world views': qualitative and quantitative). These four styles are: fieldwork (supposedly ideally suited for identifying testable and ecologically valid hypotheses); survey research (suitable for generalizations to larger populations); experimentation (suitable for identifying causal relations); and nonreactive research (as the only research style that does not involve biases introduced by data collection). As I wrote elsewhere (Bergman, 2007), there are a number of arguments that can be raised against this simplified mapping of the social science research landscape. First, it is questionable whether social science research can be divided into these four methods; second, whether the four methods have indeed the capacities attributed to them (e.g. that fieldwork 'gives access to variables and hypotheses that pertain to relatively confined natural settings' (p. 30)); and, third, whether they may be combined fruitfully across a wide range of topics, theories, data, or findings without further qualifications (e.g. that causal laws inferred from social science experiments can be generalized via surveys).

With my colleagues, I, too, predict a new era for mixed methods design. Its newness, however, will not be due to some form of dominance over mono method research. New are the emergence of critical explorations of the weaknesses of this design or elements thereof by mixed methods researchers, the active participation of mono methods specialists in strengthening the theoretical underpinnings of mixed methods design, a greater attention to what qualitative research can be contributed as a full partner of a mixed methods design, the development of more imaginative and innovative ways in combining different data and analytic strategies, and the return to the fault lines of the qualitative–quantitative divide in order to resolve mixed methods design problems, which, inadvertently, will have a profound impact on mono method theory and application. As the most significant development, mixed methods design will contribute to the deconstruction of the notion of 'paradigm' in relation to qualitative and quantitative research as the manifold applications of the specific techniques will illustrate that behind this vague grouping exist far too many dissimilarities such that a collective identity and any attempt at wholesale characterization of 'qualitative methods' or 'quantitative methods' is likely to be insufficiently applicable to some of the main strands and capacities within these families.

Chapter contributions

This book celebrates not only the advantages but, due to the diverse backgrounds and concerns of the different contributors, also the fuzziness and problems of mixed methods designs, research, and researchers. Thus, the contributions by the authors do not present a coordinated effort to 'sell' mixed methods research to the reader. Instead, the sometimes critical and admonishing voices in these pages are a demonstration of the strength of this method and design, and of its ability to bring together theorists and practitioners of such renown. Much is being said about the details of mixed methods design here but, considering the wealth of information presented in these pages from a wider perspective, it is clear that the potential for mixed methods research has not yet been reached. Some researchers interested in this design and method will become disillusioned as it is indeed not a holy grail. But the potential to excite researchers and enrich the research landscape, even to change the existing landscape for the better, is surely evident.

In my own chapter, I describe the heritage of the paradigmatic view of qualitative and quantitative methods, and how it has helped but also hindered the development of mixed methods design. I argue that it may be necessary to revisit some of the issues pertaining to the paradigm wars, rather than to retreat into some vague philosophical pragmatism – both mixed methods designs and mono method designs are likely to benefit.

Martyn Hammersley unpacks the seemingly self-evident meaning of triangulation by exploring four different forms. Mixing methods, he then argues, goes beyond the mere combination of qualitative and quantitative components as, on the one hand, such designs are not reducible to matters of technique and, on the other, qualitative and quantitative methods are neither uniform, nor stable, nor meaningful beyond a particular research context.

Nigel Fielding argues that mixed methods research has the potential to increase the degree of sophistication of research and evaluation, but also to promise results beyond their capacities. He then identifies three types of merits of this design: analytic density, linkage between divisions in the research community, and expansion of research strategies for the study of social problems.

Julia Brannen's chapter is divided into personal issues, professional issues, and project issues relating to mixed methods research. Her chapter reviews personal aspects that may explain whether and how to become involved in mixed methods design. She then describes the professional opportunities and risks for researchers engaging in this type of research, and, finally, exemplifies what it may mean to conduct mixed methods research in practice.

John W. Creswell and Vicki L. Plano Clark, known particularly for their extensive taxonomy of mixed methods designs (e.g. 2007; see also Creswell et al., 2003) address specific issues of mixed methods research, primarily focusing on concurrent and sequential mixed methods designs. Examining published work, they identify and suggest ways to address problems relating to, among others, contradictory findings, sample selection, and sample size.

Alan Bryman discusses his past and present concerns with mixed methods research, which are based in part on a content analysis of published articles using this design, as well as interviews with researchers who have employed mixed methods research. He sees in this design a danger of failing to be specific about a research question and recognizing the extent to which each research design and project has to be aware of its shortcomings. Mixed methods designs are not excluded from inherent methods-related shortcomings, even though they are often presented in this way.

Abbas Tashakkori and Charles Teddlie introduce an 'integrative framework,' which, addressing quality issues in mixed methods designs, is composed of two forms of quality: design quality and interpretive rigor. They introduce nine specific criteria for assessing the quality of mixed methods research.

Ray Pawson, exploring publications on evidence-based policy research, identifies three hypotheses in relation to current applications of mixed methods design. These hypotheses relate to an overly optimistic belief in the capacities to address the complexity of the social science research environment, an attempt to devise technical and procedural fixes for such complexity, and the vagueness and hybridity by which these results are marked. He makes a strong case for theory building and testing that may include, but go beyond combining qualitative and quantitative components in one research design.

Edith de Leeuw and Joop Hox address one of the most neglected issues in mixed methods design: the consequences of mixing different data collection methods. Using empirical evidence from social survey research, they outline a number of problems associated with mixing data collection methods in large-scale social surveys, which are also applicable to mixed methods research, but which, in the mixed methods literature, remain largely unexamined so far.

Thomas Widmer, Christian Hirschi, Uwe Serdült, and Chantal Vögeli introduce the analytical framework APES (Actor Process Event Scheme), with which they combine detailed case studies with network or dimensional analysis. They illustrate the applicability of this framework by presenting findings from a study relating to decision-making processes on foreign policy issues.

Katrin Niglas, Mauri Kaipainen, and Jaagup Kippar introduce 'exploratory soft ontology' (ESO) and related software by Mauri Kaipainen and his colleagues, which they use as a tool to explore multi-perspective knowledge construction. They provide several examples on how to use ESO.

It is a great privilege for me to have been given the opportunity to work with these authors, most of whom have shaped my own methodological understanding and research practice over the years. All errors herein are therefore entirely their fault! I would like to take this opportunity to thank them for their time and dedication to this book project. I hope the reader will draw as much inspiration from their contributions as I have.

Notes

1 Some of the chapters in this book, most notably by Martyn Hammersley, Ray Pawson, Alan Bryman, and my own, question in one way or another the appropriateness of bifurcating research methods and techniques into qualitative and quantitative approaches. It appears that many of us are forced to use such proxies in order to engage in a debate that will eventually make these terms obsolete. As long as we have researchers, who think about research approaches in these two highly heterogeneous collections of techniques and methods, mixed methods researchers are forced to use them. Mixed methods design and research, however, will outlive the simplistic qualitative-quantitative divide, albeit it will have to think of a more sophisticated definition in time.

2 Indeed, mono method research would do far better without the debilitating labels 'qualitative' and 'quantitative'.

3 However, the excellent review of far older mixed methods studies by Brewer and Hunter (2006), and the critical voices against this design, some of them are present in this book, undermine the claim that mixed methods became widely accepted from the 1960s.

4 Unfortunately, they abandon the distinction between mixed methods and mixed model research '[f]ollowing the recent developments in conceptualization of mixed methods' (Tashakkori and Creswell, 2007. 6), although they do not specify the nature of these 'developments'. Given the wide range of possibilities of mixing methods, it could be argued that this distinction remains useful, signifying at least two ends of a continuum where, on the one end, qualitative and quantitative approaches are conducted quite separately from each other (e.g. during sequential or parallel designs), whereas, on the other end, different research steps with regard to data collection and data analysis cannot be attributed easily to qualitative and quantitative components of a mixed methods design.

References

Allport, G.W. (1954) The Nature of Prejudice. Reading, MA: Addison-Wesley.

Bergman, M.M. (2007) 'Old wine in new bottles or xxx', Journal of Mixed Methods Research, 1: 1.

Brewer, J. and Hunter, A. (2006) Multimethod Research: A Synthesis of Styles, 2nd ed. Newbury Park, CA: Sage.

Creswell, J.W. (2003) Research Design: Qualitative, Quantitative, and Mixed Methods Approaches, 2nd ed. Thousand Oaks, CA: Sage.

Creswell, J.W. and Plano Clark, V.L. (2007) Designing and Conducting Mixed Methods Research. Thousand Oaks, CA: Sage.

Creswell, J.W., Plano Clark, V.L., Gutmann, M.L. and Hanson, W.E. (2003) 'Advanced mixed methods research designs', in A. Tashakkori and C. Teddlie (eds), Handbook of Mixed Methods in Social and Behavioral Research. Thousand Oaks, CA: Sage.

Guba, E.G. and Lincoln, Y.S. (1994) 'Competing paradigms in qualitative research', in N.K. Denzin and Y.S. Lincoln (eds), Handbook of Qualitative Research. Thousand Oaks, CA: Sage. pp. 105–117.

House, E.R. (1994) 'Integrating the qualitative and quantitative', in C.S. Reichardt and S.F. Rallis (eds), The Qualitative-Quantitative Debate: New Perspectives. Thousand Oaks, CA: Sage. pp. 428–444.

Maxcy, S.J. (2003) 'Pragmatic threads in mixed methods research in the social sciences: The search for multiple modes of inquiry and the end of the philosophy of formalism', in A. Tashakkori and C. Teddlie (eds), Handbook of Mixed Methods in Social and Behavioral Research. Thousand Oaks, CA: Sage.

Morgan, D.L. (2007) 'Paradigms Lost and Pragmatism Regained: Methodological Implications of Combining Qualitative and Quantitative Methods', Journal of Mixed Methods Research, 1 (1): 48–76.

Tashakkori, A. and Creswell, J.W. (2007) 'The new era of mixed methods', Journal of Mixed Methods Research, 1 (1): 3–7.

Tashakkori, A. and Teddlie, C. (1998) Mixed Methodology: Combining Qualitative and Quantitative Approaches. Thousand Oaks, CA: Sage.

Tashakkori, A. and Teddlie, C. (eds) (2003) Handbook of Mixed Methods in Social and Behavioral Research. Thousand Oaks, CA: Sage.

Part I

THE THEORY OF MIXED METHODS DESIGN

1

The Straw Men of the Qualitative-Quantitative Divide and their Influence on Mixed Methods Research[1]

Manfred Max Bergman

Qualitative researchers stress the socially constructed nature of reality, the intimate relationship between the researcher and what is studied, and the situational constraints that shape inquiry. Such researchers emphasize the value-laden nature of inquiry. They seek answers to questions that stress how social experience is created and given meaning. In contrast, quantitative studies emphasize the measurement and analysis of causal relationships between variables, not processes. Inquiry is purported to be within a value-free framework.

(Denzin and Lincoln, 1998: 8).

Quantitative research is based on observations that are converted into discrete units that can be compared to other units by using statistical analysis.... Qualitative research, on the other hand, generally examines people's worlds and actions in narrative or descriptive ways more closely representing the situation as experienced by the participants.... These two paradigms are based on two different and competing ways of understanding the world... [which] are related in the way research data is collected (words versus numbers) and the perspective of the researcher (perspectival versus objective) [and] discovery versus proof

(Maykut and Morehouse, 1994: 2–3).

In social research, examples of methodologies are positivism (which seeks to discover laws using quantitative methods) and, of course, qualitative methodology (which is often concerned with inducing hypotheses from field research)

(Silverman, 1993: 2).

Introduction

Mixed method research design is one of the fastest growing areas in research methodology today. Its aims and benefits appear rather simple: take the best of qualitative (QL) and quantitative (QN) methods and combine them. However, many debates on mixed method research design are based on methodological arguments that, upon closer inspection, are difficult, if not impossible, to sustain. This is due in part to the way in which, particularly from the early 1980s, qualitative research methods were explicitly associated with constructivism,[2] while quantitative methods continued to be linked with positivism.[3] This state of affairs led to the 'Paradigm Wars' and the 'Incompatibility Thesis'[4] (see Lincoln and Guba, 1985), which presents one of the hurdles to be overcome in order to make mixed methods designs ontologically and epistemologically viable. Many texts on mixed methods research tangentially touch upon this point but subsequently urge the researcher to be pragmatic (e.g. Creswell, 2003; Creswell and Plano Clark, 2007; Tashakkori and Teddlie, 1998; 2003). But if the differences between QL and QN methods are considered in detail, pragmatism is difficult to apply as an antidote to incompatibility. Maxcy (2003: 86; see also Maxcy, 1995), for example, suggests that

> [p]ragmatism is not interested in explanations of anomalous cause-effect cases as in the ways in which practical intelligence may push toward full and free settlement of chaos and discord. Pragmatic-oriented social-behavioral researchers join hands with rationalists as they seek better reasons for educational policies and arguments. On the other side, they link with empiricists who support a 'real world' and some matters as 'given'. Their unique contribution is to open up inquiry to all possibilities while tying that search to practical ends.

As a justification for mixing different elements within a mixed methods framework, such advice is vague and methodologically unsatisfactory. Thus, many researchers heeding such advice may incorrectly interpret pragmatism to mean that 'anything goes,' while others may wonder whether methodological concerns ought to preoccupy the researcher at all.

However, there are more elegant and consistent ways to explain apparent contradictions without having to gloss over some of the central ideas in research methodology. But even if this hurdle has been successfully overcome, it remains unclear why and how methods should be mixed. Will a mixed method design get us closer to objectivity? Should we mix different types of data or should we mix different findings? Is it possible to mix different theoretical approaches, or is it even possible to mix epistemologies? Considering these issues, one wonders whether mixing methods is indeed an improvement over mono method designs.

My aims in this chapter are to outline some of these issues in mixed method research design and then to transcend the limits of the current debates by, first, revealing inconsistencies in the literature and, second, presenting an alternative and, in my opinion, a more coherent approach to mixed methods research design. I will argue that the growth and exploitation of this fascinating research design has been hampered considerably by the ways in which QL and QN research methods have been ontologically, epistemologically, and habitually constrained by contemporary theory and application. A careful re-examination of the possibilities and limits will reveal that research design possibilities are far richer than expected, thus opening up the research process to a wealth of many new possibilities in relation to data collection and data analysis techniques. Answers to questions about why and how to mix methods will be more in line with contemporary practices. Serendipitously, this will also reveal both new and prematurely abandoned possibilities in applying mono method research designs.

Conventional divisions of labor between qualitative and quantitative methods

It is difficult to identify the origins of the idea that QL and QN methods represent fundamentally different approaches to the research process,[5] leading to the suggestion that they are best understood as separate, Kuhn-inspired[6] 'paradigms' (Guba and Lincoln, 1994). What can be observed in this regard, however, is that the focus on fundamental differences between QL and QN research methods has reached its zenith in the late 1980s and 1990s with the publication of an entire battery of influential texts (e.g. Brewer and Hunter, 1989; Danziger, 1990; Denzin and Lincoln, 1994; 1998; Flick, 1998; Lincoln and Guba, 1985; Maykut and Morehouse, 1994; Reichhardt and Rallis, 1994; Silverman, 1993; 1997; 1999). While written for different purposes and pursuing different lines of argumentation, e.g. what the differences are between QL and QN methods and whether they are compatible with each other, these texts structure our 'there-are-two-kinds-of-research-methods' perspective today and, as will be argued in this chapter, hamper a more systematic and theoretically grounded application of mixed methods design as a consequence.

Based on the heritage of these texts, numerous qualities are habitually attributed to qualitative research:

- A belief in a constructed reality, multiple (constructed) realities, or a nonexistent reality.
- An interdependence between the knower and the known, i.e. the impossibility to separate the researcher from the research subject.
- The inadvertent value-ladenness of the research process and its output, i.e. the impossibility to conduct research and interpret research findings objectively.
- The centrality of the context to the research process and findings, e.g. time-space, politics, specific situation during data production, interpretation, presentation, etc.
- The impossibility to generalize research findings beyond the limits of the immediate context.
- The impossibility to distinguish between causes and effects.
- The explicit focus on inductive, exploratory research approaches.
- The tendency to work with small, non-representative samples.
- The belief that research in this vein is or should be non-reductionistic, i.e. the belief in the ability to describe or explain in its entirety the complexity of phenomena under investigation.

In stark contrast to these qualities, the attributes of quantitative research ostensibly include:

- A belief in a single reality.
- The possibility and necessity of separating the knower from the known.
- The possibility and necessity of value-free research.
- The possibility to generalize findings beyond the contextual limits of the researched units and research situation.
- The pursuit of identifying universal, causal laws.
- The tendency to work with large, representative samples.
- An emphasis on deductive research via falsifiable hypotheses and formal hypothesis testing.

Drawing together the major distinctions between QL and QN methods, one has to wonder why these attributes are so diametrically oppositional, considering their shared subject space. In other words, should we not become suspicious by such clear and clean distinctions, especially if we reflect on the complex, messy, and compromise-laden research process itself? Examining these two lists of attributes, one ought to wonder whether the content of the lists is the result of an attempt at a truce between two factions, rather than a demarcation between two kinds of approaches. And if it is indeed a negotiated settlement between stakeholders, rather than a representation of the actual limits of the two approaches, what do QL and QN methods loose as a consequence and how does this settlement affect the possibilities and limits of mixed methods research design?

The precarious complicity of theories of mixed methods research design

Variants of such lists aiming to differentiate the so-called paradigms can be found in a number of influential books on mixed methods design or books that aim at differentiating QL and QN methods (e.g. Bryman, 1988; 2001; Creswell, 2003; 2007; Fielding and Fielding, 1986; Mertens, 2004; Tashakkori and Teddlie, 1998; 2003). They tend to reproduce previously published lists, whose elements are often categorized according to ontological, epistemological, and axiological concerns (e.g. Crotty, 1998; Denzin and Lincoln, 1994; Lincoln and Guba, 1985). As such, most theorists and practitioners concerned with mixed methods research design not only take the division of labor between the two paradigms as a given, but, more importantly, they build this division into their main *raison d'être*: whichever the prevailing definition and whichever variant is applied, mixed methods research designs are justified primarily by supposedly exploiting the strengths of each paradigm and by combining the respective strengths within one single research design.

Considering the qualities attributed to QL and QN methods more closely, however, it becomes clear how incompatible the paradigms seem to be. This is not surprising, given the main line of argumentation of its originators, i.e. an emphasis on the incompatibility thesis and the thus emergent paradigm wars (e.g. Denzin and Lincoln, 1994; Lincoln and Guba, 1985; 2000; Silverman, 1993; 1997; 1999). Accordingly, theorists and researchers engaging in mixed methods research design have to maintain a strangely schizophrenic position toward the division of labor between QL and QN methods: on the one hand, they must accept and emphasize the divergent qualities attributed to each paradigm, which, on ontological, epistemological, and axiological grounds, are clearly incompatible; on the other hand, they put forward the proposal that the strength of each paradigm can be combined fruitfully within one single research design. These two positions are irreconcilable with each other, and the fault lies not with the principle ideas behind mixed methods design but rather with its false premises, i.e. the strategic or naïve attribution of two distinct sets of qualities to the two large families of methods. Instead, QL and QN methods represent large and heterogeneous families of methods under convenient headings. The members of these two families vary tremendously within their own family to such an extent that it is difficult to identify a unique set of qualities that encompasses the characteristics of one family of methods, and that is clearly distinctive from the characteristics of the members of the other family. Most characteristics encompass either only a subgroup of members of the family or are also applicable to some members of the other family.

Examining the variety of data collection and data analysis techniques habitually sub-sumed under the QL and QN methods label, it should be asked what use such labels have and why they have established themselves so strongly and detrimentally in narratives on methodology and methods application. I argue that we must rethink the division of labor between QL and QN methods in order to better understand the possibilities and functions of methods more generally, and to better justify and apply mixed methods design specifically.

Reconceptualizing the domains of qualitative and quantitative methods

Let us return to some of the items listed earlier, which ostensibly divide the two par-adigms on ontological, epistemological, and axiological grounds (see Lincoln and Guba, 1985 for a good representative of this line of argumentation):

It is often claimed that QL research is based on the assumption that reality is either constructed or does not exist, while QN research supposedly assumes the existence of one single reality. In practice, however, this ontological proposition is often inconsistent with research applications. For example, Gilligan (1982) came to question Kohlberg's stage theory of moral development, justice, and rights (e.g. 1969). According to her own hunches, she conducted a set of qualitative interviews with young men and women from a non-representative sample to explore alternative theories and explanations. While it is not possible to generalize such findings to a wider populations (e.g. men and women in general), Gilligan nevertheless was able to formulate an alternative explana-tion to a stage theory of moral development based on her interviews. There are plenty of other examples from interview and focus group research, which aim at revealing reported thoughts, behaviors, social processes, etc. In a similar vein, modeling identity constructions statistically based on sets of responses from survey data does not necessarily mean that true identities are at the base of such survey responses. Accordingly, it is methodologically acceptable to claim that emergent identity structures are based on the co-construction between the researchers' selection and understanding of items in a questionnaire, their choice of analytic strategy, and their interpretation of the statistical output on the one hand, and the way the respondents interpreted the survey questions within the given social, political, historical, and economic context on the other hand. In contrast, it is equally acceptable to report that, based on exploratory interviews, most women who took part in a study and who are physically abused by their husbands report that the wellbeing of their children is the main reason for not leaving their partners. Here is another example against the claim that QL research must automatically reject the belief in a single reality: textual material (e.g. documents, interview transcripts, etc.) can be analyzed with regard to what was said by whom and in what particular context. The same material may be studied from a discourse or narrative analysis perspective, exploring, for instance discursive registers and strategies, agency, plots and subplots, meaning structures, etc. From a methodological perspective, it does not make sense to declare one approach more or less valid or valuable, scientific, etc. Instead, how to understand and analyze data must be based to a large extent on the consistency formed between how to understand data in conjunction with the specific research question, rationale, aims, etc. Only in connection with the specificities of the research goals does it make sense to delimit the nature of reality. Thus, in the context of their research undertaking, researchers decide (usually without being aware of it), which truth claims they make in relation to their data and findings. In other words, the research focus may well delineate ontological and epistemological constraints. A Foucauldian discourse analysis demands an interpretive approach to the research but it does not change the nature of the textual data. The same textual data can be used for other, ontologically and epistemologically different, positions, which are derived from different research agendas. The decision on whether the researcher deals (or, better, wants to deal) with one single reality, a constructed reality, multiple realities, multiple constructed realities, a co-constructed reality between the researcher and the researched, or no reality at all is unrelated to whether patterns in the data are detected via statistical analysis or otherwise.

Myths about with the QL – QN divide in relation to small versus large samples, inductive versus deductive approaches, or hypothesis generating versus hypothesis testing are even easier to dispel:

The sample size for many QN studies is often quite small and the sample size for some QL studies can indeed be rather large. For example, the findings from thousands of psychology experiments often with are based on relatively small samples (i.e., n<100), although data from these are usually analyzed statistically. Thigpen and Cleckley (1954) used one single case, a 25-year-old woman code-named 'Eve White/Eve Black' to identify "statistically, among other things," the presence of multiple personalities. Beyond that, an entire branch of statistics is concerned with the analysis of small samples (e.g. Brazzale et al., 2007; Hoyle, 2002; Pett, 2002). In contrast, there are numerous QL studies, which are based on data from hundreds of individuals. For example, Townsend and his colleagues interviewed 240 welfare officers, wardens, and proprietors of long-stay institutions (e.g. Townsend, 1962), and Thompson collected 545 open-ended interviews of between one and six hours in duration as part of a British national oral history project (Thompson, 1992; 1988; 1981).

While it is indeed not possible to formally test hypotheses with QL methods, many researchers engaging in QL research pursue hunches that are embedded either in their research question, the kind and the way they collect data, the way they analyze data, and the way they protect themselves from selective reportings of their findings. With regard to QN methods, there are many types of well-established statistical analyses, which are not primarily focused on hypothesis testing and which, therefore, do not aim primarily at generalizing findings to some population. Cluster analysis, factor analysis, correspondence analysis, multi-dimensional scaling, etc. are examples of statistical methods, in which researchers primarily are interested in exploring data structures and inductive research.[7]

Survey researchers, ethnographers, interviewers, etc. may select different positions in relation to the truth value of their data and the identified data patterns. No empirical evidence and no theoretical superstructure can determine which precise ontological and epistemological position researchers should take. Instead, researchers must and do make this decision based on their habits, training, and other concerns. Much more could be written to dispel the myths surrounding the systematic differences between QL and QN methods. This is not the place to rehearse all possible arguments but merely to demonstrate with a few examples, how problematic the division is between QL and QN methods. Indeed, the only clear statement that can be made about the distinction between QL and QN methods is that QN methods somehow relate to statistical analyses, while QL methods do not. Upon closer inspection, however, one discovers the tautology and vacuity thus uselessness of this argument.

One wonders where the myths about the divisions between QL and QN methods come from. An examination of the definitions and claims relating to them reveals a number of reasons for the widespread confusion. First, QL and QN methods are confounded with constructivism and positivism. The debates on the differences between QL and QN methods could be considerably un-muddled, if fundamental issues in the philosophy of science are separated from how data are collected and how they are analyzed. This does not mean that the philosophy of science should be neglected. On the contrary! If I could make an appeal in this regard, I would suggest a more careful consideration of primary texts on epistemology, which reveal a far more complex set of ideas on, for example, the nature of truth and whether or how it can be studied empirically. Furthermore, these texts are not easily adaptable to whether survey or experimental data should be analyzed categorically differently from interview data or a set of documents. A good grounding in this literature would also reveal that there are not 'two kinds' of methods (i.e. QL and QN) or two kinds of approaches (constructivistic or positivistic). Instead, ideas about (post-)positivism and constructivism and, particularly relevant for mixed methods, pragmatism, are tremendously varied and complex, something that most methods texts in the social sciences reproduce inadequately.

In addition to a more profound study of research-relevant topics as covered in the philosophy of science, I would also recommend adopting the following principles in order to avoid other common misconceptions and mistakes. First, it is important to clearly differentiate between data collection methods (e.g. unstructured narrative interviews, survey research based on closed-ended questions) and data analysis methods (e.g. qualitative content analysis, Foucauldian discourse analysis, quantitative content analysis, structural equation modelling),[8] at least in principle. Second, we ought to be more aware of the actual inductive and deductive aspects within the different analytic phases of our research projects as few research projects are entirely inductive or deductive. Third, we need to better distinguish between the different possibilities of data collection and data analysis methods on the one hand, and researchers habits on the other. Not all statistical analyses are about the formal testing of hypotheses with large and 'representative' datasets, and not all ethnographers embrace 'the' constructivist perspective or avoid statistical analysis. Fourth, if it is not absolutely necessary, i.e. in order to make a specific argument, we ought to refrain from creating taxonomies about, or expounding on, the possibilities and limits of QL and QN methods as such overly general classification systems are rarely useful for a specific research project. Instead, we ought to focus our efforts more explicitly on embedding and justifying our selected methods according to our research question, data needs, theoretical grounding, and research design.

Does this mean that QL and QN methods are indistinguishable? Of course not. Instead they are two large and quite heterogeneous groups of methods, which are difficult to describe such that the characteristics attributed to the methods of one family are attributable to all of its members, and that are clearly differentiable from the members of the other family of methods. From this perspective, we would have to bemoan the loss in parsimony. Even more significantly, it means that family membership in one or the other methods clan no longer points at characteristics that can be safely subsumed under either the QL or the QN label. The loss in parsimony, in my opinion, is more than compensated by, first, an increase in the flexibility with which specific techniques can be applied in the research process and, second, an increase in consistency with which specific techniques are embedded in theoretical considerations and a research design. Researchers conducting interviews do not automatically have to impose a hermeneutic perspective, if it is not suitable to their research aims. Statistical analysts do not have to link their findings to some objective and measurable reality, if it is not suitable for their purpose or perspective. This reconceptualization of QL and QN methods entails an additional consequence, which is both an advantage and a disadvantage to the conventional division: specific data collection and data analysis techniques must now be connected far more directly and explicitly to a research focus, research context, and research design.

Recasting the justifications for mixed methods research design

What may be more difficult to accept for proponents of the conventional QL or QN divide as outlined above may be quite liberating for those engaged in mixed methods research design. The latter no longer have to grapple with how to mix incompatible ontologies, epistemologies, and axiologies. For example, it is no longer necessary to search for creative ways to explain how, in the QL part of a mixed methods study, researchers explore the multiple and co-constructed realities between and within the interviewers and interviewees, while, in the QN part, they must assume that the responses to a survey are directly connected to a single and objectively assessable reality. Similarly, researchers engaged in mixed methods design no longer have to claim during one part of the research project that it is impossible to separate researchers' focus from that which is researched, that research cannot be value free, and that it is impossible to separate causes from effects, and, in another part of the project, that it is both possible and necessary for the validity of research results to separate the researchers from the researched, to conduct research value free, and to aim at identifying universal, causal laws.

This reconceptualization also no longer requires researchers engaged in mixed methods research to take on board some vague notion of pragmatism or to misuse Lévy-Strauss' notion of the research process as a bricolage and the researcher as bricoleur (Lévi-Strauss, 1966) in order to defend wobbly premises. This does not mean that pragmatism and bricolage have no place in mixed methods. Instead, with this reconceptualization, ideas behind these notions no longer have to stand for vague and inconsistent research design and its justification. From this vantage point, the interest in, and justification of, mixed methods design become better focused. Cross-validation or complementarity of results from QL and QN parts of the research project is no longer inconsistent with its premises, particularly because researchers, from this perspective, are now forced to explain, what, precisely, converges or is complementary with respect to, for example, the results of their qualitative content analysis of documents and the results from experimental data. Complementarity in particular will need further attention as it is no longer sufficient to justify mixing methods in order to 'produce a fuller picture of the empirical domain under study' (Erzberger and Kelle, 2003: 469–470; see also Brewer and Hunter, 1989; 2006). Just about any additional dataset and just about any alternative method to analyze a given dataset will 'contribute' information in one way or another to the phenomena under investigation. Whether we will get closer to an ever-elusive objectivity via many datasets and methods, or whether we will simply get into a muddle because data and findings are not as easily combined as implied by most texts on mixed methods design shall remain unanswered here. Instead, it becomes necessary to be more explicit about the embedding of specific data collection and data analysis techniques into the research design, based on explicitly stated goals. This will better focus the contribution of each QL and QN component in the pursuit of complementarity within mixed methods design.

Conclusions

I have argued in this chapter that the conventional divide between QL and QN methods is based on highly questionable premises, a form of straw man building that may be related to a considerable degree to delineating and preserving identities and ideologies rather than to describe possibilities and limits of rather heterogeneous groups of data collection and analysis techniques. The literature on mixed methods design has absorbed and is now reproducing the lines of demarcation at the cost of inconsistency and vagueness with regard to its own justification. If propositions by the defenders of the differences between QL and QN methods are taken seriously, no other possibility would exist other than to support the incompatibility thesis between the so-called paradigms. The rather feeble response by most researchers engaged in mixed methods research usually consists of being inconsistent in the premises of their research, ignoring these issues entirely, or by referring rather vaguely to pragmatism.

A far more consistent and viable solution to this problem is to critically reassess and abandon many assumptions behind the QL and QN. These assumptions not only hamper a 'paradigms' theoretically grounded application of QL and QN methods in mono method research, but unnecessarily limit the applications of the individual data collection and analysis techniques. As a result, mixed methods research will need more elaborate explanations with regard to its methods and purposes, as well as how and for what purposes the results from the different methods are being combined. Thus, mixed methods research cannot claim to bridge the unbridgeable gap between positivism and constructivism. Furthermore, it does not automatically provide better answers to research questions in principle, and it is unlikely to replace well-designed mono method research designs. But, more humbly, mixed methods design is able to provide an alternative to mono method designs, which – for specific research questions, under certain circumstances, and given enough resources – is not only one of the most exciting (and oldest!) research designs in the social sciences, but also an invitation to revisit well-established but obsolete assumptions about the possibilities and limits of qualitative and quantitative methods.

Notes

1 I would like to thank Alan Bryman, John W. Creswell, Eugène Horber, and Abbas Tashakkori for incisive comments and suggestions over the years, which have shaped my thoughts presented in this chapter.

2   Qualitative methods are often treated as synonymous with interpretive methods, both considered part of the constructivist perspective. While interpretive methods indeed emphasize the influence of convention and experience on knowledge production, the same cannot be said for many qualitative approaches, which are often conducted within a materialistic or objectivistic perspective.

3   Strictly speaking, it is not possible to engage in formal hypothesis testing and also believe in the metatheoretical notion of positivism. Rather, a formal hypothesis test, which includes a falsifiable null hypothesis, can be either rejected based on empirical evidence or the empirical evidence fails to reject it. A hypothesis can never be accepted or 'proven'. This implies that most conventional statistical research is embedded within postpositivistic metatheory. Postpositivism is a philosophical, metatheoretical position that posits that knowledge is not based on unchallengeable foundations. Instead, knowledge is fundamentally conjectural, and it is contingent and modified in light of further theoretical development or incompatible empirical evidence.

4   One could wonder whether incompatibilities between different approaches are exaggerated in order to maintain and justify separate paradigms, rather than whether incompatibilities indeed lead to paradigm wars. From this perspective, incompatibilities between QL and QN methods and the thus arising straw men building provide important identity markers for researchers.

5   It may appear that the divide originated with the different approaches between Socrates, Plato, and Aristotle on how to obtain 'true knowledge' (although a careful study of pre-Socratic thought reveals that many of the issues about the possibilities and limits of obtaining true knowledge were debated much earlier). True knowledge was usually thought to be invariant across different observers or circumstances of observation. Such knowledge is clearly separated from beliefs (or opinions), the former being infallible and unshakeable by argument, the latter being fallible but more representative of what people think they know about objects of thought. According to Plato, Socrates, in *Theaetentus*, went further by stipulating three conditions for knowledge: something must be true, it must be believed to be true, and it must be justified rationally to be true. The extent to which information from our senses and, by extension, empirical observations, played a role in acquiring knowledge has been widely debated long before and after Socrates. Alternatively, it could be argued that the division originated in the systematic epistemological differences between the so-called British empiricists and the rational philosophers on the continent in the seventeenth century. However, identifying these periods as the origin of the QL–QN divide oversimplifies and misinterprets methodological aims and concerns, then and now.

6   Kuhn (1970).

7   Exploratory research and inductive research are often but incorrectly presented to be synonymous. While an inductive research process tends to explore data for patterns that lead to the proposition of possible theories, exploratory research may simply focus on exploring patterns in the data, sometimes even avoiding explicitly a link to theory generation. Thus, exploratory research may lead to theory building, and only in this special case can exploratory research be considered in some sense similar to inductively oriented research.

8   One of the few exceptions in the methodology literature is Bernard (1999; 2005).

References

Bernard, H.R. (1999) *Social Research Methods: Qualitative and Quantitative Approaches*. Thousand Oaks, CA: Sage.

Bernard, H.R. (2005) *Research Methods in Anthropology: Qualitative and Quantitative Approaches*, 4th ed. Walnut Creek, CA: AltaMira.

Brazzale, A.R., Davison, A.C. and Reid, N. (2007) *Applied Asymptotics: Case Studies in Small-Sample Statistics*. Cambridge: Cambridge University Press.

Brewer, J. and Hunter, A. (1989) *Multimethod Research: A Synthesis of Styles*. Newbury Park, CA: Sage.

Brewer, J. and Hunter, A. (2006) *Foundations of Multimethod Research: Synthesizing Styles*, 2nd ed. Thousand Oaks, CA: Sage.

Bryman, A. (1988) *Quantity and Quality in Social Research*. London: Routledge.

Bryman, A. (2001) *Social Research Methods*. Oxford: Oxford University Press.

Creswell, J.W. (2003) *Research Design: Qualitative, Quantitative, and Mixed Methods Approaches*. Thousand Oaks, CA: Sage.

Creswell, J.W. and Plano Clark, V.L. (2007) *Designing and Conducting Mixed Methods Research.* Thousand Oaks, CA: Sage.

Crotty, M. (1998) *The Foundations of Social Research: Meaning and Perspective in the Research Process.* London: Sage.

Danziger, K. (1990) *Constructing the Subject: Historical Origins of Psychological Research.* Cambridge: Cambridge University Press.

Denzin, N.K. and Lincoln, Y.S. (eds) (1994) *Handbook of Qualitative Research.* Thousand Oaks, CA: Sage.

Denzin, N.K. and Lincoln, Y.S. (1998) 'Introduction: Entering the field of qualitative research', in N.K. Denzin and Y.S. Lincoln (eds), *The Landscape of Qualitative Research: Theories and Issues.* Thousand Oaks, CA: Sage.

Erzberger, C. and Kelle, U. (2003) 'Making inferences in mixed methods: The rules of integration', in A. Tashakkori and C. Teddlie (eds), *Handbook of Mixed Methods in Social and Behavioral Research.* Thousand Oaks, CA: Sage.

Fielding, N. and Fielding, J. (1986) *Linking Data: The Articulation of Qualitative and Quantitative Methods in Social Research.* Beverly Hills, CA: Sage.

Flick, U. (1998) *An Introduction to Qualitative Research.* Thousand Oaks, CA: Sage.

Gilligan, C. (1982) *In a Different Voice: Psychological Theory and Women's Development.* Cambridge, MA: Harvard University Press.

Guba, E. G. and Lincoln, Y. S. (1994) 'Competing Paradigms in Qualitative Research', in N. K. Denzin and Y. S. Lincoln (eds), *Handbook of Qualitative Research.* Thousand Oaks, CA: Sage. pp. 105–1 17.

Hoyle, R.H. (2002) *Statistical Strategies for Small Sample Research.* Thousand Oaks, CA: Sage.

Kohlberg, L. (1969) 'Stage and sequence: the cognitive-developmental approach to socialization', in D.A. Goslin (ed.), *Handbook of Socialization: Theory and Research.* Chicago: McNally.

Kuhn, T.S. (1970) *The Structure of Scientific Revolutions,* 2nd ed. Chicago: University of Chicago Press.

Lévi-Strauss, C. (1966) *The Savage Mind,* 2nd ed. Chicago: Chicago University Press.

Lincoln, Y.S. and Guba, E.G. (1985) *Naturalistic Inquiry.* Beverly Hills, CA: Sage.

Lincoln, Y.S. and Guba, E.G. (2000) 'Paradigmatic controversies, contradictions, and emerging confluencies', in N.K. Denzin and Y.S. Lincoln (eds), *Handbook of Qualitative Research,* 2nd ed. Thousand Oaks, CA: Sage. pp. 163–188.

Maxcy, S.J. (1995) *Democracy, Chaos, and the New School Order.* Thousand Oaks, CA: Corwin.

Maxcy, S.J. (2003) 'Pragmatic threads in mixed methods research in the social sciences: The search for multiple modes of inquiry and the end of the philosophy of formalism', in A. Tashakkori and C. Teddlie (eds), *Handbook of Mixed Methods in Social and Behavioral Research.* Thousand Oaks, CA: Sage.

Maykut, P. and Morehouse, R. (1994) *Beginning Qualitative Research: A Philosophic and Practical Guide.* London: Falmer.

Mertens, D. (2004) *Research and Evaluation in Education and Psychology: Integrating Diversity with Quantitative, Qualitative, and Mixed Methods,* 2nd ed. Thousand Oaks, CA: Sage.

Pett, M.A. (2002) *Nonparametric Statistics in Health Care Research: Statistics for Small Samples and Unusual Distributions.* Thousand Oaks, CA: Sage.

Reichhardt, C.S. and Rallis, S.F. (eds.) (1994) *The Qualitative-Quantitative Debate: New Perspectives.* San Francisco: Jossey-Bass.

Silverman, D. (1993) *Interpreting Qualitative Data: Methods for Analyzing Talk, Text, and Interaction.* London: Sage.

Silverman, D. (1997) *Qualitative Research: Theory, Method and Practice.* London: Sage.

Silverman, D. (1999) *Doing Qualitative Research: A Practical Handbook.* London: Sage.

Tashakkori, A. and Teddlie, C. (1998) *Mixed Methodology: Combining Qualitative and Quantitative Approaches.* Thousand Oaks, CA: Sage.

Tashakkori, A. and Teddlie, C. (eds) (2003) *Handbook of Mixed Methods in Social and Behavioral Research.* Thousand Oaks, CA: Sage.

Thigpen, C.H. and Cleckley, H. (1954) 'A case of multiple personality', *Journal of Abnormal and Social Psychology,* 49 (1): 135–151.

Thompson, P.R. (1988) *The Voice of the Past,* 2nd ed. Oxford: Oxford University Press.

Thompson, P.R. (1992) *The Edwardians: The Remaking of British Society,* 2nd ed. London: Routledge.

Thompson, T. (1981) *Edwardian Childhoods.* London: Routledge & Kegan Paul.

Townsend, P. (1962) *The Last Refuge: A Survey of Residential Institutions and Homes for the Aged in England and Wales.* London: Routledge and Kegan Paul.

2

Troubles with Triangulation

Martyn Hammersley

> 'Don't believe everything you hear, Nick', he advised me. I said lightly that I had heard nothing at all. They came to the door with me and stood side by side in a cheerful square of light. As I started my motor Daisy peremptorily called: 'Wait!'
>
> 'I forgot to ask you something, and it's important. We heard you were engaged to a girl out West'.
>
> 'That's right,' corroborated Tom kindly. 'We heard you were engaged.'
>
> 'It's a libel. I'm too poor.'
>
> 'But we heard it,' insisted Daisy, [...] 'We heard it from three people so it must be true.'
>
> Of course I knew what they were referring to, but I wasn't even vaguely engaged. The fact that gossip had published the banns was one of the reasons I had come East.
>
> (F. Scott Fitzgerald, *The Great Gatsby*, 1992: 22)

'Triangulation' is a term that is now very widely used. Its first appearance in the field of social research methodology seems to have been in Campbell and Fiske's (1959: 101) discussion of convergent and divergent validation of measurement instruments, being later elaborated in Webb et al.'s (1966) account of 'unobtrusive measures'. Later, it was introduced into discussions of qualitative methods by Denzin (1970), and has become one of only a small number of technical terms regularly employed by qualitative researchers. More recently, it has been central to much discussion of mixed methods and mixed strategy research (see, for example, Erzberger and Kelle, 2003). Perhaps because its use is now so common, 'triangulation' is often treated as if its meaning were clear and its value universally accepted. Yet there are divergent interpretations, and fundamental questions have been raised about its value (Blaikie, 1991; Fielding and Fielding, 1986: 33; Flick, 1992; Massey, 1999; McPhee, 1992; Silverman, 1985: 105–106).[1]

Reviewing the literature, we can identify at least four meanings, and these point to distinctive purposes and are based on varying philosophical, or at least methodological, assumptions. In this chapter I will outline, and consider the value of, these different forms of triangulation. I will suggest that at least two capture important elements of the research process, but I will also argue that these cannot be reduced to matters of technique, and do not necessarily refer to the 'mixing' of quantitative and qualitative methods. At the same time, I will raise questions about arguments to the effect that different methods are based upon fundamentally discrepant epistemological or ontological assumptions, and therefore cannot be combined.

Triangulation as validity checking

The original usage of 'triangulation', within the literature of social science methodology, referred to checking the validity of an interpretation based on a single source of data by recourse to at least one further source that is of a strategically different type. It is worth noting that this does not necessarily involve combining quantitative and qualitative approaches, or even different *methods* of data collection: for instance, it might require comparing interview data from several witnesses to an event (who played different roles within it or who have varying interests at stake in what is believed about it); or it could involve comparing observational data from various settings that bear on the same knowledge claim.[2] Of course, triangulation in this first sense *can* involve combining data produced by different methods; and these may (though they need not) span the qualitative-quantitative divide. Thus, postal questionnaire data may be used to check conclusions reached on the basis of semi-structured or unstructured interviews, or vice versa; while interpretations of interview data, produced in varying ways, might be checked through participant observation, or vice versa; and so on.

The idea behind this first concept of triangulation is that by drawing data from sources that have very different potential threats to validity it is possible to reduce the chances of reaching false conclusions. For example, it might be argued that the tendency for people to give researchers socially desirable rather than honest responses is greater in face-to-face interviews than in anonymous postal questionnaires; so that, in this respect, the latter can be used to check the validity of conclusions drawn on the basis of the former kind of data.[3] If the data from contrasting sources confirm the original conclusion, then that conclusion can reasonably be held with more confidence than before; though there needs to be some assessment of the possibility that both sources of data were biased in the same direction (perhaps by different factors). If there is a discrepancy in the data from different sources, then this requires interpretation in terms of the threats to validity likely to be involved in each type of data, and the direction and extent of error that these would tend to produce. Moreover, discrepancy will usually indicate a need for further investigation involving yet other sources of data, chosen to counter the effects of specific threats to validity.

The strategy involved in this first kind of triangulation is quite closely determined by its goal – checking the validity of descriptive inferences – as well as by the means for doing this – comparing data sources carrying distinctive threats to validity. However, a number of questions have been raised about it.

Some of these relate to the source model for the triangulation metaphor. In navigation, 'triangulation' has a quite specific meaning: it involves taking bearings on two landmarks in order to locate one's position. The angle between the two bearings, plus knowledge of the distance between the landmarks, allows the navigator to plot his or her position on a map. This lies at the point of the triangle these lines create.[4] Erzberger and Kelle have argued that 'the transfer of the notion of triangulation from trigonometry to the realm of mixed methods research [seems] to have transformed it into a somewhat fuzzy idea with a variety of possible meanings'. They continue: 'Whereas the term represents a straightforward concept in its initial frame of reference, it carries a systematic ambiguity when transferred to the domain of social research methods' (Erzberger and Kelle, 2003: 461–462). The problem, they argue, is that the meanings of the concept's components have not been defined within the new framework.

What Erzberger and Kelle are pointing to here is that the logic of methodological triangulation in social research is rather different from that of triangulation in navigation and surveying (see also Blaikie, 1991: 118-119). In the case of navigation, the second measurement does not provide verification or validation of the first, but rather is a necessary complement in order to identify relative location. By contrast, in methodological triangulation what is unknown, or at least sufficiently uncertain to need checking, is the validity of the first 'bearing', the first source of data. A complementary difference is that while in navigation a single bearing can tell us that we are on a line in a particular direction from the landmark, though not where we are located on that line, in the case of social research a single source of data can in principle tell us all we want to know: whether a particular knowledge claim is true. In short, potentially, it gives us the whole answer; we do not necessarily have to combine it with something else. Or alternatively, if it is wrong, it tells us nothing in itself. So, in this first social science version, we engage in triangulation in order to *check* our answer, not so as to gain further information in order to *produce* an answer. A third difference is that in navigational triangulation, assuming that the landmarks have been correctly identified and that the bearings have been taken correctly, the result is relatively certain; there is no need for further bearings. So, triangulation in navigation is not a device for detecting and discounting error; indeed, any error in identifying the landmarks or calculating the bearings will vitiate the triangulation process.

It is clear, then, that the meaning of the term 'triangulation' has been transformed in moving from navigation or surveying to social science. However, such transformation is characteristic of the use of metaphors. Moreover, it seems to me that the new meaning of the term has been clarified in relevant respects, through the idea that different data sources carry divergent threats to validity. Furthermore, opposition to this first version of triangulation often focuses on three features that are not essential to it: the idea that validating (rather than developing) interpretations is what is most important in research; the assumption that triangulation can provide absolute certainty; and the treatment of some sources of data as superior to others in general terms. It is worth noting that, in its original formulation, triangulation was associated with a fallibilistic conception of inquiry, one which denies the possibility of absolute certainty and does not treat any source of data as having priority. The assumption was that only by comparing data from different sources could we try to determine what is a reliable basis for inference. Those who reject this kind of triangulation must either insist that some single sources of data are always reliable, or deny that research involves the pursuit of empirically grounded knowledge.

At the same time, we should note that there are some practical difficulties in operationalizing this first form of triangulation. One of these concerns the grounds on which we attribute potential validity threats to particular data sources; often, this process is largely speculative. This is not a damning criticism, but it does point to an important issue. A second problem is that it may be difficult to meet the requirement that the different sources of information are independent of one another: for example, interview accounts produced by different informants may not be independent (see Van den Berg, 1996: 28). There is also the question of how to respond to con-flicting results; given that continuing the process of triangulation until multiple sources of information agree could be a lengthy, and possibly a never-ending, process.

The most fundamental question that has been raised about this interpretation of 'triangulation' concerns its assumption that there is a single reality whose character-istics can come to be known via the use of different data sources, methods, approaches, etc. This has led to advocacy of other forms of triangulation.

Indefinite triangulation

A second, rather less well-known, interpretation of 'triangulation' involves a different purpose and, on some formulations, abandons belief in a single reality. Aaron Cicourel proposed what he called 'indefinite triangulation', which requires collect-ing accounts of the same event from several people with a view to documenting how these accounts were 'assembled from different physical, temporal, and biographically provided perspectives [...]'. Referring to his research on school classrooms, Cicourel reports that: 'Comparing the teacher's account of the lesson before and after it was presented, and comparing the teacher's version with those of the children, produced different accounts of the "same" scene'. And he adds that: 'the children seemed to receive and organise the lesson in terms of their own orientation at the time of the event, and these conceptions do not always match the teacher's account of the lesson's purpose and conduct' (Cicourel et al. 1974: 4). The use of scare quotes around the word 'same' here indicates that for Cicourel what is involved is not an attempt to identify the truth about the scene witnessed, and therefore to assess the accounts produced by different participants in terms of how well they represent what went on. Rather, the approach adopted is closer to the sociology of knowledge: the interest is in why participants' accounts take the varying forms they do, or rather in how they have been put together. In another place, Cicourel describes indefinite tri-angulation as designed to 'make visible the practicality and inherent reflexivity of everyday accounts', in other words to show that accounts are always formulated for a purpose and in a way that is sensitive to a particular occasion, rather than simply being reflections of the world (Cicourel 1974: 124). Built into the ethnomethod-ological position drawn on here is a denial that there can be only one true statement about relevant features of the situation to which various accounts relate, and (even more significantly) a rejection of the idea that social science can or should adjudicate amongst informants' accounts in terms of their truth.

A slightly different version of this second interpretation of 'triangulation' was gen-erated by Clem Adelman and his colleagues on the Ford Teaching Project. They were influenced by Cicourel, but their purpose was a more practical educational one. They elicited different perspectives about teaching situations, and then communicated these to the participants, this then producing *second-order* accounts of the first-level accounts, and so on, potentially without end. Adelman writes:

> The underlying idea here is that no action is self-contained; people can have intended actions which are constrained by context. No actions are untrammelled, all actions in the social world are interactions. Interaction necessarily involves a reciprocation and thus a reciprocal viewpoint. Triangulation, then, does not treat the speech act as self-contained action. A speech act is seen

as incomplete, needing reciprocal interpretations to complete its meaning in a social context. (Adelman, 1981: 79–80)[5]

What is involved here is a kind of educational development work: the aim seems to be to induce all parties to the interaction to overcome the restraints of politeness and to say honestly what they thought about what had taken place, and to take notice of the honest accounts of others; thereby illuminating the meanings which were involved in the original events, and enhancing mutual understanding and future practice.

Both versions of this second interpretation of 'triangulation' treat it as a device for generating divergent interpretations, rather than for checking the validity of inferences from data. Moreover, in each case the research concerned was governed by a distinctive orientation. With Cicourel and his colleagues, the approach was one in which the focus of inquiry has been transformed from that which governs most social science: the concern is entirely with how accounts of social phenomena are constructed differently by different participants, in the belief that the social world is constituted in and through such accounting practices. How one evaluates this notion of triangulation depends upon an assessment of the sociological approach involved, either ethnomethodology in general or Cicourel's particular interpretation of it.[6] In the case of the Ford Teaching Project, this second interpretation of 'triangulation' is also linked to an approach that is very different from most social science, this time geared very closely to educational improvement. Here an assessment would have to take into account not just what knowledge about the social world is produced by this approach but also its value in educational terms.

Rather more recently, an argument very similar to that of Cicourel has been central to what has been referred to as the 'radical critique of interviewing' (Murphy et al., 1998). For example, Silverman has claimed that 'counterposing different contexts [triangulation, in the first sense discussed in the section 'Triangulation as validity checking'], ignores the context-bound and skilful character of social interaction and assumes that members are "cultural dopes", who need a sociologist to dispel their illusions [...]' (Silverman, 1993: 158). The inference drawn here is that as researchers we should not be concerned with assessing the validity of the accounts that informants provide, but rather with analyzing how they produce these accounts and what functions are served by them. This argument usefully emphasizes the situated nature of all accounts, and offers an important caution against assuming that one source of data is always superior to others (whether a researcher's observations as against informants' own accounts, or the views of people in official positions versus the opinions of those at the bottom of the credibility hierarchy, or vice versa, and so on). However, there is little sign of most social scientists abandoning assessments of the validity of informants' accounts. More importantly, it is not clear why the fact that accounts occur in contexts, are skilfully produced, and may serve various functions should be taken to mean that they cannot be valid, or should be treated as expressions of multiple realities or of situational variation, and therefore have some sort of intrinsic validity. The fact that informants' accounts can be analyzed for the interpretative work they involve, and the interactional work they do, does not disqualify them as sources of information on which social scientists can draw (see Hammersley, 2003b). And, contrary to what Silverman claims, following Garfinkel, using them in this way does not turn social scientists into 'ironists' any more than a concern with the validity of competing accounts in a court of law has this effect on jury members.

Triangulation as seeking complementary information

A third interpretation of 'triangulation' has been outlined by Erzberger and Kelle, amongst others, and is perhaps today the most common meaning of the term routinely employed by qualitative researchers. These authors comment that:

> the use of different methods to investigate a certain domain of social reality can be compared with the examination of a physical object from two different viewpoints or angles. Both viewpoints provide different pictures of this object that might not be useful to validate each other but that might yield a fuller and more complete picture of the phenomenon concerned if brought together.

And they add a further metaphor to clarify what they have in mind: '[...] Empirical research results obtained with different methods are like the pieces of a jigsaw puzzle that provide a full image of a certain object if put together in the correct way' (Erzberger and Kelle, 2003: 461).[7]

This interpretation of 'triangulation' taps into older discussions about the strengths and weaknesses of different research methods and the value of combining them (for example Sieber, 1973 and Zelditch, 1962), and about how complementary data can be derived from diverse informants (Dean et al., 1967). In early responses to these arguments, questions were raised about whether data sources should be judged in terms of their 'fitness for purpose' or in terms of 'completeness' (Becker and Geer, 1957; see also Trow, 1957 and Becker and Geer, 1957). Here, there is a parallel to the problem (that arose in the case of the first version of triangulation) of identifying the biases characteristic of particular sources of data: how do we know which data sources will provide the most desirable kinds of complementary information? There are also problems with the idea, sometimes drawn on here, that we can have complete knowledge of a phenomenon.

It is also worth emphasizing that using triangulation to produce complementary data and using it to serve validation are not incompatible. Indeed, gaining further information about a phenomenon, through drawing on multiple sources of data, could lead us to change the category into which we originally placed it, on the grounds that it no longer looks like an X but appears to be a Y. Here, while the purpose for which the new data were collected was gaining complementary information, what has resulted is a correction of the initial interpretation, one that is analogous to what may occur in triangulation for checking validity. This reflects the fact that this third interpretation, like the first, assumes a single reality.[8]

More recently, it has been argued that particular methods involve divergent assumptions about the very nature of the social world (ontology) and about how it can be understood (epistemology) (Blaikie, 1991; Flick, 1992). These arguments challenge not just the first interpretation of 'triangulation' but also this third one; and they point to some further interpretations of the term.

Triangulation as epistemological dialogue or juxtaposition

Flick has put forward a formulation that might, at first sight, seem to be an example of the third type of triangulation, just discussed in the upper section. However, it suggests a significant new element. He writes: 'Triangulation was first conceptualized as a strategy for validating results obtained with the individual methods. The focus, however, has shifted increasingly toward further enriching and completing knowledge and towards transgressing the (always limited) epistemological potentials of the individual method' (Flick, 1998: 230; see also Flick, 1992 and 2004; Sale et al., 2002). Flick argues that different methods do not simply provide varying kinds of information about the same object, but constitute the world in different ways.[9] And the shift he is reporting here has been associated with the growing influence of constructionism and postmodernism, with their focus on the way in which social phenomena are created in and through social interaction or discourse. Crucially, if we apply this idea to the research process itself, we are led to conclude that different methods construct the social world in divergent ways, so that combining them may not lead either to validation or to increasing the completeness of the picture.

This shift could imply, not so much a reinterpretation of 'triangulation', as an abandonment of it. The triangle is, after all, a modernist image, and drawing metaphors from technical occupations like navigation and surveying might be rejected for the same reason. More generally, if the data sources to be combined involve conflicting epistemological assumptions, then issues emerge about what 'combination' could mean, and whether it is legitimate. Perhaps research should operate strictly within the confines of a single epistemological paradigm? Some qualitative researchers would advocate this (see for instance Lincoln, 1990).

However, other responses are possible. It might be argued that we need to set up some form of dialogue between the epistemological positions built into various research methods, interpreting data from different sources with a view to resolving or transcending epistemological divides. A source here might be philosophical hermeneutics (see Warnke, 1987). This is what we might call the dialogical strategy; and it is perhaps what Flick had in mind.

Alternatively, it could be argued that data produced by methods having different epistemological assumptions must simply be juxtaposed. For example Denzin and Lincoln adopt Richardson's argument that the model for 'mixed-genre texts in the postexperimental moment' should be a crystal not a triangle. They write: 'Like crystals, Eisenstein's montage, the jazz solo, or the pieces in a quilt, the mixed-genre text "combines symmetry and substance with an infinite variety of shapes, substances, transmutations .... Crystals grow, change, alter ....Crystals are prisms that reflect externalities and refract within themselves, creating different colors, patterns, arrays, casting off in different directions" (Richardson, 2000, p.934)' (Denzin and Lincoln, 2005: 6). This position perhaps reflects a refusal to choose among epistemological paradigms, or to let the reader do this easily. Instead, the goal is to put, and to keep, methods and epistemologies both in tension and in question, along with throwing doubt on any idea that one or other approach is correct, or that the differences between them can be overcome. We might call this 'postmodernist triangulation'.

In relation to these arguments, however, we should ask whether it is true that different sources of data, or even different methods, do involve conflicting ontological or epistemological assumptions; and if they do, whether this implies incorpatibility. A number of writers assert this; for example, Blaikie (1991) identifies empiricism, interpretivism, and realism as fundamentally different philosophical orientations that underpin various social research methods. And he and other critics ascribe 'ignorance or misunderstanding' to those who fail to 'recognize' the ontological and epistemological differences built into different methods (Blaikie, 1991: 126 and 128; see also Massey, 1999: 183). However, these authors do not effectively establish that conflicting epistemological and ontological assumptions are *necessarily* built into the use of specific methods.

One of the problems with many discussions of triangulation is that distinctions are not drawn between combining data from different sources, using different methods, and integrating different methodological approaches.[10] And, in part, this reflects the fact that discussion of triangulation has been caught up in debates about the relationship between quantitative and qualitative research traditions, as well as in disputes among competing qualitative traditions.

The relationships between philosophy and method are much more complex and open to change than these discussions suggest (see Hammersley, 1992: chap 9; 1996). There are not just three philosophical positions that have been influential in social science. Moreover, particular philosophical ideas are almost always open to divergent interpretations, and are combined with others to shape the influence they have. For instance, positivism is by no means univocal (Halfpenny, 1982; Hammersley, 1995: chap 1), and while a positivist conception of science has often encouraged the use of highly structured methods, it has not always done so. For example, in anthropology, it led Malinowski to rely on participant observation (see Leach, 1957 and Strenski, 1982) and the 'naturalism' that informed the thinking of some qualitative sociologists in the twentieth century drew on nineteenth-century positivism, with its inductivist notion of science (Hammersley and Atkinson, 2007). Similar diversity is revealed if we examine the methodological implications that have been derived from phenomenology: this has encouraged both primary reliance on introspection and in-depth interviews and the restriction of data to transcripts of 'naturally occurring conversation' (see Frank, 1979; Heritage, 1984; Maso, 2001).

In specific terms, we need to ask, for example: to what extent is it the case that in combining data from interviews with multiple witnesses – in order either to validate inferences about events they observed or to provide a more complete picture of those events – we are conflating divergent ontological or epistemological assumptions? While people may have different perspectives on the world, and we do of course need to take this into account, in practice they will rarely act on fundamentally discrepant assumptions about the nature of what exists in the relevant domain, or about how we can gain knowledge of it. Rather, what we generally find are sets of accounting practices that involve overlapping as well as discrepant assumptions, the degree of overlap and discrepancy varying considerably across cases.

Nor is any such difference in fundamental assumptions automatically involved when researchers combine data from different methods, even when data are combined from methods associated with qualitative and quantitative approaches, for example participant observation and structured observation. While one of these methods seeks to avoid making prior judgements about what is likely to be observed, whereas the other relies on previously defined categories, there is a continuum between the two. Furthermore, there is no fundamental epistemological or ontological discrepancy here. Both methods depend upon looking and listening. Both usually emphasize the need to minimize the inferences built into the data. And while structured observation is often seen as reducing the danger of idiosyncratic reporting, the use of audio- and video-recording in much contemporary qualitative research largely reflects the same concern. Of course, we could dress up these two methods as deriving from contrasting epistemological positions – a methodism which treats following procedures as the way to truth and an intuitionism that insists on the priority of researcher insight – but it is doubtful that use of these methods usually reflects commitment to these positions, and it does not logically imply them.

Much the same point could be made about diverse kinds of interviewing. If we take life history interviews and the administration of attitude scales, while there are certainly differences in assumption here about the nature of attitudes and how they can be identified, it is not clear that these are either epistemological or ontological in any strict sense. To contrast attitudes as unique complexes of evaluations and orientations built up by a person over the course of life with the view that they are more specific in character and can be categorized in terms of a standard typology is to outline different *psychological* theories rather than different philosophical positions.[11] While the boundary between psychological theory and philosophical viewpoint is not a clear-cut one, it is important nonetheless. And it is not obvious that different psychological theories must be treated as competitors, except (sometimes) when they are being used to explain specific phenomena happening in particular contexts.

There is a tendency to assume that because, at a particular point in time, some philosophical ideas and research methods have been associated with one another this indicates a logical connection between them; whereas usually the connection is much looser and less stable. This is not to deny that particular epistemological and ontological assumptions can be taken to have significant methodological implications. For example, a commitment to standpoint epistemology, for which (at least within a certain kind of social formation) one social category of person has more direct insight into the nature of the world than others, implies an asymmetrical approach to understanding the accounts of informants from different social classes or genders. Similarly, some kinds of relativism or scepticism perhaps imply that research findings cannot or should not be assessed in terms of whether they correspond with reality, but must rather be judged in political, moral or aesthetic terms (Smith and Hodkinson, 2005). But by no means all philosophical differences have major methodological implications, and it is rare for these to be entirely determinate in character.

In fact, it is hard to know how to interpret some claims about epistemological/ ontological differences. As we have seen, the main failing that is ascribed to the first interpretation of 'triangulation' (though it also applies to the third) is that it assumes that there is one reality and that this is knowable. Some commentators deny these assumptions, on the grounds that people have different perspectives on the world, and that social researchers need to document these, and not simply judge those perspectives in terms of whether they correspond to reality (as determined by researchers). Yet this still involves describing a single world, albeit one in which there are multiple perspectives; and researchers are still claiming validity for their own accounts of those perspectives, or of the discursive practices that produced them.

Conclusion

The case of triangulation illustrates, in part, how relatively straightforward practical research strategies can become caught up in the philosophical debates that now plague social inquiry. Checking other sources of information – both for the purposes of testing the validity of one's initial interpretation and to provide complementary information – is a routinely used practice in everyday life; and one that was incorporated into scholarly work in history and the human sciences long before the triangulation metaphor was developed.[12] Given this, we should hesitate to reject it on philosophical grounds.

This is not to say that there are no problems with how 'triangulation' has often been interpreted. One reason for opposition to it is that it has been treated in some of the methodological literature as a validation *technique*. While Campbell's own position was fallibilist, there has long been a tendency in some quarters, especially in discussing quantitative method, to reduce the social research process to the application of techniques or the following of rules. On this interpretation, triangulation comes to be treated as a feature of research design that can be included in checklists designed to evaluate the quality of studies (Seale, 1999: 56). To some degree, qualitative researchers' criticisms of triangulation are a negative reaction against this technicism, an insistence on the interpretative judgement necessarily involved in the research process.

Yet, as we have seen, these criticisms often go well beyond challenging a technical orientation, apparently rejecting the idea that there is a single reality which it is the aim of social research to understand. Embedded in what I referred to as the postmodernist version of triangulation, for instance, is the belief that there are multiple realities or forms of life, and that research is itself necessarily implicated in these, able at best only to draw attention to their incommensurability. While this line of argument highlights some difficult philosophical problems, I am not convinced that these have much significance for the practice of social research. Indeed, it seems to me that deciding to engage in research of any kind necessarily assumes that there is a single reality and that aspects of it can be known. It is difficult to see what other distinctive goal inquiry could have than the production of knowledge; and in everyday usage 'knowledge' implies true understanding of something, where truth (though not relevance) is independent of perspective. While we must certainly recognize that there are variations among people and groups in what is taken to be true, and that all knowledge is fallible, we need not and should not reduce 'truth' to 'what is believed to be true'.[13] In fact, it has long been recognized that any sustained effort to use the concepts of truth or knowledge (and their synonyms) in this fashion ends in contradiction; and also that any attempt to avoid using those concepts fails. Moreover, these constitutive assumptions of inquiry, far from being restricted to one epistemological perspective, such as positivism, are shared by almost all of them, including those that have most shaped social research: for example, empiricism, Kantianism, Hegelianism, and pragmatism. The only philosophical positions that reject these assumptions are strong forms of relativism or scepticism; and there are only a few philosophers who have advocated these, or claimed that this can be done consistently.[14]

If the aim of research is to produce knowledge of the social world, and specifically of the kind that most social scientists have traditionally pursued, then the most fruitful interpretations of the term 'triangulation' are the first and third ones distinguished in previous sections. Furthermore, as already noted, these interpretations are complementary rather than in competition. In other words, using data of different types can help us both to determine what interpretations of phenomena are more and less likely to be valid *and* to provide complementary information that illuminates different aspects of what we are studying. Triangulation of these sorts also helps us to recognize the limits to what any particular type of data can provide. Of course, even if we concentrate on these two kinds of triangulation, there are still important questions to be asked about what 'combining' data from different sources means, and how we should go about it. In relation to 'triangulation-as-validity-checking', these concern how we should seek to identify predominant threats to validity associated with various data sources, and how far we should pursue the process of triangulation. In relation to triangulation-as-seeking-complementary-information, one problem is how we should decide what additional information is and is not relevant to our study. Fortunately, though, these are questions that, in themselves, do not raise fundamental philosophical problems. It *is* important to remember, though, that these forms of triangulation are investigative strategies that offer evidence to inform judgements, not techniques that provide guaranteed truth or completeness.

Let me turn, finally, to the question of the role of triangulation in so-called mixed methods research. The position I have taken on the nature and value of triangulation here is similar to that of many advocates of this approach. However, I want to caution against conflating triangulation with the combining of quantitative and qualitative approaches. One argument against this is that, as I emphasized earlier, triangulation may involve using different qualitative sources of data (from participant observation, interviewing, documents, etc.), or various quantitative methods, rather than crossing the divide between the two. A more fundamental concern, however, is that the very notion of mixed methods research preserves the quantitative-qualitative division even while seeking to bridge it.

The problem is not that this distinction does not refer to significant variation in how researchers go about their work. To the contrary, the problem is that it refers to very many sorts of variation. And just as it is best to see triangulation operating at a more micro level than the combining of different broad approaches – for example, we should think of it in terms of using data from interviews with different people or observations in different settings, combining different forms of interviewing or observation, and so on – so too it is better to see the differences between qualitative and quantitative as operating at a more specific level. The qualitative-quantitative distinction can refer to variation in at least the following aspects of the research process: the specification and development of research problems (a more 'inductive' versus a more hypothetico-deductive approach), the planning of research (more emphasis on initial or on recurrent planning), the collection of data (more versus less structured approaches), data analysis (use of counting, tables, statistical techniques versus reliance on qualitative and discourse analysis), and writing research reports (standard format versus a flexible format depending upon what is being reported, what audience is being addressed, etc.). Now, the point is that there is no automatic link between most of the choices made about each of these aspects of the research process and the choices that are made about others. It is possible to combine a relatively inductive approach with using quantitative data; to collect unstructured data and then turn it into quantitative form; to report qualitative research in terms of the standard format, and so on. The spirit of much advocacy of mixed methods research, which I applaud, is to undermine the tendency to assume that there are impermeable boundaries between the quantitative and the qualitative. The danger of such advocacy is that it nevertheless treats the distinction between quantitative and qualitative methods as if it were more uniform, stable, and meaningful than it is.

Notes

1 For useful brief accounts of triangulation, see Bryman (1988: 131–134 and 2004: 447). Kelle (2001) provides a discussion of different types or interpretations of triangulation that covers some of the same ground as I do here. Seale (1999: chap 5) offers a good review of epistemological criticisms of triangulation.

2 This relates to Denzin's distinction between within-method and between-method triangulation (Denzin, 1970: 301). In fact, there is considerable scope for within-method variation. With regard to interviews, this may concern not just differences in degree of structure but also in where interviews are carried out, who is interviewed, and in what manner (for example, single or group interview, face-to-face versus phone or internet, etc.). In relation to observation, there can be variation in structure, but also in the role of the observer, whether it is overt or covert, and so on.

3 Here and elsewhere in this chapter I am using 'validity' as a synonym for 'truth'. It is worth noting that it could be argued that in some cases people may be less likely to offer socially desirable responses in interviews than in questionnaires, and this points to the potentially problematic nature of assumptions about the validity threats associated with particular data sources. Also, of course, socially desirable responses need not be false.

4 A similar method is employed in surveying, though here the aim is not to discover one's location but to document the physical relations amongst various points on a site.

5 This seems to be at odds with Garfinkel's (1967) ethnomethodological account of meaning-in-social-interaction, since he treats asking for clarification when there is no interactionally obvious need for it as both socially disruptive and as potentially endless (because there is no possibility of 'completing' the meaning of an event or action). See Heritage (1984).

6 I have attempted a general assessment of ethnomethodology elsewhere, specifically in relation to conversation analysis: see Hammersley (2003a). It is worth noting that there is no need to reject the idea of a single reality in order to study how people put together accounts. All that is required in studying this important research topic is to suspend any concern with evaluating the validity of the accounts in order to understand how they were constructed, and perhaps also why they were constructed in the ways that they were. This need not be in competition with an orientation towards the validity of various accounts; though it is often seen this way.

7 For other versions of this notion of complementarity, drawing on the metaphors of a mosaic and of binocular vision see Becker, 1970 and Gorard and Taylor, 2004: 44, respectively. The latter authors insist that triangulation can *only* be about providing complementary information not about validation, appealing to what they refer to as the 'true meaning' of the metaphor (p. 45).

8 For interesting and useful discussion of the affinities and conflicts between the first and third forms of triangulation, within the field of research on families, see Perlesz and Lindsay, 2003 and Ribbens McCarthy et al., 2003.

9 Much the same position is advocated by Fielding and Fielding (1986). It is worth noting that Denzin partially anticipated his critics in 1970: 'I have attempted to indicate that [...] research methods represent different means of acting on the environment of the scientist. Surveys, for example, dictate a stance toward the invariant and stable features of this reality, while participant observation assumes a reality continually in change and flux. [...] Each research method reveals peculiar elements of symbolic reality' (Denzin, 1970: 298). He goes on to use the metaphor of a kaleidoscope, but argues that: 'this is not to imply that reality has the shifting qualities of the colored prism, but that it too is an object that moves and that will not permit one interpretation to be stamped upon it' (pp. 298–299). His later championing of Richardson's metaphor of a crystal (Denzin and Lincoln, 2005: 6) seems close to this in some, but not all, respects.

10 Indeed, there are problems about how we should differentiate among sources, among methods, and among approaches. The nature of the 'combination' or 'integration' is also often obscure: Bryman, 2006; Moran-Ellis et al., 2006.

11 This reflects wider slippage in the use of 'epistemological' and 'ontological' to refer to what would more appropriately be identified as methodological and theoretical differences.

12 For example, writing in 1898, Langlois and Seignobos declare that: 'It is a principle common to all sciences of observation not to base a scientific conclusion on a single observation; the fact must have been corroborated by several independent observations before it is affirmed categorically. History, with its imperfect modes of acquiring information, has less right than any other science to claim exemption from this principle' (Langlois and Seignobos, 1898: 196). It is clear that what the authors are referring to here is the first interpretation of 'triangulation' outlined above. Seale also notes that the idea of comparing data from different sources was common in the writings of Becker and others before this was explicitly labelled 'triangulation' within the qualitative tradition by Denzin (Seale, 1999: 55).

13 For a recent argument against this tendency from someone who previously was open to the accusation of encouraging it, see Habermas (2003: Introduction). And for challenges, from very different perspectives, to the idea that the work of Nietzsche, commonly appealed to in this context, provides a justification for this kind of perspectivism, see Clark (1990) and Sadler (1995).

14 For illuminating discussion of these issues, see Haack (1993; 1998; 2003).

References

Adelman, C. (1981) 'On first hearing', in C. Adelman (ed.), *Uttering, Muttering: Collecting, Using and Reporting Talk for Social and Educational Research*. London: Grant McIntyre.

Becker, H.S. (1970) 'Life history and the scientific mosaic', in H.S. Becker (ed.), *Sociological Work*. Chicago: Aldine.

Becker, H.S. and Geer, B. (1957) 'Participant observation and interviewing: a comparison', *Human Organization*, 16: 28–34.

Blaikie, N.W.H. (1991) 'A critique of the use of triangulation in social research', *Quality and Quantity*, 25 (2): 115–136.

Bryman, A. (1988) *Quantity and Quality in Social Research*. London: Allen and Unwin.

Bryman, A. (2004) 'Triangulation', in M. Lewis-Beck, A. Bryman and T.F. Liao (eds), *Encyclopedia of Social Science Research Methods*. Thousand Oaks: Sage.

Bryman, A. (2006) 'Integrating quantitative and qualitative research: how is it done?', *Qualitative Research*, 6 (1): 97–113.

Campbell, D.T. and Fiske, D.W. (1959) 'Convergent and discriminant validation by the multitrait-multimethod matrix', *Psychological Bulletin*, 56 (2): 81–105.

Cicourel, A.V. (1974) *Cognitive Sociology*. Harmondsworth: Penguin.

Cicourel, A.V., Jennings, K.H., Jennings, S.H., Leiter, K.C.W., MacKay, R., Mehan, H. and Roth, D.H. (1974) *Language Use and School Performance*. New York: Academic Press.

Clark, M. (1990) *Nietzsche on Truth and Philosophy*. Cambridge: Cambridge University Press.

Dean, J.P., Eichorn, R.I. and Dean, L.R. (1967) 'Fruitful informants for intensive interviewing', in Doby, J.T. (ed.), *An Introduction to Social Research*, 2nd ed. New York: Appleton-Century-Crofts

Denzin, N.K. (1970) *The Research Act in Sociology*. Chicago: Aldine.

Denzin, N.K. and Lincoln, Y.S. (eds) (2005) *Handbook of Qualitative Inquiry*, 3rd edition. Thousand Oaks CA: Sage.

Erzberger, C. and Kelle, U. (2003) 'Making inferences in mixed methods: the rules of integration', in A. Tashakkori and C. Teddlie (eds), *Handbook of Mixed Methods in Social and Behavioral Research*. Thousand Oaks CA: Sage.

Fielding, N.G. and Fielding, J.L. (1986) *Linking Data*. Thousand Oaks, CA: Sage.

Fitzgerald, F. Scott (1992) *The Great Gatsby: the Authorized Text*. London: Abacus.

Flick, U. (1992) 'Triangulation revisited: strategy of validation or alternative?', *Journal for the Theory of Social Behaviour*, 22 (2): 175–197.

Flick, U. (1998) *An Introduction to Qualitative Research*. London: Sage.

Flick, U. (2004) 'Triangulation in qualitative research', in U. Flick, E. von Kardoff, and I. Steinke (eds), *A Companion to Qualitative Research*. London: Sage.

Frank, G. (1979) 'Finding the common denominator: a phenomenological critique of life history method', *Ethos*, 7 (1): 68–94. (Reprinted in N. Fielding (ed.) (2003) *Interviewing*, Volume 1. London: Sage.)

Garfinkel, H. (1967) *Studies in Ethnomethodology*. Englewood Cliffs, NJ: Prentice-Hall.

Gorard, S. with Taylor, C. (2004) *Combining Methods in Educational and Social Research*. Maidenhead: Open University Press.

Haack, S. (1993) *Evidence and Inquiry: Towards a Reconstruction in Epistemology*. Oxford: Blackwell.

Haack, S. (1998) *Manifesto of a Passionate Moderate*. Chicago: University of Chicago Press.

Haack, S. (2003) *Defending Science – Within Reason: Between Scientism and Cynicism*. Amherst, NY: Prometheus Books.

Habermas, J. (2003) *Truth and Justification*. Cambridge, MA: MIT Press.

Halfpenny, P. (1982) *Positivism and Sociology*. London: Allen and Unwin.

Hammersley, M. (1992) *What's Wrong with Ethnography?*. London: Routledge.

Hammersley, M. (1995) *The Politics of Social Research*. London: Sage.

Hammersley, M. (1996) 'The relationship between qualitative and quantitative research: paradigm loyalty versus methodological eclecticism', in J.T.E. Richardson (ed.), *Handbook of Qualitative Research Methods for Psychology and the Social Sciences*. Leicester: British Psychological Society.

Hammersley, M. (2003a) 'Conversation analysis and discourse analysis: methods or paradigms?', *Discourse and Society*, 14 (6): 751–781.

Hammersley, M. (2003b) 'Recent radical criticism of interview studies: any implications for the sociology of education?', *British Journal of Sociology of Education*, 24 (1): 119–126.

Hammersley, M. and Atkinson, P. (2007) *Ethnography: Principles in Practice*, 3rd edition. London: Routledge.

Heritage, J. (1984) *Garfinkel and Ethnomethodology*. Cambridge: Polity Press.

Kelle, U. (2001) 'Sociological explanations between micro and macro and the integration of qualitative and quantitative methods', *Forum Qualitative Sozialforschung/Forum: Qualitative Social Research* [On-line journal], 2: 1. Available at: http://qualitative-research.net/fqs-texte/1-01/1-01kelle-e.htm (Accessed 11 December 2007).

Langlois, Ch.V. and Seignobos, Ch. (1898) *Introduction to the Study of History*, English translation. London: Duckworth. 1913.

Leach, E. (1957) 'The epistemological background to Malinowski's empiricism', in R. Firth (ed.), *Man and Culture: an Evaluation of the Work of Bronislaw Malinowski*. London: Routledge and Kegan Paul.

Lincoln, Y.S. (1990) 'The making of a constructivist: a remembrance of transformations past', in E.G. Guba (ed.), *The Paradigm Dialog*. Newbury Park, CA: Sage.

Maso, I. (2001) 'Phenomenology and ethnography', in P. Atkinson, A. Coffey, S. Delamont, J. Lofland and L. Lofland (eds), *Handbook of Ethnography*. London: Sage.

Massey, A. (1999) 'Methodological triangulation, or how to get lost without being found out', in A. Massey and G. Walford (eds), *Studies in Educational Ethnography, Vol. 2, Explorations in Methodology*. Stamford, CT: JAI Press.

McPhee, G. (1992) 'Triangulation in research: two confusions', *Educational Research*, 34 (3): 215–219.

Moran-Ellis, J., Alexander, V.D., Cronin, A., Dickinson, M., Fielding, J., Sleney, J. and Thomas, H. (2006) 'Triangulation and integration: processes, claims and implications', *Qualitative Research*, 6 (1): 45–59.

Murphy, E., Dingwall, R., Greatbatch, D., Parker, S. and Watson, P. (1998) 'Qualitative research methods in health technology assessment: a review of the literature', *Health Technology Assessment*, 2 (16): 1–260. Available at: <http://www.hta.nhsweb.nhs.uk/execsumm/summ216.htm> (Accessed 14 August 2002).

Perlesz, A. and Lindsay, J. (2003) 'Methodological triangulation in researching families: making sense of dissonant data', *International Journal of Social Research Methodology*, 6 (1): 25–40.

Ribbens McCarthy, J., Holland, J. and Gillies, V. (2003) 'Multiple perspectives on "family" lives of young people: methodological and theoretical issues in case study research', *International Journal of Social Research Methodology*, 6 (1): 1–23.

Richardson, L. (2000) 'Writing: a method of inquiry', in N.K. Denzin and Y.S. Lincoln (eds), *Handbook of Qualitative Inquiry*. Thousand Oaks, CA: Sage.

Sadler, T. (1995) *Nietzsche: Truth and Redemption*. London: Athlone Press.

Sale, J., Lohfeld, L.H. and Brazil, K. (2002) 'Revisiting the quantitative-qualitative debate: implications for mixed-methods research', *Quality and Quantity*, 36: 43–53.

Seale, C. (1999) *The Quality of Qualitative Research*. London: Sage.

Sieber, S.D. (1973) 'The integration of fieldwork and survey methods', *American Journal of Sociology*, 78: 1335–1339.

Silverman, D. (1985) *Qualitative Methodology and Sociology*. Aldershot: Gower.

Silverman, D. (1993) *Interpreting Qualitative Data*. London: Sage.

Smith, J.K. and Hodkinson, P. (2005) 'Relativism, criteria, and politics', in Denzin, N.K. and Lincoln, Y.S. (eds), *Handbook of Qualitative Research*, 3rd edition. Thousand Oaks, CA: Sage.

Strenski, I. (1982) 'Malinowski: second positivism, second romanticism', *Man*, 17: 766–777.

Trow, M. (1957) 'Comment on "Participant observation and interviewing: a comparison"', *Human Organization*, 16: 33–35.

Van den Berg, H. (1996) 'Frame analysis of open interviews on interethnic relations', *Bulletin de Methodologie Sociologique*, 53: 5–32.

Warnke, G. (1987) *Gadamer: Hermeneutics, Tradition and Reason*. Stanford: Stanford University Press.

Webb, E.J., Campbell, D.T., Schwartz, R.D. and Sechrest, L. (1966) *Unobtrusive Measures: Nonreactive Research in the Social Sciences*. Chicago: Rand McNally.

Zelditch, M. (1962) 'Some methodological problems of field studies', *American Journal of Sociology*, 67: 566–576.

3

Analytic Density, Postmodernism, and Applied Multiple Method Research

Nigel Fielding

The developmental trajectory of multiple method research is a somewhat curious one. Combining methods is at least as old as Thucydides' account of the Peloponnesian wars, in which the speeches constituting a quarter of the History offer insight into the Greek political mind, the motives of contemporaries, and the arguments they used, so that, blended with the descriptive chronicle, the work balances detailed documentation of events with insights into what they meant to those involved. However, the modern origin of methodological combination is commonly dated to Campbell's 'multi-trait, multi-method matrix' in psychology (Campbell and Fiske, 1959), which rendered the concept in highly formal terms. Methodological combination was to be systematic and carefully orchestrated. Approaches following Campbell's inspiration were based on 'triangulation', an objective aiming to test and prove relationships. The goal was causal explanation with predictive adequacy and the mechanism was 'convergent validation'. By combining independent measures susceptible to characteristic and dissimilar forms of error it would be possible to isolate relationships between factors and outcomes with confidence that the findings were not artefacts of any of the methods being combined or their interaction.

However, subsequent approaches have strayed from this path. Whether due to the encounter with disciplines like sociology that are less beholden to control designs, new theoretical currents that elevate relativism, such as feminism and postmodernism, or whether reflecting pressure to throw everything in the methodological toolkit at applied research problems, voices such as Blaikie's (1991) are increasingly isolated in insisting either on triangulation's original objectives or on the idea that certain combinations are epistemologically unsound. Blaikie's view that methodological combination is particularly ill-suited to providing explanatory social science because different methods provide different results that offer different answers to the same question, is a principled perspective against a tide that sometimes seems to uncritically endorse methodological combination. This risks a practice of multiple method research that is either trite, with methods combined without much reflection on rationale, or weak, with a single method dominant and researchers paying lip service to the other methods.

It would be tempting to attribute such problems to multiple method research having become an orthodoxy, except that empirical evidence on actual practice suggests confusion over what constitutes a genuine multiple method research design (Niglas, 2004), over-claiming of the mantle of multiple method research design

('MMRD') when judged against what is actually done, and backsliding from MMRD when the demands of delivering it prove too great (Bryman, 2006). Bryman found that in studies ostensibly employing multiple methods there was substantial divergence from the considered use of MMRD we might expect if it was securely established in the methodological canon. Researchers sometimes employed multiple methods without any rationale for why it was necessary or superior to using a single method, while other researchers who gave a rationale did not use multiple methods in the study itself, and yet other researchers declared both a rationale and deployed multiple methods but relied on a single method for their analyses. This is not to deny that there is also a small industry of multiple method doyens earnestly promulgating legitimate combinations of methods and endeavouring to lay down rules and standardize procedures.

However, it is hard to survey the kaleidoscope of work done in the name of multiple method research without concluding that it is marked by turbulence. That is both a good and a bad thing, as turbulence has elements both of vigour and uncertainty. Recognizing that there are many schools of thought about the practice may help us gain benefit from the former without succumbing to the latter. This chapter explores three aspects of contemporary multiple methods practice: the move away from convergent validation towards multiple method research for 'analytic density', the engagement of (moderate) postmodernism with multiple method research, and the role of multiple method research in evaluating programmes of social intervention.

Convergent validation and analytic density

Campbell's original conceptualization aimed to reveal not only connections between knowledge from different sources but to seek the truth of given relationships in those connections. The social and behavioural sciences of his time held a strict understanding of the strengths and weaknesses of particular methods (Sieber, 1973), and Campbell participated in an inquiry into 'unobtrusive methods' (Webb et al., 1966) which was framed in terms of revealing hidden truths masked by mainstream methods. Campbell and Russo (1999) suggest that Campbell continued to valorize convergent validation but acknowledged that a more flexible practice suited newer schools of thought that were centrally informed by relativism. Whatever Campbell's personal journey, it is undeniable that conceptions of the objectives of MMRD have substantially changed in recent years.

Classical triangulation sought confirmation of conclusions from the convergence of findings from different methods. This amounted to conducting multiple studies in the hope that each reached the same conclusion, showing that the conclusion was not an artefact of method, provided each method had predictable and measurable sources of error. This condition was necessary to ensure that the methods being combined did not share blind spots that would mean that bringing them together might multiply error. Current thinking is that triangulation is only one of three possible approaches to MMRD. Kelle (2001) identifies the convergent validation approach as the first of three models, the 'validity' model. In the second, MMRD is a way to get a wider, more comprehensive perspective on the phenomenon ('the complementarity model'). Kelle regards the third model as triangulation in its original land surveying sense, where one has to combine methods to get a view of the phenomenon at all (the 'trigonometry model'). This heuristic is serviceable, provided we recognize that the distinctions are overdrawn for clarity's sake. For instance, even triangulation for convergent validation does not preclude the idea that different methods reveal different 'dimensions' of a phenomenon, even if its main purpose is to seek points where findings converge, and it often produces multi-factored accounts with each factor accounting for different amounts of variance rather than identifying a single causal factor.

The model in Kelle's typology that is especially relevant here is that of complementarity. This relates epistemologically to the idea of multiple perspectives on reality, which is associated with Lesniewski's (1992) demonstration that a given phenomenon can be perceived from multiple conceptual schemes. Lesniewski argues that this does not rule out the possibility of there ultimately being a single empirically adequate understanding. Crucially, he further argues that while the outcome may be a single adequate understanding, we may need multi-faceted data to derive it. There is a link here with Kelle's position that simply combining methods does not guarantee we will solve analytic puzzles. Our analysis of findings from combined methods must be informed by theory.

Empirical research like Bryman's (2006) suggests that multiple method work is increasingly oriented to Kelle's second and third models, getting a fuller picture or getting any picture at all, in line with Trend's (1978: 353) observation that the virtue of MMRD is not so much analytic closure through convergence but that it 'give(s) different viewpoints the chance to arise, and postpone(s) the immediate rejection of information or hypotheses that seem out of joint with the majority viewpoint'. Using multiple methods increases the likelihood that weak empirical evidence and gaps in argument will be exposed. In contending with disparate findings from multiple methods the effect is often to challenge taken-for-granted assumptions, promoting more sophisticated analyses that result from deeper engagement with the phenomenon. For example, a researcher may set out to study 'job satisfaction' in a given occupation on the (reasonable) basis that many studies use the concept, but, having examined findings from several methods, come to appreciate that the concept could be rendered differently and reach very different conclusions. Researchers may find that what seemed a stable, empirically observable concept does not register with members of that particular occupation, or that the items they took as indicators of the concept are not linked in the way they supposed.

Such circumstances may lead researchers to suspect that what the field takes as a valid, well-established observation, such as job satisfaction being related to autonomy and occupational status, is an epiphenomenon behind which stands a quite different reality. Thus, the criminologist who finds indications in job satisfaction survey measures that judges derive satisfaction from having the final say and from the respect received in court may hear in interviews with judges about instrumental satisfactions concerning more limited and regular working hours when they move from the Bar to the bench, and have to reconcile the judges' survey answers and interview narratives with observations of lawyers and judges quarrelling in closed session like spouses, with judges no more likely to have the final say than anyone else.

The effect of MMRD may thus be to problematize what researchers originally conceived as a straightforward research topic. Assuming no technical flaws, when findings differ amongst methods the productive response is to reconceptualize the

analysis to better accommodate what has been learned. This will yield greater analytic density than would have resulted from the uncritical application of an established concept by way of a single method. When Deacon et al. (1998) found apparent
contradictions between quantitative and qualitative findings in their study of social
scientists' relations with the media, rather than resolve it by 'epistemic prioritisation'
of one method over another they re-analyzed the data, found elements that had been
overlooked, and produced a more complex analysis offering a better understanding
of journalist/academic relationships.

It is useful to embed this idea of analytic density in an analogy to scientific fields. At
any one time the research community associated with a field is likely to be marked by
debate over contested findings, disagreements about priorities, and competition for
resources. Despite this, research communities regularly pull together differently committed researchers and perspectives into a best sense of the current 'state of the art', often
in annual conferences. This does not mean that all researchers suddenly suspend their
commitments and think the same, but that it is possible to produce an overview that
assigns the various perspectives a place while keeping as its unifying core the phenomenon motivating those who study it. Difference is the base from which knowledge
develops. Hermeneutics maintains that community standards of knowledge emerge
from a practice of dialogic perspectives. Knowledge advances by the dialogue between
differently committed minds. Research fields thus display analytic density. By the same
token, multiple method research puts findings from different methods in dialogue and
this stimulates more fine-grained and sophisticated knowledge.

An example of how MMRD helps build analytic density comes from Allen's
(2001) work on the gendered fear of crime. Fear of crime is regarded as lower in
males than females but Allen suspected this reflected essentialist assumptions and
inadequate methods. Crime surveys often combine proportions of those reporting
they are 'very' or 'fairly afraid'. When this is done the male response is much lower,
suggesting men are less fearful. Allen took nationally representative British Crime
Survey data and examined the 'very' afraid response, leaving out the 'fairly' category,
which is more often selected by women for all crimes. This suggested the inaccuracy
of male fearlessness. Allen then designed a survey questionnaire whose items finely
discriminated 'very' or 'fairly' anxiety-provoking situations. It gauged fear levels and
secured an interview sub-sample. Interview guides for each respondent were based
on their survey responses, focusing on the determinants of fear of crime they identified and asking them to discuss experiences informing their responses. Pronounced
similarities became apparent between male and female responses, along with second
thoughts behind men's original survey ratings of perceived risk. The overall inquiry
indicated that fear of crime is not as gendered as was thought.

Does this example represent successful MMRD or simply that we always need
qualitative methods to interpret quantitative findings? A complementarity case
would be that, without quantitative survey data providing one version of social reality we would not know how to configure the interviews. To see that interviews
might illuminate the issue we had to have the quantitative data from more finely discriminating 'very' and 'fairly' worrying situations. Where Kelle's theoretical considerations come in was Allen's incorporation of a feminist criminological analysis
suggesting that gendered fear of crime would converge following experience of
criminal victimization. Allen's articulation of methods drew on this theory, without

which there would have been less inclination to re-work and challenge the official crime survey. While a multiple method approach enabled conclusions attracting more confidence we might argue that its real value was in promoting a critical stance towards the data that afforded more clarity about what the findings demonstrated.

We now have a more flexible approach to methodological combination than in classic triangulation. The original literature usually involved one method taking precedence (Creswell, 1994) although more recent constructions have elaborated research design options in a way that is sometimes helpful (Creswell et al., 2003). More even-handed combinations favour analytic density, as findings from given methods are less likely to be subordinated simply because of their intrinsic nature. Thus, Caracelli and Green (1997) offer two main groups of mixed method designs, 'component' designs (including complementary or comparative designs) and 'integrated' designs (including iterative designs, nested designs and holistic designs). What have been called 'transformative technologies' (Lee, 1995) have also facilitated methodological interrelation and analytic density. While what now seem straightforward technologies have had significant influence, such as tape recorders, which enabled recording of larger numbers of interviews than could be handled by note-taking and thus improved accuracy and sample sizes (Lee, 2004), most technologies that have been transformative in the social sciences are computational.

A recent technologically based means of more closely integrating qualitative and quantitative data is the development of quantification features in qualitative software (Computer-assisted qualitative data analysis, or 'CAQDAS'). Such software provides counts of 'hits' from specified retrievals, basic quantification facilities, and ports to export results to SPSS and import quantitative data as data tables. The potential for methodological integration has been increasingly acknowledged (Bazeley, 1999), as in Richards' (2000) 'pattern analysis', a quasi-variable analysis where patterns are pursued by sorting qualitative data by reference to imported demographic or other descriptive data.

Tabular import and export functions enable manipulation of data either as information about codes that have been applied to the text or a matrix built from 'cross-tabulated' coded data. Quantitative data can be imported to inform interpretation before detailed coding, such as divisions within an interview sub-sample apparent from response to a survey questionnaire. Possibilities for data integration include sorting qualitative data extracts by categorical or scaled criteria, and deriving variables from qualitative data by dividing responses into binary categories or ordinal response sets. Once variables have been derived numerous quantitative procedures become available, including correspondence analysis, logistic regression and other multi-variate techniques (Bazeley, 2006). Since qualitative research emphasizes interpreting data by reference to context, it is important that the categorized response sets exported to statistics software for analysis are still linked to the qualitative data from which they originated. For example, a table in the N-Vivo package provides access to qualitative data from each cell of the matrix produced when a cross tabulation-type search is performed across data files. Colour graduation of matrix table cells indicates the density of coding in each cell. Users can show socio-demographic characteristics against selected codes by entering the socio-demographics as additional rows (where columns are, e.g. individual respondents and rows are code categories). Analytic searches can thus combine interpretive coding and coding representing socio-demographic details.

When we conceptualize a social phenomenon we must generally address its historical, structural and cultural dimensions to achieve a full account covering all the
relevant factors (although each analyst may have their own notion of the priority
between these standard dimensions). A final example of how analytic density is built
up by reference to these various dimensions is taken from research on the career paths
of female science graduates. The case of physics is an analytically important anomaly
in the gender gap in recruitment, retention and advancement in scientific occupations. Recruitment to science discipline first degrees and first destination employment
has steadily become more equitable, but there have only been limited gains in the proportion of female physicists. In several developed countries, including the US and
UK, women have exceeded parity in biology and biochemistry at degree level and are
close to it in chemistry and mathematics. Women gaining qualifications and working
in mathematics have increased substantially. Physics being mathematically based, one
might assume more women could enter physics if they wished.

International comparison reveals variations pointing towards explanations.
Table 3.1 shows that while the US and UK have similar profiles, Hungary, with substantially dissimilar economic circumstances, has a high representation of women
with first degrees in physics and in academic employment. Attrition between the
two stages is also low.

Rossiter's (1982) structural analysis employed historical data. Some 30% of women
scientists in US government employment in the late 1930s were in biology, but only
1% were in physics. In research employment, 51% of women scientists were in biology, only 6% in physics. Differences in the 'quantitative feminization' (Glover and
Fielding, 2000) of scientific disciplines are therefore long established. Rossiter's
account rests on whether a discipline needs research associates for repetitive work
like data processing and classification. She shows that women clustered in these posts
and were welcome in such roles even in all-male universities. Sciences needing
extensive classification work, like biology, biochemistry and chemistry, gained efficient, self-effacing labour. Physics did not need this sort of work. The principal
opportunities for female physicists were confined to women's colleges. These seldom
had the resources and facilities necessary for big science physics. Women thus struggled to research the areas and produce the publications needed for career advancement into the discipline's top positions. This is an effective analysis suggesting that
the low representation of women in physics has long-standing structural roots.
However, we might ask why the patterns of the 1930s are still with us.

TABLE 3.1   *Cross-national women's representation at different educational
and employment levels in physics, 1990*

Country	(a) First degrees (%)	(b) Doctorates (%)	(c) Academic employment (%)	Difference between (a) and (c)
France	24	21	23	−1
Hungary	50	27	47	−3
Italy	29	21	23	−6
USA	15	9	3	−12
UK	16	12	4	−12

Source: Selected data from Megraw's work cited in Dresselhaus et al., 1994.

The data in Table 3.1 can be explained in other ways at macro level, for example, working from the observation that countries with a large public sector are those where women's attrition in physics is lowest. But we might also observe that countries with large physics establishments, high industrial development, and strong women's movements had the lowest numbers of female physicists. Concluding that macro-level analysis could not solve the puzzle, Dresselhaus et al. (1994) conducted qualitative interviews with female scientists in countries with a high representation of female physicists. Explanations emerged linked to national circumstances. For example, simply because Portuguese women represent 35% of physics faculty does not mean Portugal is strong on equal opportunities. Portugal has a relatively recent history of institutional science. Newly industrialized countries offer more opportunities for women since science begins to be developed when many women are already in employment and there are thus fewer institutional barriers to negotiate. But this is not a complete answer, because the interviews also established that in recently industrialized countries like Portugal and Hungary, academic science is unpopular with men compared to business and industry due to pay and career advancement prospects (Keeves and Kotte, 1996).

However, these country-specific accounts tied to stages of economic development are too indirect for some, and cannot explain the long-term rigidities observed in cases like the US. A more generic explanation emphasizes the culture of scientific disciplines. For example, Wertheim (1997) argues that physics is seen as a pseudoreligious belief system akin to Catholicism. Both feature a male-only 'priesthood' intent on 'transcendent abstractions'. Wertheim wants physics to adopt new goals and argues that women's self-reflexivity, based on their reproductive role, can offer them. She notes that female scientists brought to biology an emphasis on cooperation among organisms, explaining their evolutionary features in a way contrasting with the competitive mechanism generated by male biologists.

Critics argue that Wertheim, and other cultural analysts, make essentialist assumptions about women's nature and imply these can unproblematically be imported to scientific disciplines. Wertheim assumes scientific agendas are determined by scientists rather than material interests, and that women lack men's hierarchical world view or would not acquire it if they held top disciplinary positions. Wertheim's account thus begs a lot of questions. But so do the other single-cause explanations. We only get the rounded picture when we have studies of the historical, structural and cultural dimensions. Research into gender and scientific patents surveyed and interviewed male and female scientists; the survey revealed females were awarded fewer than half the number of patents awarded males, while the interviews suggested the reason was lack of an 'old girls network'. The latter finding led the researchers to revisit their panel dataset and apply Inverse Probability of Treatment Weight procedures to account for the dynamics of self-selection into patenting (Ding et al., 2006), confirming the network factor but adding that female scientists had more traditional, commercial risk-aversive constructions of academic careers. The analytic density marking mature research fields requires both attention to several analytic dimensions and use of a variety of methods, bearing in mind the productive interplay between historical data, macro-level structural data, field data and interpretivist cultural analysis.

Postmodernism and multiple method research

The foundations of social science have recently been challenged by perspectives associated with postmodernism, creating a substantial cleavage with little communication across the divide. Since critics have long argued that social science knowledge is not cumulative in the way that prevails in the natural sciences, it seems counter-productive if the field further divides itself. However, without engaging in a general assessment of postmodernism, we can remark a connection between it and the more mainstream methodological practice of multiple method research. One element of 'affirmative postmodernism' (Rosenau, 1992) or 'moderate postmodernism' (Kvale, 1995) can be reconciled with multiple method research. The common ground may be limited but affords one point of connection that may enable a more productive dialogue and increase the cumulative derivation of social science knowledge. Such cumulation necessitates the building of bridges between accounts that are motivated by different problematics, epistemologies, and methodologies. That is precisely the task that any serious engagement with MMRD also necessitates. It is therefore important to understand that postmodernism is not a single conceptualization but, like interactionism, conflict theory or structural functionalism, a jostling array of competing positions beneath a broad, roughly unifying rubric. Amongst these, some positions are more amenable to a project of conciliation in the interests of achieving satisfactory (if necessarily always incomplete) explanation and some are less so.

It is easy to find postmodernist statements suggesting lack of belief in social 'reality', such as Derrida's statement that 'there is nothing outside the text' (1976: 158). This is generally taken to mean 'there is no truth, no reality, no history, no actual flesh-and-blood people in the world' (Lucy, 1995: 1), because texts do not neutrally report the facts of people's lives. If language is merely a distorting screen that only projects experience out of the speaker's categories, and there are no overweening criteria with which to judge a statement's correctness, we have a position where all accounts must be deemed equally legitimate (Spence, 1988: 68). But this is to misrepresent Derrida's intention. Derrida advanced his view in arguing that language and interpretation are central to all human experience, against an orthodoxy that dismissed such concerns as trivial. Arguing that we should rethink our knowledge of empirical objects in light of the complexity of the interpretive process is not to argue that language has no connection with empirical objects. Indeed, arguing that language intrinsically distorts implicitly concedes that behind language is a stable object that can be distorted. Moreover, postmodernists overdraw opposing positions in suggesting that others take language to be transparent and unproblematically providing accurate testimony.

Criticizing postmodernism's exaggerated relativism is facile. Huber (1995: 205) gives a particularly stark statement of this perspective: 'postmodernists are complete relativists who see science as an intellectual device to further the ends of those paying for research rather than a way to discover truth about the universe'. Postmodernism undoubtedly highlights scientific motives other than the dispassionate quest for understanding, questions claims to objective knowledge and problematizes the notion of an observer-independent reality. But there are many others who see a degree of logic in relativism, and the sociology of scientific knowledge provides compelling accounts of cases where science has been corrupted by ulterior motives. The more sophisticated postmodernist accounts do not aim to deny the existence of reality but to demonstrate the obstacles in the way of achieving absolute truths in all fields of knowledge. Thus, Denzin's assertion (1992: 120) that we should 'seriously question' the 'ontological status' of the empirical world is not an attempt to deny the reality of the social but to be reflexively aware of the interpretive processes through which empirical realities are created.

Extreme postmodernism is certainly antithetical to the notion of method but moderate variants can be applied to empirical research, employing methods like deconstructionism. Thus, 'affirmative postmodernism' (Rosenau, 1992) does not reject the possibility of cumulative social knowledge, despite severe doubts about the foundational assumptions of research methodology. In fields like socio-technological studies postmodernist work is oriented both to previous postmodernist and non-postmodernist work. 'Sceptical postmodernism', the other pole of Rosenau's typology, certainly asserts the impossibility of truth, but the hallmark of 'affirmative' postmodernism is an orientation to process that is consonant with the tenets of much longer-established positions such as symbolic interactionism.

Contrary to sceptical postmodernism's famous 'death of the subject', affirmative postmodernists do not find it necessary to eliminate the concept of the subject in the subject/object distinction simply to be cautious about generalization. Sceptical postmodernism rejects the idea that social science can achieve axiomatic knowledge, but the affirmative position concedes the possibility, simply criticizing the idea that social science understandings of society should be privileged. Affirmative postmodernists are hostile to 'the intellectual hegemony implicit in grand theory' (ibid: 83) but do not consequently hold that all theories are equivalent. Importantly for our interest in its position on multiple method research, affirmative postmodernists maintain that generalization and theoretical conclusions can be derived from close study of every-day life, using conventional qualitative methods. The focus on daily life is 'empiricist in character [and] is offered as a basis of generalisable statements' (ibid).

Affirmative postmodernism is not dissimilar to previous perspectives that endorse a reflexive rather than positivist epistemology, are cautious about claims to objectivity, and found comparative analysis on an interest in difference rather than sameness. Even the postmodernist concept of 'intertextuality', the connection of everything with everything, can be read not as obviating causal explanation but as highlighting causal complexity. Intertextuality may complicate the disentangling of dynamic temporal processes but that has long been a focus of mainstream systems theory (Buckley, 1967). Rather than rejecting all methods, affirmative postmodernism seeks techniques that capture complexity, 'methods that apply to a broad range of phenomena, focus on the margins, highlight uniqueness [and] concentrate on the enigmatic' (Rosenau, 1992: 117).

Affirmative postmodernists hold a constructivist theory of social reality. As Edelman (1988) demonstrated, it is implicit in the idea of reality construction that some accounts are valid and others are not. Arguing that obdurate social realities cannot be directly represented does not preclude assessing the relative validity of different analyses. Moderate postmodernists may doubt claims to axiomatic knowledge but they accept 'specific, local, personal and community forms of truth' (Kvale, 1995: 21). Postmodernism highlights the location of research within social and political structures, the historically bound nature of research, and the changing, inconsistent nature of social phenomena. These are hardly unique or groundbreaking concerns.

Bogardus (1924) problematized the relationship of research to its socio-political context, Whyte (1953) highlighted the location of research in its own micro-history so that knowledge of the social always lagged behind the phenomenon's current development, and Lazarsfeld (1944) engaged with the multi-dimensional and ambiguous nature of social reality.

The hysterical tenor of responses to postmodernism by mainstream social scientists, particularly those working in a narrowly algebraic approach to modelling social behaviour, must be motivated by something other than sincere engagement with postmodernist arguments, in that founding figures like Bogardus, Whyte and Lazarsfeld were regarded as entirely mainstream by the social science establishment of the day and yet these authorities freely engaged with the complexities that make social science something more interesting than a cut-and-dried application of modelling software. If the considered reservations and qualifications these and other venerable social scientists readily introduced into the discipline are really so unacceptable, postmodernism's more prejudiced critics must not be aiming at postmodernism but at qualitative methodology in general.

Methodologists pursued a middle path between extreme relativism and uncritical objectivism long before moderate postmodernism (Southgate, 2003). The argument is not that there is anything new or better about postmodernism's critique. Indeed, Weber's moderate perspectivist position on objectivity, the concept from hermeneutics that community standards of validity mediate understandings of social reality (Bernstein, 1983), and symbolic interactionism and phenomenology, offer more helpful advice on negotiating problems of subjectivity and perspective through reflexive self-monitoring. However, postmodernism indisputably celebrates the idea of multiple perspectives and this is a clear point of connection with contemporary understandings of multiple method research in the pursuit of analytic density. That connection offers a means to reconcile postmodernist work with work done in other traditions, and thus the prospect not only of finer-grained methodological interrelation but of a more cumulative social science.

Grey's study (1994) of accountancy careers illustrates the postmodernist approach. Instead of analyzing detailed career patterns and influences on career choices, Grey's Foucauldian theoretical orientation focuses on the political and control functions of the 'career' that disciplines accountants to conform to the requirements of the firm. Adopting a postmodernist approach helps Grey question realities taken for granted by accountants and show how these are produced through discourses of power. However, Grey imputes this characteristic of the profession rather than derive it from his respondents – there are no member checks here. Indeed it is likely that many accountants would disagree with his interpretation.

Without member checks on authenticity, what evaluative criteria do postmodernists use? Denzin's criteria of 'credibility, transferability, dependability and confirmability' (1994: 14) are consonant with the earlier positivist criteria of internal and external validity, reliability and objectivity, but elsewhere postmodernist writings elevate an 'empowerment' criterion, where research is evaluated by its potential to empower those it studies (Kinchloe and McLaren, 1994). That criterion begs obvious political and ethical questions. It would either prevent direct study of 'unloved groups' such as paedophiles or racists, or require that a sympathetic perspective be applied to them. Also problematic is the basis on which deserving groups would be selected, as is how to measure whether a group was better off post-research or that it was the research that improved things. But there is an overtone to these problems. Simply to raise them obliges researchers to engage with the idea that research has a political dimension and can be seen from different perspectives, and that any consensus on validity is based on values, purposes and interests. Postmodernism's reminder of such concerns is not without value. But it is possible to acknowledge postmodernist concerns without abandoning reliability, validity and generalizability. We simply need validity criteria that accommodate competing perspectives.

Reflecting multiple perspectives is only problematic when taken too far. Postmodernism's threat is 'that of transgression, of excessive skepticism, and of a paralysing relativism – of a crossing of limits beyond which "anything goes"' (Marcus, 1994: 403). Relativism's fundamental problem is that it is self-refuting (Hammersley, 1992). Consistency of argument requires that relativists must accept that their own claim that all truth is relative is itself true only relatively, and that it may therefore be false in terms of some frameworks. This produces the perverse conclusion that relativism is itself both true and false.

Taking the view that there is no single valid description of a situation because validity is a matter of perspective need not mean there is no valid description or that every description is valid. Acknowledging that there are multiple perspectives does not mean that all perspectives are equal. 'Multiple valid descriptions and explanations of the same phenomenon are always available. But this is not to say that there can be multiple, *contradictory*, yet valid accounts of the same phenomenon' (emphasis in original, Hammersley, 1992: 199). While acknowledging multiple perspectives is fundamental to the achievement of analytic density, absolute relativism cannot arbitrate between perspectives. Rather than celebrating difference, this 'epistemological relativism' prevents researchers engaging with it, by holding that 'difference' proves all knowledge claims are impossible. For postmodernism to serve as a system of explanation it requires validity criteria beyond 'empowerment' and it cannot treat all accounts as equal.

Moderate or affirmative postmodernism's emphasis on reflecting different constructions of social reality, and the practice of multi-method research, come together around multiple perspectives. Documenting multiple perspectives suggests that we have looked at the research issue from 'all angles'. Research that uses different methods to capture different aspects of the phenomenon, draws samples purposively to contrast different participants' perspectives and so on, encourages explanations that better accommodate the complexity of social phenomena, which are often multi-causal, displaying conditions that make for an outcome in one combination but not another (Ragin, 1987). We are not required to enter the methodological dead-end of epistemological relativism in order to acknowledge that the process of achieving analytic density is likely to include a relativist element so we can fruitfully engage with difference.

Multiple method research in evaluating programmes of social intervention

The world of multiple method research oddly combines orthodoxies and heresies. One dimension of this is apparent when we contrast its status in academic and applied research. It remains controversial in the academic sphere, in contrast with applied research, where many regard it as a practical necessity. It is Kelle's (2001) emphasis on theory as guiding empirical inquiries using MMRD that is of interest here. In particular, in application to applied research we might argue that an elaboration of 'theory' is required. We have discussed how MMRD can add 'analytic density' to research inquiries. This has the effect of turning research 'projects' into research 'programmes', because it makes for more sophisticated analyses. While the importance of 'theory' and the virtues (and timeframe) of complex analyses are readily accepted in academic research, where the idea of the research programme as a series of coordinated investigations of a research problem is a mark of the scientific approach, this is less the case in applied research. What might stand in applied research in the place of 'theory' as animating inquiry and dictating the research design?

One starting point would be an understanding of the different context in which applied research operates. The 'policy community' is a major and growing consumer of social science research. We need to understand the policy environment and political frame of reference in which applied research is done in relation to the needs of government, voluntary organizations and interest groups. There is a sense in which any inquiry, even that which explicitly declares itself to be a-theoretical, contains an implicit theory. This idea of theory as 'default' shows that even for members of the policy community who do not want their research to come with conceptual strings attached, some engagement with the wider implications of research is necessary. Members of the applied research community therefore need to have a 'theory' of the policy environment in which their research will be placed, and members of the policy community need to have a 'theory' of the research world which allows them to understand and evaluate research.

The policy communities of developed societies have become increasingly sophisticated, as the interaction between academic research elites and policy elites demonstrates (not least by the research internship systems operating in many countries). However, this is not matched by growth in the sophistication of academic understandings of the policy community. When they engage in policy-related research, academic researchers seek to do so on their own terms, and there is little concern with what happens to the research once the report is written and, in commissioned work, accepted by the sponsor. There is certainly a drive by bodies concerned with the interface between academic research and policy to encourage greater engagement by academics with the requirements of the policy community, but there is seldom the kind of determined follow-through that is necessary to promote the application and ongoing refinement of research findings, nor are academics naturally inclined to adopt the tactics of 'political animals' that are needed to establish their research programmes as part of the government agenda. We might argue that an understanding of the policy community as a research environment is necessary if rigorous and conceptually oriented work is to be achieved in applied research.

One mark of that community is that those engaged in commissioning research have increasingly displayed a predisposition in favour of multiple method research. This may result from the commonsense appeal of the underlying logic (combined with indifference to the epistemological differences between methods), but the trend also relates to some significant institutional moves amongst policymakers and evaluation researchers. In tune with the recent promotion of 'evidence-based policy', an emphasis on MMRD is apparent in official documents such as invitations to bid to conduct research on programmes or policies implemented or planned by government departments, and in reviews of research capacity, such as the Rhind Report (2003). In the former, those commissioning research increasingly specify the research design and this increasingly involves MMRD. In the latter, one endemic criticism of research capacity is that the diminishing skill base in respect of quantitative methods causes an incapacity to conclusively address major social problems in multiple method research.

While one consequence of policymakers' embrace of research combining quantitative and qualitative methods is a campaign to improve quantitative skills, another is a drive to overcome constraints on the representativeness and generalizability of qualitative research. Government has initiated topic-specific reviews of quality standards for qualitative research (such as in the field of health) and generic reviews of quality standards for qualitative research (such as Spencer et al., 2003, commissioned by the UK Cabinet Office). Qualitative research may have 'arrived' but it is welcome only provided its findings can be associated with findings from research using other methods.

A substantial impetus to MMRD in applied research has come from similar initiatives to those motivating the exercises in quality standards for qualitative research. Long before quality standards emerged for qualitative research they were a familiar part of the environment for quantitative researchers, where criteria derive from benchmarks that are intrinsic to statistical data. A prominent application of large-scale quantitative research is in health research and many of the quality standards for quantitative research were laid down in the context of epidemiological research, which involves large (even whole population) samples and experimental/control designs (often looking at only one variable, those receiving and not receiving given interventions). This approach has taken institutional form in the 'Campbell collaboration' and its criminal justice equivalent, the 'Cochrane collaboration'. Membership represents a kind of official seal of approval and members must produce research adhering to inflexible quality standards. This is more a 'club' than a checklist in both senses of the English word 'club' (a closed organization, and a big stick to beat people with).

To overstate the case, the embrace of social research by policymakers is both welcome as a sign of enhanced legitimacy and worrying in that it appears to bring with it a particular construction of social research. Recognizing why policymakers commission research, how policymakers use research and the place of research in the political process, is the beginning of a more sophisticated understanding of the policy/research interface. Such considerations inform some problematic issues that emerge where MMRD has been adopted in applied research.

For example, the situation where policymakers accept that qualitative research has a real contribution to make, but chiefly as part of a multiple method research design, can lead to methodological dilemmas. We might take two examples from the health field. The first concerns the UK controversy over the combined Measles, Mumps and Rubella (MMR) vaccine. A small sample, but highly publicized, study by a practising doctor suggested a link between the vaccine and autism in children. As a result there was substantial parental resistance to MMR vaccination and many parents demanded that single vaccines be provided against each disease or refused vaccination altogether. Parental resistance had the effect of increasing the incidence of the diseases, mumps seriously so. Health policy researchers were asked to address the issue. Their background was in epidemiology and their medical school did not include staff with qualitative research expertise. They wanted to add qualitative understanding to large-scale survey and epidemiological data by a 'meta-analysis' of qualitative studies. The idea was to simply add together the samples from small qualitative studies of parental resistance until they had a large enough sample size to draw inferences. The danger was that simply 'adding together' a cluster of qualitative studies would be to ignore differences in modes of eliciting parental views, analytic techniques, degrees of experience of vaccination amongst respondents, and so on. 'Adding together' could multiply error.

The second example emerges from the first. Faced with the epistemological problems mentioned, a large meeting of policymakers, health researchers, statisticians and methodologists was convened. The lead researchers briefed the meeting on the problem of parental resistance. They declared that they had open minds and wanted to learn from the meeting how qualitative studies could best be included in a multi-method effort. They then suggested that Bayesian statistics could be used to back-estimate the validity and reliability of predictions based on the qualitative studies of parental resistance (and indeed of predictions based on small sample studies of the links between the vaccine and autism). Bayesian methods would be used to progressively fine-tune predicted frequencies of the fit between particular parental characteristics and the likelihood of consent to vaccination. In discussion, methodologists pointed out that the original studies had not been designed to enable prediction, and in few cases were there items in the research instruments that would reliably allow such inferences to be drawn.

Following this, the meeting divided into groups to discuss how qualitative and other small sample research could be incorporated alongside other methods. However, when it came time for the discussion groups to report back, it became clear that the researchers directing the programme were not interested in the variety of approaches and solutions the groups had generated. For example, a view had emerged in two groups that using methodological integration facilities in qualitative software would enable more highly specified conclusions to be extracted from the data than in the original studies, which had pursued other analytic purposes. Qualitative secondary analysis using qualitative software would help identify conclusions relevant to the programme's agenda. This, and several other approaches, received noncommittal responses. The lead researchers returned to the idea of applying Bayesian statistics and there was no further consultation.

Concluding remark

The use of multiple method research in applied work is both welcome for its potential to increase the sophistication of the evaluation and reason for caution in that it subjects component parts of multiple method research designs to pressures to produce results beyond their innate capacities. However, multiple method research is also part of the solution to the latter problem, because it is intrinsic to it that methods can be chosen to compensate for the defects associated with other methods. Such flexibility is best understood as reflecting the fact that MMRD is not a technique, like calculating tests of significance in statistical software, but an attitude of inquiry, an approach to research quality and to what makes for adequate explanations of social phenomena.

Multiple method research appears therefore to offer several merits. It can bring greater sophistication to our understanding of social phenomena (the business of analytic density), it can reach out across divisions in the research community (the linkage between postmodernism and multiple method research), and it can strengthen the methodological armoury of researchers when they apply social science to real-world social problems. Whether these are benefits naturally depends on one's perspective. The matter should not be decided because MMRD is a growing orthodoxy but because it more effectively solves problems that compel social science and the societies to whom social science is responsible.

References

Allen, J. (2001) *Going Boldly: an Exploratory Investigation of Male Fear of Crime*, unpublished dissertation. Guildford: University of Surrey

Bazeley, P. (1999) 'The bricoleur with a computer', *Qualitative Health Research*, 9 (2): 279–287.

Bazeley, P. (2006) 'The contribution of computer software to integrating qualitative and quantitative data and analysis', *Research in the Schools*, 13 (1): 63–73.

Bernstein, R. (1983) *Beyond Objectivism and Relativism*. Philadelphia PA: University of Pennsylvania Press.

Blaikie, N. (1991) 'A critique of the use of triangulation in social research', *Quality and Quantity*, 25: 115–136.

Bogardus, E. (1924) 'Methods of interviewing', *Journal of Applied Sociology*, IX: 456–467.

Bryman, A. (2006) 'Integrating quantitative and qualitative research', *Qualitative Research*, 6 (1): 97–113.

Buckley, W. (1967) *Sociology and Modern Systems Theory*. Englewood Cliffs, NJ: Prentice Hall.

Campbell, D. and Fiske, D. (1959) 'Convergent and discriminant validity by the multi-trait, multi-method matrix', *Psychological Bulletin*, 56(2): 81–105.

Campbell, D. and Russo, M.J. (1999) *Social Experimentation*. Thousand Oaks, CA: Sage.

Caracelli, V. and Green, J. (1997) 'Crafting mixed method evaluation designs', in J. Green and V. Caracelli (eds), *Advances in Mixed Method Evaluation*. San Francisco CA: Jossey Bass.

Creswell, J. (1994) *Research Design*. Thousand Oaks, CA: Sage.

Creswell, J., Tashakkori, A., Jensen, K. and Shapley, K. (2003) 'Teaching mixed methods research:practices, dilemmas and challenges', in A. Tashakkori and C. Teddlie (eds), *Handbook of Mixed Methods in Social and Behavioral Research*. Thousand Oaks, CA: Sage. pp. 619–638.

Deacon, D., Bryman, A. and Fenton, N. (1998) 'Collision or collusion', *International Journal of Social Research Methodology*, 1 (1): 47–63.

Denzin, N. (1992) *Symbolic Interactionism and Cultural Studies*. Oxford: Blackwell.

Denzin, N. and Lincoln, Y. (1994) 'Introduction', in N. Denzin and Y. Lincoln (eds), *Handbook of Qualitative Research*, London: Sage.

Derrida, J. (1976) *Of Grammatology*. Baltimore: Johns Hopkins University Press.

Ding, W., Murray, F. and Stuart, T. (2006) 'Gender difference in patenting', *Science*, 313: 665–667.

Dresselhaus, M., Franz, J. and Clark, B. (1994) 'Interventions to increase the participation of women in physics', *Science*, 263: 1392–1393.

Edelman, M. (1988) *Constructing the Political Spectacle*. Chicago: University of Chicago Press.

Glover, J. and Fielding, J. (2000) *Women and Scientific Employment*. London: Macmillan.

Grey, C. (1994) 'Career as a project of the self', *Sociology*, 28 (2): 479–497.

Hammersley, M. (1992) 'Some reflections on ethnography and validity', *International Journal of Qualitative Studies in Education*, 5 (3): 195–203.

Huber, J. (1995) 'Institutional perspectives on sociology', *American Journal of Sociology*, 101 (1): 194–216.

Keeves, J. and Kotte, D. (1996) 'Patterns of science achievement: international comparisons', in L. Parker (ed.), *Gender, Science and Mathematics*. Dordrecht: Kluwer Academic.

Kelle, U. (2001, February) 'Sociological explanations between micro and macro and the integration of qualitative and quantitative methods [43 paragraphs]'. *Forum Qualitative Sozialforschung / Forum: Qualitative Social Research* [On-line Journal], 2(1). Available at: http://www.qualitative-research.net/fqs-texte/1-01/1-01kelle-e.htm (Accessed 11 December 2007).

Kinchloe, J. and McLaren, P. (1994) 'Rethinking critical theory and qualitative research', in N. Denzin and Y. Lincoln (eds), *Handbook of Qualitative Research*. London: Sage.

Kvale, S. (1995) 'The social construction of validity', *Qualitative Inquiry*, 1 (1): 19–40.

Lazarsfeld, P. (1944) 'The controversy over detailed interviews', *Public Opinion Quarterly*, 8: 38–60.

Lee, R.M. (ed.) (1995) *Information Technology for the Social Scientist*. London: UCL Press.

Lee, R.M. (2004) 'Recording technology and the interview in sociology, 1920-2000', *Sociology*, 38 (5): 881–901.

Lesniewski, S. (1992) *Collected Works*. Dordrecht: Kluwer.

Lucy, N. (1995) *Debating Derrida*. Melbourne: Melbourne University Press.

Marcus, G. (1994) 'What comes (just) after "post"?', in N. Denzin and Y. Lincoln (eds), *Handbook of Qualitative Research*. London: Sage.

Niglas, K. (2004) *The Combined Use of Qualitative and Quantitative Methods in Educational Research*. Tallinn, Estonia: Tallinn Pedagogical University.

Ragin, C. (1987) *The Comparative Method*. Thousand Oaks, CA: Sage.

Rhind, D. (2003) *Great Expectations*. London: Academy of Learned Societies in the Social Sciences.

Richards, L. (2000) 'Integrating data: can qualitative software do it?', *Social Science Methodology in the New Millenium: Proceedings of the Fifth International Conference on Logic and Methodology*. Koln: Zentralarchiv fur Empirische Sozialforschung.

Rosenau, P.M. (1992) *Post-modernism and the Social Sciences: Insights, Inroads, and Intrusions*. Princeton, NJ: Princeton University Press.

Rossiter, M. (1982) *Women Scientists in America*. Baltimore: Johns Hopkins University Press.

Sieber, S. (1973) 'The integration of fieldwork and survey methods', *American Journal of Sociology*, 78 (6): 1335–1359.

Southgate, B. (2003) *Postmodernism in History*. London: Routledge.

Spence, D. (1988) 'Tough and tender-minded hermeneutics', in S. Messer and L. Sass (eds), *Hermeneutics and Psychological Theory*. London: Rutgers University Press.

Spencer, L., Ritchie, J., Lewis, J. and Dillon, L. (2003) *Quality in Qualitative Evaluation*. London: Cabinet Office.

Trend, M.G. (1978) 'On the reconciliation of qualitative and quantitative analyses', *Human Organization*, 37: 345–354.

Webb, E.J., Campbell, D.T., Schwartz, R.D. and Sechrest, L. (1966) *Unobtrusive Measures*. Chicago: Rand McNally.

Wertheim, M. (1997) *Pythagoras' Trousers*. London: Fourth Estate.

Whyte, W.F. (1953) 'Interviewing for organisational research', *Human Organization*, 12 (2): 15–22.

4

The Practice of a Mixed Methods Research Strategy: Personal, Professional and Project Considerations

Julia Brannen

In this chapter I focus on three issues that are relevant and of concern to researchers in embarking on mixed methods research. First, I focus on personal issues drawing upon my own research biography and consider the factors that may influence engagement in mixed methods research. Second, I consider professional issues: the opportunities and risks for researchers in engaging in mixed methods research strategies. Third, I consider some project issues: what mixing methods means in practice in carrying out a research project. It is necessary before doing so to say something about the definition of the term and how I use it in this chapter.

In order to address a research question or set of research questions, researchers must devise a strategy or, as Bryman suggests, 'a general orientation to the conduct of social research' (Bryman, 2004: 20). Mixed methods research means adopting a research strategy employing more than one type of research *method* (Fielding and Fielding, 2008; Tashakkori and Teddlie, 2003). The methods may be a mix or qualitative and quantitative methods, a mix of quantitative methods or a mix of qualitative methods. Some researchers have distinguished between mixed methods used within a single project and mixed method designs (Morse, 2003), the point being that their separateness will have implications not only for analysis but also for how the data are written up.

If mixed methods research is a research strategy does it represent a particular type of research design? The answer is both yes and no. Adopting a mixed methods strategy may constitute a strategy in its own right or it may be subsumed within another research strategy, as in the case of adopting a case study design in which a number of different methods are embedded. Ethnography (Coffey and Atkinson, 1996) and action research (Reason and Bradbury, 2001) are also research strategies that may also employ more than one method (Lykes, 2001).

Mixed methods research also means working with different *types of data*. It may also involve using *different investigators* – sometimes different research teams working in different research paradigms. For these reasons mixed methods research is often referred to as multi-strategy research (Bryman, 2004) implying the application of a number of different research strategies related to a complex range of research questions and a complex research design. On the other hand, mixed methods may form part of a long-term strategy (several years) as in the case of a research programme that is pursued over time by a group of researchers applying different methods and approaches consecutively (see Kelle, 2005 who cites the example of using ethnographies at a later point in a research programme to help explain statistical associations from an earlier study). In this chapter I use the term to mean a combination of qualitative and quantitative methods within a single research project in the collection of data.

How I came to engage in mixed methods research

I started my research career as a sociologist using qualitative methods, methods in which I still feel myself to be more skilled. The story of my engagement in mixed methods occurred at a particular time and place and with particular people. In the 1980s when research funders were more generous in the amount of time they allocated for methodological development than they are today, I was working in a research unit that saw its work as having policy relevance, and with co-researchers who were open to different ideas and paradigms. At this time I joined a research programme which proposed to use largely quantitative methods and was fortunate in being allowed to make a considerable contribution in influencing its development, indeed changing its methodological direction to encompass a mixed methods research strategy. The programme that I joined was designed to explore longitudinal changes in women's employment and wellbeing after childbirth. While the size of the cohort of women was not compromised and much of the data were coded for entry onto SPSS the interview was adapted to explore the meanings that women attributed to their situations and experiences with consequences for the analysis. In fact qualitative and quantitative analysis proceeded side by side with some interesting results (Brannen, 2004). I recall finding this change of direction quite unremarkable at the time until the government funder of the programme invited me to write a paper on the subject of mixed methods research (a paper that was largely intended to convince the government Office of the Chief Scientist of the value of qualitative as well as quantitative data but also led to a training seminar for funded researchers and a text on mixed methods research (Brannen, 1992)).

So why did I go on working in this way? First, I would say that the research questions I sought to address and the samples I wanted to select required a mixed methods strategy. In addition, I think it also had something to do with the fact that in the research unit where I worked quantitative and qualitative methods were used so well that I did not feel one approach was likely to be compromised at the expense of the other. In Bryman's terms (Bryman, 1988) I was influenced initially by situated pragmatic reasons and over time the approach became a taken-for-granted part of my methodological repertoire.

The opportunities and risks for researchers engaging in a mixed methods research strategy

I turn now to the wider context in which research is done and methodological developments take place. A mixed methods strategy represents to researchers an apparent opportunity for advancement in methodology. It also presents possible risks.

First, a mixed methods strategy presents an opportunity for *skills enhancement*. In striving to create a 'knowledge society' (the goal set by the European Council for Europe for 2010), Western societies have sought to increase the numbers of young people in formal training as greater emphasis is placed upon skills and their accreditation through courses and qualifications. In learning social science methodologies, this emphasis is similarly visible as students and researchers increasingly undertake training courses. The UK's Economic and Social Research Council's huge investments in recent years into developing research skills and methods is a case in point. It is also now mandatory for doctoral students funded by the UK's Economic and Social Research Council to undergo training across the spectrum of research methods, while many graduates take Masters courses in social research methods before they enter doctoral programmes. Such methods of learning how to do research have overtaken former pathways notably vocational apprenticeships conducted within a particular discipline, research centre and project.

There is much to commend these new pathways into and within research, in particular the opportunity to learn about a range of methods and thus to stay open to new ways of addressing research questions. Broadening one's methodological repertoire mitigates against 'trained incapacities', as Reiss (1968) termed the issue – the entrenchment of researchers in particular methods or types of research. On the other hand, training is not the same as learning. Knowledge soon fades if not put into practice fast. As methodology acquires a higher status in the social sciences and more emphasis is placed on *displaying* methodological rigour, there is also the need to be mindful of Coser's admonition to the American Sociological Association in 1975 against producing young researchers 'with superior research skills but with *a trained incapacity to think* in theoretically innovative ways' (Coser, 1975).

Second, mixed methods research is an opportunity to encourage thinking 'outside the box'. In the UK social sciences, we have seen the growing importance of *substantive fields* bringing together researchers across disciplinary boundaries. Reflecting the general fragmentation that has gone on within particular disciplines such as sociology (Platt and Hopper, 1997), increased funding has been allocated by the UK's Economic and Social Research Council to programmes of research within substantive fields in which researchers bid for money for projects in those fields: for example, programmes on work, childhood, youth, migration, social exclusion. While there are undoubted benefits for researchers and other stakeholders in learning about and integrating research evidence across disciplines and within a substantive field, there may be some disadvantages, especially for researchers. It can distract attention from theoretical questions. This can happen if research is reduced to a set of skills acquired outside disciplinary boundaries, so that researchers are less exposed to the traditions of a particular discipline and may fail to acquire a secure identity within a discipline. While theoretical eclecticism may be no bad thing, such an approach risks researchers being insufficiently schooled in theoretical issues and traditions. Such weak schooling is apparent in the way grand theory in particular is imported at the writing up stage of a research project in order to strengthen or confirm research findings rather than being used in 'sensitizing' ways (Blumer, 1954) in earlier stages of the research process.

However, there remain strong pressures for researchers to remain securely within their own disciplines. In Britain, as increasingly elsewhere, publishing in scholarly journals has become mandatory. It remains the case that many of the most prestigious journals are discipline based while journals devoted to methodology tend to attract particular types of method. Two journals that attract research that uses mixed methods are the *International Journal of Social Research Methodology* and the newly launched *Journal of Mixed Methods Research*.

Third, developing a mixed methods strategy fits with the political currency accorded to 'practical enquiry' that speaks to policy and policymakers and which informs practice, as distinct from scientific research (Hammersley, 2000). As noted above, my own initiation into mixed methods research occurred in a policy-informed research environment. In today's world, researchers are required to address the needs of research stakeholders and users, with funders often framing our research questions for us and sometimes even our methods. On the other hand, research has always been subject to political climates and persuasions (Finch, 1986; Platt, 1996). In Britain we have seen a whole industry of mixed methods research created around evidence-based policy and over a longer timeframe in the evaluation of policy (Ritchie, 2003; Tashakkori and Teddlie, 2003). However the downside to this is that researchers have less and less leeway to define their own research questions and to follow their own ideas.

Fourth, opportunities for mixed methods research strategies are occurring with the increasing importance paid to cross-national research in the context of sizable research budgets provided by the European Union (EU) and the escalation in the size of the research projects they fund. Many EU projects typically comprise context mapping exercises, involving the synthesis and secondary analysis of quantitative data together with policy analysis involving documentary methods and intensive research methods that address the micro level (Hantrais, 2005). This contextualizing work is essential to cross-national research. However, there is a danger that such datasets are collected but are not integrated into a comparative analysis nor sufficiently inform research outputs.

Finally, with the growth of strategic and practically oriented research which meets the needs of users, there is increased emphasis upon dissemination. Researchers must speak at least two languages – the technical language of research and a language which makes research results accessible to a wide variety of audiences. Thus words become as important as numbers. Mixed methods research allows for both. However the different presentational modes of presenting quantitative and qualitative data can sit awkwardly together in the written outputs or may prove too unwieldy to be put together.

Mixed methods research strategies offer therefore both opportunities and risks. They offer creative possibilities for addressing research questions in terms of a range of methods. However these possibilities should not take the place of creative thinking. Mixed methods may come into their own at a time in which social science research has first and foremost to be of practical relevance and applicable to policy fields. Practical relevance should not substitute for theoretical relevance. The opportunity to learn new research skills is to be welcomed and is particularly encouraging of cross-disciplinary collaboration but should not undermine disciplines and theoretical concerns.

What mixing methods means in practice in a research project

To understand what a mixed methods strategy involves it is necessary to be attentive to the points in the research process at which qualitative and quantitative methods are brought to bear (Brannen, 2004; 2005); the outcomes in terms of what researchers make of the different kinds of data in the analysis and writing up their research; and the epistemological assumptions underpinning the choice of each method and their intended use (Moran-Ellis et al., 2006).

This involves working backwards: from the accounts of the outcomes of mixing methods to how they were intended to be used. What researchers claim on behalf of their methodological practice is not always what they deliver. As Bryman (2006) has described, there is likely to be a slippage between researchers' research plans and their execution. Practices may belie the person's intentions. While researchers may initially justify their approach in terms of tailoring methods to research questions, in practice they may make references to the *outcomes* of the research. So that while the choice of methods may start off as central to the research design being chosen in relation to research questions and their epistemological framing, the possibilities and constraints of the research process, including those encountered during the data analysis phase, may divert the original plan or intention. For example, a researcher may decide during the interpretation of the data to address a theoretical debate that was not considered at the time of writing the research proposal. A researcher may decide during analysis that there is no time to exploit fully all the data and so on. This is not necessarily to criticize the work but merely a point of methodological reflection that needs to be explored in writing about methodological practice, one's own or those of others.

In exploring how researchers apply a mixed methods research strategy, I have focused upon some of my own work and some studies discussed in the 2005 Special Issue of *The International Journal of Social Research Methodology: Theory and Practice (IJSRM)* that was devoted to mixed methods research. This small sample of mixed methods studies cannot be seen to be representative of mixed methods research but straddles much, though far from all, of the continuum of different types of mixed methods strategies. The mixed methods studies are of three types:

(a) Mixed methods studies where the quantitative component of the study was more dominant and the researchers specialized in quantitative work; in these cases this preceded the qualitative component (four studies).
(b) Mixed methods studies where the qualitative component had priority and the researchers identified themselves primarily as qualitative researchers; the qualitative component similarly followed on from the quantitative component (two studies).
(c) A study in which the quantitative component came second and where neither approach appeared to dominate (one study).

In discussing these studies I have tried to unpick how qualitative and quantitative methods were justified, how the data from each method were used and how they contributed to explanations and understandings generated by the research. On this basis I propose some general issues to explore in assessing the value of mixed methods studies.

Studies where the quantitative component dominated and preceded the qualitative

In this group of studies, the quantitative method involved large-scale longitudinal research. Not surprisingly, the main rationale given rested on the usefulness of the longitudinal design for assessing change rather than that of a mixed methods research design (Plewis and Mason, 2005: 188; Sammons et al., 2005: 213). Other rationales given related to the need for particular statistical techniques such as regression analysis, clustered samples and multi-level modelling. The additional use of qualitative methods in these studies to look at particular groups or sites was likewise justified in terms of another research design – case study – rather than focusing upon the benefits of mixed strategy design *per se*. The qualitative case studies were selected on the basis of the quantitative findings collected from the longitudinal study in order to assist in their clarification.

Thus Hoyles et al. (2005) in their study of children's mathematical reasoning took as their main method longitudinal quantitative methods in order to track progress in mathematics – in terms of attainment and reasoning – of children attending randomly selected schools within nine geographically diverse English regions. They also strategically selected samples – particular groups of pupils from the quantitative study – for qualitative investigation, notably those whose progress in mathematics reasoning decreased over time (lower at Time 2 than at Time 1) and where the children's ability to calculate mathematically increased. They employed interviews with students to explore these findings further. Similarly, Sammons et al. (2005) employed a longitudinal quantitative design to explore the effects of pre-school education on children's attainment and development at entry to school (the sample was drawn from six English local authorities and six types of pre-school provision). They selected a small number of the early education centres from their original sample on the basis of their contrasting profiles.

A second feature of these studies is also apparent. At an early stage of the research process there appears to have been a transformation of the data: data from the qualitative case study were transformed into a quantitative form during data processing. Thus Hoyles et al. in their study of pupils' mathematical reasoning turned their qualitative data into four types of 'reasoning' signalled by mathematical symbols c_1 to c_4 (p. 229). Similarly, Sammons et al. (2005) who carried out qualitative case studies of early education centres coded the qualitative data so that the 'reduced data' (p. 219) were used to provide statistical explanations for the outcome data produced in the quantitative longitudinal study. Thus a key concept that was derived from the qualitative data analysis appears to have been transformed into a quantitative variable and correlated with outcome variables.

In this latter case, it seems that qualitative data were used to explain the quantitative results. Indeed in this latter study the considerable extent to which the quantitative component dominated this study is evident in the strategy whereby the fieldworkers doing the qualitative case studies were required to 'protect' themselves from knowledge of the quantitative results in order to avoid bias. This suggests that the study in question while using qualitative methods analyzed the data within a set of assumptions typically associated with positivistic research concerning bias and neutrality rather than using all the data to inform understanding, as is required in case study designs (Yin, 2003a; 2003b) and ethnographic and qualitative research (Delamont, 2004).

Yet, in justifying their research strategy, it is interesting that the rationale given for different methods is in terms of offering 'complementary strengths' and minimizing weaknesses 'associated with reliance on only one paradigm' (p. 221). That is the researchers in reflecting upon mixed methods seek to identify themselves *less* in terms of a single cluster of epistemological assumptions while their practice suggests the methods are applied very much from *within* a particular cluster or paradigm.

In a third example, Blatchford (2005) justifies using a mixed methods strategy and also a longitudinal design to investigate the relationship between classroom size and pupils' educational achievement. (The quantitative sample consisted of 10,000 children from a random selection of schools.) Blatchford's rationale is framed in terms of the power of mixed methods to 'reconcile inconsistencies in previous research'. Quantitative information was required to examine associations or relationships statistically – class size, adult-pupil ratios, teacher time and pupil behaviour etc. He also noted that qualitative methods were needed to assess such relationships, in particular, case studies. However he suggested that in the analysis phase 'priorities had to be set and some areas of investigation received more attention than others' (2005: 204). In this study the analysis sought statistical links between class size and educational achievement. This latter type of quantitative analysis dominated despite the researchers having collected 'fine grained data on classroom processes' that lend themselves to other kinds of analysis, for example to do with understanding processes of learning in different classroom environments. The qualitative data are put to limited use, as Blatchford himself notes: the qualitative data could have been analyzed both qualitatively and quantitatively. Again transformation of the qualitative data into quantitative data took place during the data processing phase.

Studies where the quantitative component preceded but was subsidiary to the qualitative component

These exemplars are taken from my own research. In an article in the Special Issue I gave an example of a study in which a more highly resourced qualitative study (in terms of researcher time) was preceded by a questionnaire survey (Brannen, 2005). I have used several such designs. The study quoted there concerned children's concepts of care and their contribution to family life (Brannen et al., 2000). The first phase was a self-completion questionnaire survey of school-based populations in mixed ethnic areas of London – of around 1,000 children aged 11–12. The second phase involved a sub-sample drawn from the survey of groups of children and their parents living in different types of family/household (63 households). This second phase employed a semi-structured interview with children and separately with mothers or main carers, with other methods embedded in the interviews with the children. The primary rationale for doing a survey was the purposive sampling of cases to be studied qualitatively – children living in different types of household structures. Gaining access to children via schools was considered the only feasible method. A second rationale is also given, namely to provide *contextual* information about the populations of children from which the cases were selected. The rationale for the qualitative study concerned the main aims of the study, namely to understand children's experiences of living in different types of families and to explore their own concepts of care.

Although not reported in the paper in question, the data analysis stuck mainly to these aims. However, an examination of the main publication (Brannen et al., 2000) shows that the survey was used to provide extensive data on reported behaviour on particular items that were listed in the questionnaire such as children's contribution to family work and their views and reports of parental practices carried out by mothers and fathers, issues that were *not systematically* explored though covered in the interviews. However, in reflecting upon the methodology of the study the authors focus upon the way the different data work together to give a holistic picture of children's concepts and experiences of care. Significantly, though, they concluded that children even when their perspectives were accessed via a range of methods, do not emerge as authors of their own stories of family life. Rather children's understandings have to be pieced together in a way that researchers have to read between the lines, drawing upon multiple sources of data, including the reports of the children's mothers, and also a number of different qualitative methods that were linked to the interviews. In the book no play is made of the fact of the mixed methods design while the transformation of data was limited, for example the use of questionnaire survey data as a basis for classifying the household types which in the interviews were found in most cases to provide similar information.

A recent study (Brannen et al., 2007) that was not discussed in my article in the journal's Special Issue focuses on how four groups of workers who care for vulnerable children 'come to care'. The study adopted a complex iterative approach in which biographical case studies were sandwiched between surveys (a postal survey from which respondents were later followed up in a telephone survey). The different methods broadly addressed different timeframes including two surveys of the same four sets of childcare workers conducted at an interval of a year and a subset of biographical case studies sandwiched between the surveys that provided insight into workers' perspectives over time and their own life course. Each method therefore had a different purpose. A strength of the first (postal) survey was, among other things, to provide a sampling source for the biographical case studies and for a follow-up telephone survey a year later to determine the work destinations of childcare workers over time. In addition the surveys and a set of interviews with managers sought to provide contextual information on large groups of childcare workers and the local authorities and services in which they were located. The surveys therefore provided extensive data on *group* characteristics patterns, for example the work experiences of the different groups and their management of work-family responsibilities. While the survey questions were in general designed to address different research questions from the biographical interviews, inevitably it was necessary to ask some that were similar. However, the contexts in which the particular data were collected were taken into account in their analysis and interpretation, including the timeframes adopted by informants and the specific contexts in which questions were posed and responses given.

The data sources were integrated largely in two ways as suggested in the methodological literature (Brannen, 1992; 2004; Greene et al., 1989). The main mode of integration was complementarity in which each data source and data analysis addressed rather differently framed research questions. A second mode of integration was also relevant, namely the use of survey evidence as a basis for further exploration and to initiate new questions to be explored in the biographical and telephone interviews.

Some contradictions arose between different types of evidence notably between the survey evidence and the biographical interviews. The postal survey questionnaire was designed to generate extensive data on each childcare group and across the groups: the responses to the set questions were pre-coded and no account could therefore be taken of what respondents had in mind when they answered the questions. Thus the postal survey data concerning care workers' future employment intentions were difficult to interpret and in some cases proved unreliable predictors of later actions as reported in the telephone survey. This is not an issue of reliability as normally understood in the methodological literature but to do with the way in which present time infuses perceptions of the future so that workers' experiences of their present jobs shaped how they presented their future work intentions at a particular moment in time.

The case material was also used to generate *new themes* that were not therefore reflected in the survey evidence. Hence it was necessary to carry out analysis not envisaged in the design of the project. For example, a number of problematic aspects were raised by childcare workers in their biographical interviews concerning coping with work-family responsibilities which related to the particularities of their occupations. These were not reflected in the survey evidence. Indeed the survey evidence suggested a more positive picture in that most respondents suggested that they managed their work-family responsibilities successfully. Of course the two sets of evidence may not necessarily be seen to conflict but rather to suggest that while most people present themselves 'getting by' on an everyday basis, challenges and tensions remain.

However, although the survey data were drawn upon in writing up these data, in much of the analysis the main thrust lay in the qualitative material either used as individual case studies to extrapolate about the social processes involved in becoming a care worker or as exemplars to illustrate the thematic analysis carried out across the case material (the latter being the more common type of qualitative analysis).

Studies where the qualitative component precedes the quantitative

Examples where qualitative methods precede quantitative methods as an explicit form of mixed methods research design appear less easy to find. In practice, however, in survey research it is commonplace for a qualitative pilot study to be carried out to test the meaning of questions to be used in the survey instrument. Also, in psychology, most personality scales are based on prior clinical research. Hammond's mixed methods study reported in the IJSRM Special Issue is justified as part of a new programme of research on the wider benefits of adult learning (Hammond, 2005). It claims to use qualitative research as a way of establishing significant variables for subsequent isolation and examination in an existing national longitudinal dataset. The rationale for the qualitative phase (biographical interviews) was that the research area was under-researched and the research questions relatively unformulated (p. 241). The quantitative study was an existing cohort study (the 1958 National Child Development Study – NCDS) and the main justification for doing the research and gaining the funding, given the emphasis currently placed upon exploitation of these expensive datasets. The qualitative component was conceived as a 'mapping' exercise carried out to inform the research design and implementation of the quantitative phase: the identification of variables for the quantitative analysis (p. 243). This has parallels with qualitative pilot work as a prologue to a survey, although in this case the qualitative material was to be analyzed in its own right.

Interestingly, despite its use of large-scale longitudinal survey data, this article contrasts with others in this Special Issue that draw upon similar datasets. This author is insistent that causal outcomes should not be inferred from the quantitative evidence. While suggesting that the qualitative data were used to identify appropriate analysis for the quantitative part of the research project, she also insists that these data should *not* be used to explain quantitatively arrived-at outcomes, as in the other studies discussed above, but to interrogate them further (Hammond, 2005: 244).

Unusually, for studies in educational research this author goes on to cite results found in the quantitative analysis that are contradicted by evidence from the biographical interviews. For example, Hammond reports that the effect of adult learning on life satisfaction found in the NCDS cohort analysis was greater for men than for women while women reported themselves in the interviews to be positive about the courses they had taken. On this issue the biographical interviews were regarded as being 'more sensitive' than the quantitative measure. She also suggests that the interview data showed that improved sense of wellbeing in the present was not necessarily incompatible with a negative view of the future. The quantitative data are found wanting in having conflated satisfaction with 'life so far' and with 'life in the future' (see for a similar critique of quantitative data by Brannen and Nilsen, 2007).

Similarly, another finding from the cohort study suggesting marginal benefits to individuals of taking several adult education courses was modified by the earlier qualitative evidence: that taking courses may act as a replacement activity for those who lacked informal support networks, thus balancing out the additional beneficial effects of courses. By contrast, further contradictions are explained in terms of the lack of representativeness of the qualitative study.

One factor that may explain why Hammond took up the contradictions between the survey and interview evidence is the priority she gave to the biographical interviews and the identification of the researcher in question with a qualitative approach (although the latter is not explicitly stated). In any event the biographical interviews were conducted *before* the quantitative analyses and were used to shape which analyses were done in the quantitative part. Hence the qualitative data threw up hypotheses while the quantitative dataset could be used to reject or confirm the qualitative evidence. Another factor perhaps is that the researcher in question had no stake in creating or shaping the quantitative dataset (since these data had already been collected). Indeed while the research design was shaped by the existence of this cohort study, there was no protocol suggesting the ways in which it might be useful in pursuing this programme of research.

However, what is interesting about the rationale given for this iterative use of qualitative work to test quantitative evidence (that in turn may be refuted by the qualitative evidence) is the rationale given: namely the way mixed methods strategy can pose new lines of questioning (Greene et al., 1989) – a result not necessarily anticipated at the outset of the research project.

Conclusions

This chapter considered some issues that shape whether researchers use a mixed methods research strategy and also some that they may wish to take note of in deciding to do so.

In this chapter, I have sidestepped deliberately issues around the commensurality of qualitative with quantitative data (as in notions of triangulation) as contrasted with the separate treatment approach in which it is assumed that the methods address different research questions and the data are seen as irreducible. Such issues are typically discussed in terms of paradigm differences. For example, Smith and Heshusius (1986) take the view that qualitative and quantitative data cannot be combined because they arise from different paradigms. Rather I have started from the standpoint of the researcher, that is from their own 'research habitus' (in Bourdieu's meaning of the term – Bourdieu, 1990), their own biographies, skills, interests and research environments, the kinds of research questions they seek to address, together with the kinds of analyses they expect to generate from their data. The chapter began with reference to my own research biography showing how a qualitative researcher is drawn into mixed methods through force of circumstance while retaining an allegiance to particular types of research question and particular styles of research. It then went on to suggest a number of opportunities posed by mixed methods research strategies which arise in the wider context in which funded research is currently carried out (in the UK), and pointed to the risks as well as the opportunities for researchers' professional development.

The last section of the chapter moved to the project level and the practice of a mixed methods research strategy involving both qualitative and quantitative methods within a single project. It emphasized that assessing the application of a mixed methods strategy is problematic given that methodological reflections and claims take place at the end of the research process when the results are being written up. Three types of studies were considered in relation to the ordering of the methods, the primary identification of the researcher writing about methodological practice, and the dominant assumptions that appeared to influence the work. The three types of mixed methods research considered here appeared to use the different types of data they collected in different ways. In the first group of studies where the quantitative component was dominant, the qualitative data and their manipulation were shaped by the nature of the research questions that were set in the (first) quantitative part of the project. The qualitative data were moreover treated and transformed in effect into quantitative variables and into a quantitative mode with the purpose of fleshing out the explanations required for the quantitative results. While this also seemed to be true in part at least in the study in which equal weight was given to the qualitative phase that preceded the quantitative phase (analysis of a national cohort survey), in this study the discrepancies found in posing similar questions to both the qualitative and quantitative datasets led to further interrogation of both datasets. However, any methodological issues concerning the differences between the methods (in terms of the types of knowledge generated) were downplayed in favour of the new research questions suggested in this process.

In the studies in which the subsidiary quantitative component preceded the qualitative phase, the modalities of the different types of data were maintained and were not treated as commensurate. Instead they were intermeshed in presenting a synthesized analysis in the writing up of the studies (Pawson, 1995). As Moran-Ellis et al. (2006) suggest, this integration of data arising from a mixed methods strategy takes place as part of the *interpretative process*, referred to as 'analytic or interpretative integration'. By contrast, integration in the dominating quantitative mode happens during *data processing* when the data are transformed in ways that allow the researchers to use the data to address the same issue or set of issues.

In conclusion, in considering whether to undertake mixed methods research it is important first of all to take into account the research questions we seek to address. Second, we should take account of our biographies, past and current methodological resources and the *potential* resources available to us and how far these are likely to support the use of such a strategy. The latter should not deter us from trying out different approaches, however. In this latter case, it is therefore important to give due consideration to the building of research teams and research environments in order to engage in mixed methods research strategies. Third, the wider policy and practical context in which research is carried out is an important influence upon the kinds of research that we do and the methods that we use.

Mixed methods research should not be considered a tool kit, a technical fix or belt and braces approach. Mixed methods research is challenging in the justification or research design phase of research and in becoming skilled in different methods. It is also challenging in the discovery phase in which we have to make sense of our data in relation to the questions we sought to ask, the methods used and the type of data generated, and in making claims about our research findings. It requires a great deal of reflectivity throughout the research process.

References

Blatchford, P. (2005) 'A multi-method approach to the study of school class size differences', *International Journal of Social Research Methodology: Theory and Practice*, 8 (3): 195–207.

Blumer, H. (1954) 'What is wrong with sociological theory?', *American Sociological Review*, 19: 3–10.

Bourdieu, P. (1990) *The Logic of Practice*. Cambridge: Polity Press.

Brannen, J. (ed.) (1992) *Mixing Methods: Qualitative and Quantitative Research*. London: Gower.

Brannen, J. (2004) 'Working qualitatively and quantitatively', in C. Seale, G. Gobo, J. Gubrium and D. Silverman (eds), *Qualitative Research Practice*. London: Sage.

Brannen, J. (2005) 'Mixing methods: the entry of qualitative and quantitative approaches into the research process', *International Journal of Social Research Methodology: Theory and Practice*, 8 (3): 173–185.

Brannen, J., Heptinstall, E. and Bhopal, K. (2000) *Connecting Children: Care and Family Life in Later Childhood*. London: Falmer.

Brannen, J. and Nilsen, A. (2007) 'Young people, time horizons and planning: a response to Anderson et al.' *Sociology,* 41: 153–160.

Brannen, J., Statham, J., Mooney, A. and Brockmann, M. (2007) *Coming to Care: The Work and Family Lives of Workers Caring for Vulnerable Children*. Bristol: Policy Press.

Bryman, A. (1988) *Quantity and Quality in Social Research*. London: Unwin Hyman.

Bryman, A. (2004) *Social Research Methods*. Oxford: Oxford University Press.

Bryman, A. (2006) 'Paradigm peace and the implications for quality', *International Journal of Social Research Methodology*, 9: 111–126.

Coffey, A. and Atkinson, P. (1996) *Making Sense of Qualitative Data: Complementary Research Strategies*. London: Sage.

Coser, L. (1975) 'Presidential address: Two methods in search of a substance', *American Sociological Review*, 40 (6): 691–700.

Delamont, S. (2004) 'Ethnography and participant observation', in C. Seale, G. Gobo, J. Gubrium and D. Silverman (eds), *Qualitative Research Practice*. London: Sage.

Fielding, J. and Fielding, N. (2008 in press) 'Ways of mixing qualitative and quantitative data', in P. Alasuutari, L. Bickman and J. Brannen (eds), *The Handbook of Social Research*. London: Sage.

Finch, J. (1986) *Research and Policy: The Uses of Qualitative Methods in Social and Educational Research*. Lewes: Falmer Press.

Greene, J.C., Caracelli, V.J. and Graham, W.F. (1989) 'Toward a conceptual framework for mixed method evaluation designs', *Educational Evaluation and Policy Analysis,* 11: 255–274.

Hammersley, M. (2000) 'Varieties of social research: a typology', *International Journal of Social Research Methodology: Theory and Practice*, 3 (3): 221–229.

Hammond, C. (2005) 'The wider benefits of adult learning: An illustration of multi-method research', *International Journal of Social Research Methodology: Theory and Practice*, 8 (3): 239–257.

Hantrais, L. (2005) 'Combining methods: A key to understanding complexity in European societies?' *European Societies*, 7 (3): 399–421.

Hoyles, C., Kuchemann, D., Healy, L. and Yang, M. (2005) 'Students' developing knowledge in a subject discipline: Insights from combining quantitative and qualitative methods', *International Journal of Social Research Methodology: Theory and Practice*, 8 (3): 207–225.

Kelle, U. (2005) 'Mixed methods as a means to overcome methodological limitations of qualitative and quantitative research'. Paper given at an ESRC Research Methods Programme Seminar on Mixed Methods, Manchester.

Lykes, M. (2001) 'Creative arts and photography in participatory action research in Guatemala', in Reason, P. and Bradbury H. (eds), *Handbook of Action Research: Participative Inquiry*. London: Sage.

Moran-Ellis, J., Alexander, V.D., Cronin, A., Dickinson, M., Fielding, J. Sleney, J. and Thomas, H. (2006) 'Triangulation and integration: processes, claims and implications', *Qualitative Research*, 6 (1): 45–69.

Morse, J. (2003) 'Principles of mixed method design', in A. Tashakkori and C. Teddlie (eds), *Handbook of Mixed Methods in Social and Behavioural Research*. Thousand Oaks: Sage.

Pawson, R. (1995) 'Quality and quantity, agency and structure, mechanism and context, dons and cons', *Bulletin de Methodologie Sociologique*, 47, 4–48.

Platt, J. (1996) *A History of Sociological Methods in America 1920 -1960*. Cambridge: Cambridge University Press.

Platt, J. and Hopper S. (1997) 'Fragmentation, social theory and feminism', *Contemporary Sociology*, 26 (3): 283–285.

Plewis, I. and Mason, P. (2005) 'What works and why: Combining qualitative and quantitative approaches in large-scale evaluations', *International Journal of Social Research Methodology: Theory and Practice*, 8 (3): 185–195.

Reason, P. and Bradbury H. (2001) *Handbook of Action Research: Participative Inquiry*. London: Sage.

Reiss, A.J. (1968) 'Stuff and nonsense about social surveys and participant observation', in H.S. Becker, B. Geer, D. Reisman and R.S. Weiss (eds), *Institutions and Persons: Papers presented to Everett C Hughes*. Chicago: Aldine.

Ritchie, J. (2003) 'The applications of qualitative methods to social research', in J. Ritchie and J. Lewis (eds), *Qualitative Research Practice: A Guide for Social Science Students*. London: Sage.

Sammons, P., Siraj-Blatchford, Sylva, K., Melhuish, E., Taggart, B. and Elliott, K. (2005) 'Investigating the effects of pre-school provision: Using mixed methods in the EPPE research', *International Journal of Social Research Methodology: Theory and Practice*, 8 (3): 207–225.

Smith, J. and Heshusius, L. (1986) 'Closing down the conversation: The end of the quantitative-qualitative debate among educational enquiries', *Educational Research,* 15: 4–12.

Tashakkori, A. and Teddlie, C. (eds) (2003) *Handbook of Mixed Methods in Social and Behavioural Research*. Thousand Oaks: Sage.

Yin, R.K. (2003a) *Case Study Research. Design and Methods*, 3rd edition. London: Sage.

Yin, R.K. (2003b) *Applications of Case Study Research*, 2nd edition. London: Sage.

5

Methodological Issues in Conducting Mixed Methods Research Designs

John W. Creswell, Vicki L. Plano Clark and Amanda L. Garrett

Introduction

A need exists in the mixed methods literature to go beyond the types of designs available to researchers and to begin exploring issues and strategies in conducting these designs. This chapter advances potential concerns that need to be anticipated by researchers in conducting mixed methods research designs. It begins by locating these concerns within two broad categories of designs (i.e. concurrent and sequential designs), identifying potential concerns researchers might anticipate in using these designs, and citing published mixed methods studies that illustrate not only the issues but also potential strategies, expressed or implied, for addressing them. The methodological problems we explore relate to finding contradictory evidence between quantitative and qualitative data, the integration of data, sampling, introducing bias, participant selection, selection of results to use, and the sequence of implementing data. Understanding these issues and exploring alternative strategies to address them will enhance our understanding of mixed methods procedures and encourage rigorous, thoughtful designs.

In the literature on mixed methods research, considerable attention has been directed toward organizing and classifying types of mixed methods designs (e.g. Creswell and Plano Clark, 2007; Greene et al., 1989; Morse, 1991; Tashakkori and Teddlie, 2003). In our review of these classifications, we have located 12 configurations developed by authors from nursing, evaluation, public health, education, and social and behavioral research (Creswell and Plano Clark, 2007). Although the names differ for the types of designs, two characteristics emerge that are common to many classifications: either the purpose of the design is to merge (or bring together) the qualitative and quantitative data in a parallel or concurrent way, or to have one type of data (quantitative or qualitative) build on or extend the other type of data (qualitative or quantitative) in a sequential way. These two major design options seem to hold whether the research is presented as a single study, such as found in many doctoral studies, or in a multi-phase project, such as found in the evaluation literature and in large-scale funded projects.

Our investigations examining the application of mixed methods in many disciplines resulted in the collection of numerous studies that fit into this concurrent or sequential schemata (e.g. in family medicine, Creswell et al., 2004; in counseling psychology, Hanson et al., 2005; in physics education, Plano Clark, 2005; and in family science, Plano Clark et al., in press). As we reviewed these mixed methods studies, we found few authors discussing potential methodological issues that might limit the findings of their studies. Discussing procedural limitations that might influence the outcomes is not new in research methodology or in quantitative or qualitative discussions. For example, in the classic treatise on experimental and quasi-experimental designs, Campbell and Stanley (1966) identified 16 types of designs, and discussed eight threats to internal validity and four threats to external validity. In qualitative research, Jacob (1988) classified the traditions of qualitative research and discussed issues in the traditions, such as the foci of the types and their levels of analysis. In addition, as we presented workshops and discussions about mixed methods research in the U.S. and internationally, participants began raising questions about potential flaws or challenges that might emerge in using different mixed methods designs. Building on these perspectives, we suggest that as mixed methods emerges as a field of study and the types of designs become clearer to researchers, a discussion about the methodological problems likely to arise in implementing these designs and potential strategies that researchers might use to address them is timely.

As we wrote our recent book on mixed methods research (Creswell and Plano Clark, 2007), we began to enumerate some of the challenges that would likely occur in different types of designs. Some methodological problems were mentioned as we discussed each design; others we integrated into the data collection and the data analysis discussions. Although authors have mentioned particular methodological problems, such as sampling and contradictory findings, their work was not centered on particular mixed methods designs (Collins et al., 2006; Erzberger and Kelle, 2003; Kemper et al., 2003; Teddlie and Yu, 2007; Trend, 1979). Thus, there was little information to help us recognize and address the issues inherent in the designs within the mixed methods literature. We did not find any discussions in this literature that directly spoke to these issues, aside from the general comment in Tashakkori and Teddlie (2003) that the design issues and logistics in conducting mixed methods research were two unresolved issues.

The purpose of this chapter is to identify methodological problems and advance potential strategies for planning and conducting mixed methods designs. Our intent is to present a pool of ideas from which researchers can draw in their efforts to overcome methodological problems and craft rigorous studies. To this end, we start with the issues that we specified previously (Creswell and Plano Clark, 2007), issues largely based on conversations with U.S. and international researchers. A useful heuristic for thinking about these methodological problems in designs occurred as we mapped the core ideas for this chapter: to organize the issues and seek out strategies for addressing the issues using designs clustered into concurrent or sequential designs. We therefore organized the issues into distinct themes, related them to either concurrent or sequential designs, and looked extensively in published, empirical mixed methods articles reported in the journal literature, for example that would illustrate the challenges as well as present potential strategies for addressing them. As we reviewed the articles, we were also careful to identify challenges that we had not previously anticipated.

Methodological framework

We discuss in our book four major designs, two of which can be conducted concurrently (Triangulation, Embedded) and three that are conducted sequentially

I. Triangulation Design

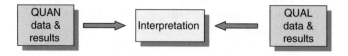

II. Concurrent Embedded Design

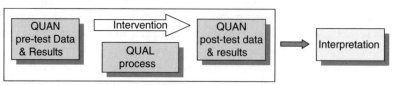

Figure 5.1 Concurrent mixed methods designs

(Explanatory, Exploratory, Embedded) (see Figures 5.1 and 5.2) (Creswell and Plano Clark, 2007).

The Triangulation Design is a one-phase design in which quantitative and qualitative data are collected and analyzed in parallel and then merged together to develop a more complete understanding or to compare the different results. Although this design is the most popular mixed methods design, it is also probably the most challenging of the four major types of designs. Researchers use a second type of concurrent design, an Embedded Design, when they want to enhance a study based on one method by including a secondary dataset from the other method. This design is often used when researchers need to embed a qualitative component during an

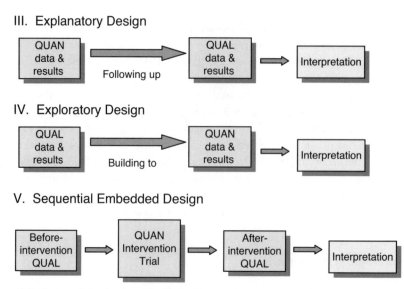

III. Explanatory Design

IV. Exploratory Design

V. Sequential Embedded Design

Figure 5.2 Sequential mixed methods designs

intervention in an experimental study. In this case, the qualitative data are collected concurrent with the implementation of the intervention, and the qualitative information typically focuses on exploring how the experimental participants experience the intervention while the quantitative arm addresses the outcomes of the trial (see Creswell et al., 2006, for additional reasons for embedding qualitative data within experiments).

Turning to the sequential Explanatory, Exploratory and Embedded Designs, the quantitative and qualitative data collection are implemented in different phases and are connected in some way. Researchers use the Explanatory Design when they start with quantitative methods and then follow up with qualitative methods, usually to help explain the initial quantitative results. Researchers using an Exploratory Design begin by exploring the topic with qualitative methods and then build to a second quantitative phase where the initial results may be tested or generalized. The sequential Embedded Design typically involves collecting qualitative data before an intervention begins or after it is complete. When collected before the intervention, researchers use the qualitative data to help recruit participants, to help test the treatment before the actual experiment, or to select participants that can be best suited for the experimental and control conditions. When collected after the intervention, the qualitative data help to explain why different outcomes resulted.

Method

These types of designs provided a framework for analyzing published mixed methods studies. We conducted literature reviews using major databases including ERIC, PsycInfo, and PubMed. We located studies that met our basic criterion of mixed methods research: studies in which the authors collected, analyzed, and merged or connected both quantitative and qualitative approaches of data in a single study or in multiple studies in a program of inquiry (Creswell and Plano Clark, 2007). Next, we classified these studies as either concurrent or sequential designs. To accomplish this we closely examined the articles, paying particular attention to the methods section to determine a) if the authors of the study included both quantitative (i.e. close-ended) and qualitative (i.e. open-ended) data; b) how they integrated both sets of data (either concurrently or sequentially); and c) if they mentioned the type of mixed methods design they were using. Based on these factors, we identified nearly 160 articles spanning the last 15 years. The articles were drawn from fields in the social sciences and the health sciences. Then, we examined two sections of the studies in depth: the methods and the results/discussion sections to find occurrences of methodological issues. We were chiefly interested in determining if the authors mentioned specific issues or challenges in carrying out their designs and whether the authors identified procedures (or strategies) to address the issues. We began to organize the issues and the solutions into a table that would provide practical suggestions for conducting each of the four mixed methods designs and provide researchers with references they could use for their procedures (see Table 5.1). We were also open to identifying issues not in our original schema.

TABLE 5.1 *Problems and strategies for concurrent and sequential designs*

	Challenges	Strategies	References
Concurrent Designs	Contradictory findings	– Help uncover new theories	Erzberger and Kelle (2003)
		– Collect additional data	Creswell (2005)
		– Reanalyze original data	Padgett (2004)
		– Use as springboard for new inquiry	Bryman (1988)
		– Give priority to one form of data	Chesla (1992); Russek and Weinberg (1993)
	Data integration	– Design study to address same topics or questions for both strands	Knodel & Saengtienchai (2005)
		– Transform one type of data to be compared with the other	Caracelli and Greene (1993); Witcher et al. (2001); Crone and Teddlie (1995)
		– Compare using a matrix of both quantitative and qualitative data	McEntarffer (2003); Teno et al. (1998)
	Sampling	– Have same individuals participate in both arms or use a subset of the original sample	Creswell and Plano Clark (2007); Phinney and Devich-Navarro (1997); Capella-Santana (2003)
		– Select sub-sample for qualitative from larger quantitative sample	Hossler and Vesper (1993)
		– Use a small random sample for both strands	Tolman and Szalacha (1999)
		– Use same research sites in both arms	McVea et al. (1996)
		– Use different participants	Whittemore et al. (2000)
		– Have unequal sample sizes in both strands	Hendrix et al. (2001)
		– Enlarge the qualitative sample	Luzzo (1995); Idler et al. (1999)
	Introducing bias	– Collect unobtrusive data during trial	Victor et al. (2004)
		– Sample equally from both experimental and control groups	Creswell and Plano Clark (2007)
		– Postpone qualitative data until after trial	Rogers et al. (2003)
		– Alternate administration of quantitative and qualitative data collection	Luzzo (1995)
Sequential Designs	Sampling	– Select same participants (or subset) to explain initial results (Explanatory Design)	Miller et al. (1998); Way et al. (1994)
		– Select different participants for follow-up when initially exploring (Exploratory Design)	Kutner et al. (1999)
		– Use the same participants but enlarge the quantitative follow-up (Exploratory Design)	Weitzman and Levkoff (2000)

TABLE 5.1 *Problems and strategies for concurrent and sequential designs*—cont'd

	Challenges	Strategies	References
	Participant selection	– Use criteria for participant selection (Explanatory Design), such as building on significant results, non-significant results, outliers, extreme cases, strong predictors, distinguishing demographics or individuals from different comparison groups, or some combination	Creswell and Plano Clark (2007); Way et al. (1994); Thøgersen-Ntoumani and Fox (2005); Ivankova et al. (2006)
		– Follow up with volunteers (Explanatory Design)	Baumann (1999)
	Selection of results to use	– Use quotes, codes, themes from first phase in follow-up instrument development (Exploratory Design)	Creswell and Plano Clark (2007)
		– Use rigorous procedures to demonstrate psychometric properties	Tashiro (2002); DeVellis (1991)
		– Use same domains of interests in both strands	Weitzman and Levkoff (2000)
	Implementing qualitative data collection	– Collect qualitative data before intervention (Embedded Design)	Donovan et al. (2002)
		– Collect qualitative data after intervention (Embedded Design)	Rogers et al. (2003)
	Contradictory findings	– Identify and discuss them	Umberson (1995)
		– Add additional data collection phase to the study	Waysman & Savaya (1997)
All Designs	Skills to conduct mixed methods studies	– Use a research team with skilled members	Shulha & Wilson (2003); Weitzman & Levkoff (2000)
		– Have all members trained in both qualitative and quantitative	Miall & March (2005a)
	Length of time to conduct studies	– Have one phase as less of a priority than the other phase	Creswell (2003)
		– Collect both strands of data on single questionnaire	Webb et al. (2002)
	Accommodating funders	– Change design to preferred approach of funding agency	Miall & March (2005b)

Examples of issues and strategies

Our search of the literature yielded several issues and numerous strategies either implied or expressed by authors. We discuss these issues and strategies for both concurrent and sequential designs, providing examples drawn from the examined studies.

Concurrent design issues and strategies

We begin with a discussion of the concurrent designs and explore how authors of published mixed methods articles addressed contradictory findings, integrated or combined the quantitative and qualitative data, chose participants for the samples and the size of the samples, and limited the potential bias of data collection in their designs.

Contradictory findings

This issue may emerge during a concurrent type of design when the quantitative and qualitative results do not agree. Disconfirming findings may indicate flaws or inconsistencies in the research design. Erzberger and Kelle (2003) explain that discrepancies between quantitative and qualitative data may be the result of researcher's errors in data collection and analysis or poor application of theoretical propositions. Divergent findings, however, can also be thought of as a means to uncovering new theories or extending existing theories.

Disagreement between the quantitative and qualitative strands may be a minor or a major difference in the results. These differences may be difficult to resolve and may require the collection of additional data to resolve the differences (Creswell, 2005). This strategy, however, raises a further question about what type of additional data will be needed, analyzed, or given priority.

Padgett's (2004) study recounts how a team of researchers returned to their initial database for more insights after contradictory findings emerged. This occurred during the Harlem Mammogram Study, which was funded by the National Cancer Institute to examine factors that influenced delay in response to an abnormal mammogram among African-American women living in New York City. The research team had collected both structured quantitative data and open-ended interview data. After data analyses, the team concluded that the women's decisions to delay were not driven by factors in their quantitative model. The researchers then turned to their qualitative data, highlighted two qualitative themes, and reexamined their quantitative database for support for the themes. To their surprise, the quantitative data confirmed what the participants had said. This new information, in turn, led to a further exploration of the literature, in which they found some confirmation for the new findings. Used in this way, researchers could also view the contradiction as a springboard for new directions of inquiry (Bryman, 1988).

To resolve contradictory findings, authors may also give priority to one form of data over the other. Chesla (1992) advised comparing the data from each strand by 'weighing the evidence' and deciding on priority by determining which method was more fully developed (p. 684). Russek and Weinberg (1993) prioritized their data in their study of the use of technology materials within elementary school classrooms. These authors measured teachers' anxiety levels in implementing lessons involving calculators and computers through quantitative questionnaire data and qualitative interviews and observations. When these data were evaluated, the results from the two strands were inconsistent. The authors reported that the two forms of qualitative data had more validity than the one quantitative measure.

Data integration

It can be challenging to integrate two sets of different forms of data and their results in a meaningful way (Bryman, 2007). Erzberger and Kelle (2003) offer researchers a series of guidelines on the integration of two strands of data. Based on studies in the literature, three strategies are used to integrate data: (1) designing and implementing comparable topics or questions for both arms; (2) transforming the data so that it can be more easily compared; and (3) using matrices to organize both sets of data into one table.

The first strategy is to design both the quantitative and qualitative strands of the study to address the same questions or concepts. In their effort to merge and corroborate two distinct datasets in a triangulation design, Knodel and Saengtienchai (2005) offered a solution to facilitate data comparison. These authors studied the caregiving and support systems available to adults with HIV or AIDS in Thailand between adult children and their older parents. Both quantitative and qualitative data were collected through the administration of structured, closed-ended surveys, and open-ended interviews with parents. The qualitative data permitted elaboration of the quantitative survey measures. In order to simplify the merging of the qualitative and quantitative data, these authors utilized a range of comparable question topics (health insurance, welfare assistance, parental caregiving, support from others, economic support, and care of the children orphaned by AIDS) for both strands of the study. In this way, the authors were better able to integrate the two sets of data.

A second data-integration strategy is to transform one form of data so that it can be more easily compared with the other form (Caracelli and Greene, 1993). In general, it is more intuitive for researchers to quantify their qualitative data by transformation than to transform their quantitative data into qualitative data. Witcher et al. (2001) transformed their qualitative data into quantitative results in a study of pre-service teachers' perceptions of characteristics of effective teachers by counting themes and calculating frequencies or 'endorsement rates' (p. 49). In this way, the authors determined which themes were more commonly mentioned by teachers in their study. Crone and Teddlie (1995) carry this idea a step further by quantifying their qualitative themes and then conducting statistical analyses on these data. These researchers gathered data from teachers and administrators and then computed chi square tests on the themes in order to compare data from schools with varying levels of effectiveness.

Another method for merging quantitative and qualitative data is to develop a matrix that combines the information. The study by McEntarffer (2003) explored how 16 undergraduates in teacher education (eight junior-senior mentors and eight freshman mentees) developed positive working relationships. Qualitative data collection consisting of documents, interviews, and observations led to three qualitative themes. In addition, the researcher collected quantitative information on individual strengths of the students through the StrengthsFinder instrument, developed by The Gallup Organization (Clifton and Anderson, 2002). McEntarffer created a matrix that combined both forms of data by comparing individuals with certain personal strengths with the qualitative themes that had been reported. In another study by Teno et al. (1998), the authors sought to understand the barriers and aids of living wills in decision-making for hospitalized, seriously ill adults. They collected quantitative data from medical record reviews and structured interviews with patients, their surrogates, and physicians and qualitative data from narratives written by intervention nurses. They identified 14 cases for analysis and reported, in tables, information that included both qualitative and quantitative data. They described the case in the first column (i.e. male, age 65, with non-Hodgkin's lymphoma), provided quotes in the second column to indicate the barriers and aids of the living wills (i.e. caused minor problems), and then reported quantitative scores for the patients (i.e. a comatose score, length of days in the hospital, and days in the intensive care unit (ICU)). In this way, they combined both qualitative and quantitative profiles of cases in a single table.

Sampling

Researchers need to consider the consequences of having different samples and different sample sizes when merging quantitative and qualitative datasets (Creswell and Plano Clark, 2007). Different sample sizes are common in mixed methods designs because quantitative and qualitative data are usually collected for different purposes. Strategies for addressing sample selection and size issues in concurrent designs are to (a) use the same individuals in both samples or (b) collect large qualitative samples for comparison with the large quantitative samples.

When selecting samples in a concurrent design, it is preferred to have the same individuals participate in both samples in order to make the data and results more comparable (Creswell and Plano Clark, 2007). There are ample illustrations of the use of the same individuals or sites in Triangulation and concurrent Embedded Designs. Phinney and Devich-Navarro (1997) used the same participants in both strands of their triangulation study of bicultural identification for African-American and Mexican-American adolescents. The authors administered questionnaires and conducted interviews with their entire sample (N=98). In a convergence study of teacher candidates' multicultural attitudes and knowledge, Capella-Santana (2003) gathered quantitative questionnaire data from 90 undergraduate elementary education teacher candidates. She also invited all participants to be interviewed 'to corroborate the information obtained through the questionnaires' (p. 185). Although the author of this study may have sought to use the entire sample, only a few teachers chose to participate in the interviews (N=9). Hossler and Vesper (1993), in their research on parental saving behaviors for postsecondary education, offered yet another sampling strategy in which the same participants are utilized. These authors reported selecting a sub-sample of qualitative participants (N=56) from a larger, longitudinal sample (N=4923) in order to compare their data. While the quantitative survey data were used to identify the factors associated with parental saving, the qualitative data (multiple interviews with parents and students) allowed for a more detailed description of these behaviors and plans and how they changed through time. Tolman and Szalacha (1999) also employed the same participants in their study of female adolescent sexuality. These authors opted to use one small random sample (N=30) with the knowledge that their data would be subjected to both quantitative and qualitative analyses. Furthermore, the authors' choice of sample size for this study was unique. They selected this sample size because it would allow for both detailed descriptions and statistical analysis. The authors described their choice of sample size as 'an important compromise in the overall study design' (p. 35). McVea et al. (1996) evaluated family practices that had adopted prevention materials in a Triangulation Design. They gathered both quantitative data (e.g. using a structured observation checklist) and qualitative data (e.g. through key informant interviews) from the same eight practices (or research sites). Another strategy is to use different participants. For example, in a concurrent Embedded Intervention Design, Whittemore et al. (2000) studied how social support from peer advisors decreased complications following myocardial infarction through a randomized controlled trial. Within this larger trial, the authors also qualitatively explored the perceptions of peer advising. Data were collected during the trial from 10 peer advisors providing social support to 45 myocardial infarction patients. The 10 peer advisors were not subjects in the trial but were individuals providing the intervention during the trial.

Turning more directly to the question of sample size, one approach is to have unequal sample sizes in the quantitative and qualitative strands of a study for the purpose of providing a full picture of the situation. An example of unequal sample sizes was found in the multi-level mixed methods study on co-therapy by Hendrix et al. (2001). These authors collected quantitative outcome data from 402 clients and qualitative, focus group data from 12 therapists about their experiences. Both forms of data from the two distinct samples contributed to a fuller depiction of the effects of a co-therapy arrangement for both clients and student therapists.

An example of enlarging the qualitative sample size was found in Luzzo's (1995) triangulation study. His quantitative sample consisted of 401 students and his qualitative sample consisted of 128 of those 401 students, a large number for interviews or for establishing any depth of detail from any single student. Idler et al. (1999) also included a large qualitative sample in their study of participants' self-ratings of health. Their study was distinctive in that they gathered information from a single sample (N = 159) for both their quantitative (medical history survey) and qualitative data (ethnographic interviews). Undoubtedly, collecting qualitative data from such a large sample is time and labor intensive. These authors, however, inform us of the 'feasibility of obtaining detailed qualitative data ... that are of sufficient size for statistical analysis' (p. 474).

Introducing bias

If data are collected concurrently, will one form of data bias the other? In all of the concurrent data collection procedures, it is possible that one form of data might introduce bias that would confound the results from the other form of data if collected from the same participants. Bias can be a particular problem in intervention trials in which the investigators introduce a qualitative arm during the trial. One approach to address this issue is to collect unobtrusive qualitative data. This was the approach used by Victor et al. (2004) in an intervention trial of individuals with osteoarthritis of the knee. They asked individuals in the intervention group to maintain diaries during the intervention to review their symptoms, use of medication, and goals for treatment during the trial. The investigators then collected these diaries after the intervention and reviewed them. Another strategy could include sampling equally from both the experimental and control groups so that the potential bias is the same across groups (Creswell and Plano Clark, 2007). In some cases investigators might postpone the qualitative data collection until after the intervention and employ a sequential design of data collection to avoid introducing bias or alternate the order that participants completed the quantitative and qualitative data collection (Luzzo, 1995).

Sequential design issues and strategies

For the sequential designs, the methodological issues relate to selecting a sample, to building on results, to implementing forms of data collection, and to resolving contradictions.

Sampling

In a sequential design, the issue arises as to whether the same or different participants need to be selected for the two phases of the project. Further, the question arises as to whether the number of participants will be the same or different for the two phases. On the issue of sample size, the sizes of the quantitative and qualitative samples may be unequal given the nature of quantitative research to generalize to a population whereas the qualitative sample is to provide an in-depth understanding of a small group of individuals. Further, since the two samples are not being directly compared as in concurrent designs, the sample sizes in a sequential design do not need to be of equal sizes (Creswell and Plano Clark, 2007).

Turning to the issue of using the same or different participants, researchers need to consider the intent of the sequential design. If the intent of the study is for the second phase to help explain the first phase (Explanatory Design), then a strategy would be to select the same or a subset of the participants from the initial, quantitative phase for the second qualitative follow-up phase. In the Explanatory Design study by Miller et al. (1998), the authors collected data from the same pairs of alternatively and traditionally prepared teachers in both the quantitative and qualitative phases of the study. In the study of depression and substance use in high schools, Way et al. (1994) followed up in the qualitative stage of their Explanatory Design with a subset of students who had completed the quantitative questionnaire used in the initial data collection stage of the study. In contrast, when Exploratory Designs are used, the individuals in the first stage of data collection are typically not the same participants as those in the second stage. Because the purpose of the second, quantitative phase is to generalize the results to a population; different and more participants are used in the second phase. In their study on the information needs of terminally ill patients, Kutner et al. (1999) conducted interviews with 22 terminally ill patients in the first phase and administered a quantitative instrument to a second, distinct population of 56 patients in the second phase. Another strategy is to enlarge the qualitative sample to have an adequate number of participants for statistical analysis for a follow-up quantitative phase. Weitzman and Levkoff (2000) offered yet another solution for selecting participants in their exploratory study of health research on minority elders, to use the same core sample of participants in both arms of the study. These authors then added to their original qualitative sample of 40 to arrive at a larger quantitative sample of 120.

Participant selection

In a two-phase project in which the second phase builds on the first, the issue arises as to how to select participants for the second phase. Many options emerge for selecting participants for the second phase. Even when researchers carefully consider various options, limitations in choosing participants may still exist. There may be ethical dilemmas and other challenges that hinder selection of participants such as a need to protect the anonymity of participants from the first phase or unknown participant identities from anonymous survey data (Leahey, 2007; Ting et al., 2006).

In an Explanatory Design, the researcher needs to determine which quantitative results from the first phase will be the basis for selecting participants in the second, qualitative phase. Selection can be based on identifying qualitative participants using significant quantitative results, unexpected non-significant quantitative results, outliers, extreme cases, strong predictors in a correlational study, distinguishing demographic characteristics, or individuals from different comparison groups. Way et al. (1994) found suburban and urban high school students to differ in their depression and substance use scores. They used this quantitative result as a basis for studying in qualitative follow-up interviews with students in the top 10% of depression scores from both types of schools.

Researchers may also choose participants based on a combination of strategies building on the results. In their Explanatory study, Thøgersen-Ntoumani and Fox (2005) decided to include participants based on self-interest (as indicated from the first phase), cluster (self-assured, unhappy, exercising happy, physically unhappy), and demographic characteristics in their research on physical activity and mental health among corporate employees. Ivankova et al. (2006) also utilized multiple levels of selection in a study of persistence in a distance-learning program among doctoral students. These authors chose one participant from each of the four groups (beginning, matriculated, graduated, withdrawn) and then applied maximal variation sampling strategies to include participants with a wide variety of demographic features.

Aside from examining the results as a basis for participant selection, another strategy is to follow up with individuals who volunteer to participate. For these volunteers, the questions in the qualitative interviews, for example could probe the quantitative findings in more depth. In an Explanatory Design study of adoptive fathers and birthfathers, Baumann (1999) simply asked the fathers completing the questionnaire whether they would be interested in being interviewed for the follow-up qualitative arm of the study.

Selection of results to use

Researchers using an Exploratory Design need to determine what results from the qualitative first phase exploration to use in the second, follow-up quantitative phase. One instance in which this situation arises is where the researcher wants to use the first, qualitative phase to explore in order to develop an instrument that will be tested with a large sample of a population. What results do mixed methods researchers use from the initial exploratory phase when they want to develop an instrument for measurement?

One strategy for instrument development is to analyze the qualitative findings and identify key quotes, form codes, and then group the codes into themes. The procedure for constructing an instrument entails using the quotes as items on the instrument, the codes as variables, and the themes as scales (Creswell and Plano Clark, 2007). Another approach is to employ a rigorous set of procedures recommended for designing a sound psychometric instrument so that scores will be reliable and valid. Tashiro (2002), in a cross-cultural study of the lifestyle behaviors of Japanese college women, used detailed procedures to develop her instrument. She began by collecting qualitative focus group data. She formed a questionnaire using data from the focus groups, as well as from other unpublished sources. The focus group participants were then asked to evaluate the clarity of the questions, and the resulting questionnaire was used in a pilot test with participants similar to those in the study. The questionnaire's content was validated by a number of research experts and checked for inter-item reliability and test-retest reliability. These procedures closely follow those recommended by DeVellis (1991) for designing an instrument with solid psychometric properties. Another way to facilitate the development of a valid instrument using an Exploratory Design is to use the same general topics for both the qualitative and quantitative inquiries. Weitzman and Levkoff (2000) utilized the same 'domains of interest' (p. 198) to develop and tailor a protocol (consisting of a battery of instruments) through qualitative techniques for four cultural/ethnic groups in a study of health among minority elders.

Implementing qualitative data collection

Issues with implementing data collection arise in all forms of sequential Embedded Designs in which the researcher needs to place qualitative data within the context of a largely quantitative intervention design (or quantitative data within a largely qualitative design). Does the researcher collect qualitative data before the trial (the quantitative phase) begins or after the trial concludes? One answer to this question is to consider the purposes for collecting the qualitative data. Donovan et al. (2002) provided an example of embedded qualitative data before a randomized controlled trial of men and prostate cancer. They decided to gather the qualitative data before the trial so that they could better recruit men to a trial on a sensitive topic. They interviewed men after they received results of their prostate tests and before their randomization to different treatment groups in the experiment. In this way, they enhanced their recruitment efforts for different treatment conditions by learning what issues might arise for the men when considering whether to participate in the study. An example of an after-trial Embedded Design comes from Rogers et al. (2003). They conducted a randomized controlled trial of two interventions to improve the management of anti-psychotic medication. After the trial, they followed up by collecting qualitative data to better understand the quantitative results. They selected individuals after the experiment who had scored positively and negatively on the major outcomes measures and they were able to learn about the effectiveness of the interventions. Thus, in these two examples, we learn that a secondary data source can be embedded sequentially within a larger study and that the issue of when to collect the supporting data will vary depending on its purposes in a study.

Contradictory findings

Contradictory findings may also emerge in Exploratory and Explanatory Designs when the data are inconclusive or in opposition to each other. There are several strategies researchers can use to address divergent results in sequential studies. One strategy in addressing conflicting findings in sequential studies is to identify and discuss them. By clearly articulating these differing results, researchers can open new avenues of research. This is the approach Umberson (1995) adopted in her Explanatory study of marital quality after the death of a parent. This author found the qualitative data she collected did not address aspects of the quantitative data it was to explain. She discovered that, while parental death was related to negative partner behaviors in the quantitative analysis, this was not found as a theme in the qualitative data. Although she did not explore this discrepancy in her data further, she suggests that more direct questions regarding the topic of negative behaviors be included in future studies on filial bereavement.

Authors advance other ideas for attending to discrepant findings, including adding an additional phase to the study in order to obtain a comprehensive, inclusive set of results. Waysman and Savaya (1997) utilized this idea in their exploratory evaluation of a nonprofit agency. These authors began with interviews and focus groups in order to construct survey questions which were used to measure outcomes. Above and beyond these two techniques, these authors implemented a third phase, consisting of focus groups, in order to explain the divergent responses to the instrument. This final phase centered on the outcomes (satisfaction and dissatisfaction) with the agency. Two focus groups, composed of participants with extreme scores (those most and least satisfied with the nonprofit agency as indicated by their responses to the instrument) were conducted. Each group discussed specific factors which contributed to their respective perception of the agency.

Other design-related issues

As we reviewed the studies, several challenges surfaced that did not fit into our list of nine concurrent and sequential issues. These were the findings that skills in both quantitative and qualitative research are needed to appropriately conduct studies, that some designs are more time-consuming than others, and that researchers may need to accommodate funding agencies in the designs of their studies.

Skills to conduct mixed methods research

Mixed methods research requires that individual researchers have expertise in both quantitative and qualitative research, or that they join a team with diverse expertise in both areas. Shulha and Wilson (2003) discussed the concept of team or collaborative mixed methods research. These authors offer a definition, rubric, and example cases for conducting collaborative mixed methods research projects. Collaboration may be especially important in a concurrent type of design in which both strands (quantitative and qualitative) go forward at the same time. Without combining expertise, there is the inclination of investigators to use either quantitative or qualitative in isolation rather than in combining 'differing methodological viewpoints' (Weitzman and Levkoff, 2000: 205). Several studies have made the recommendation that the research team be composed of individuals with high levels of expertise in quantitative and qualitative methods, respectively (Weitzman and Levkoff, 2000). In this way, there is a combination of skills from which to draw upon (Waysman and Savaya, 1997). Miall and March (2005a) suggested that graduate students working on the research project have training in both quantitative and qualitative traditions. Thus, it may be important for all members of the research team to have some training in both methods. Without such diverse skills, the mixed methods project, already requiring extensive time to complete, should be slowly implemented (Waysman and Savaya, 1997).

Length of time to conduct studies

The sequential designs especially require extensive time to conduct because the procedures are sequenced over two or more phases. One strategy to address this is to not treat both phases (assuming two phases) as equal in treatment (Creswell, 2005). An initial large survey in the first phase can be followed by a smaller qualitative phase consisting of three or four interviews. This unequal treatment of phases is especially helpful to graduate students with limited time to conduct their masters theses and doctoral dissertations. Another strategy to address time constraints is to substitute an open-ended questionnaire to elicit qualitative responses rather than to conduct face-to-face or phone interviews. This was the approach used by Webb et al. (2002) in their study of the psychological effects of mass casualty events on those in the forensic odontology field.

Accommodating funders

Another challenge to using a particular mixed methods design is that it may not be the preferred approach of the funding agency. In Miall and March (2005b), the authors made a comment in a footnote on sampling about changing their entire research design. At the outset, the authors wanted to pursue an Explanatory Design, but they were compelled to use an Exploratory Design by their funding agency. 'We had intended to draw an interview sample from the larger telephone survey. In reviewing our research proposal, the funding agency mandated a qualitative study followed by a survey' (p. 407).

Discussion

In this chapter, we attempted to identify and discuss issues and potential strategies that authors might use when they conduct mixed methods designs. To discuss these challenges, we found it useful to categorize the designs into concurrent and sequential designs. A review of many concurrent and sequential published studies indicated that authors did not tend to specifically mention or reflect on the types of issues they may have encountered in implementing their studies. We did find, however, limited evidence in the methods discussions and the limitation sections of the studies that issues were present. Even more elusive were the identification of strategies for how to address these methodological problems. Thus, we began to examine the published articles using issues that we developed in our discussion of different types of designs (Creswell and Plano Clark, 2007), and we sought to enlarge our understanding through careful inspection of published mixed methods studies.

This review resulted in a more expanded list of potential issues and strategies for addressing them. Looking across the issues we found, it now appears that there is some overlap between concurrent and sequential designs. In both types of designs, the potential of contradictory findings exists as well as issues related to sample selection and sample size. Other issues, however, were unique to the type of designs, such as the bias issue that tends to surface during concurrent designs and when qualitative data might be used during sequential intervention trials. We did not find certain strategies that we had expected to find, such as the case of unequal sample sizes in a concurrent design where the qualitative cases were weighted to enhance the numbers of participants or where unequal sample sizes were reported as a limitation in the study. Also, issues about the skills of the team members and the pressure from funding agencies to adopt specific designs were not anticipated prior to our study.

Still, as shown in Table 5.1, we identified many strategies that might be considered by researchers conducting concurrent and sequential mixed methods designs.

The methodological issues and strategies we reviewed are not an exhaustive list of possibilities but are meant to provide a starting point for future discussion. Simple strategies for addressing these methodological challenges are not easily applied or recommended (Chesla, 1992). Researchers must display ingenuity in building customized solutions to their methodological dilemmas using their research experiences. We based our analysis on the major types of designs we have advanced in our writings, and on the mixed methods studies we had gathered. Other published studies would undoubtedly reveal additional challenges and strategies that would add to the methodological complexity of potential considerations for researchers to contemplate.

Based on our findings, however, we encourage mixed methods researchers to write about methodological problems and detail their strategies for addressing them. Further, they need to consider that options exist for addressing these issues, and that by stating the issues and their approaches, they help readers plan and conduct mixed methods studies. With such discussion and that found in this chapter, we foreground methodological issues that relate to mixed methods designs and point readers in the direction of discussing these strategies. In this way, we hope to advance the mixed method literature beyond the available research designs and into the complexities of conducting the designs.

References

Baumann, C. (1999) 'Adoptive fathers and birthfathers: A study of attitudes', *Child and Adolescent Social Work Journal,* 16 (5): 373–391.

Bryman, A. (1988) *Quantity and Quality in Social Research.* London: Routledge.

Bryman, A. (2007) 'Barriers to integrating quantitative and qualitative research', *Journal of Mixed Methods Research,* 1 (1): 8–22.

Campbell, D.T. and Stanley, J.C. (1966) 'Experimental and quasi-experimental designs for research on teaching', in N.L. Gage (ed.), *Handbook of Research on Teaching.* Chicago: Rand McNally. pp. 1–80.

Capella-Santana, N. (2003) 'Voices of teacher candidates: Positive changes in multicultural attitudes and knowledge', *Journal of Educational Research,* 96 (3): 182–190.

Caracelli, V.J. and Greene, J.C. (1993) 'Data analysis strategies for mixed-method evaluation designs', *Educational Evaluation and Policy Analysis,* 15 (2): 195–207.

Chesla, C.A. (1992) 'When qualitative and quantitative findings do not converge', *Western Journal of Nursing Research,* 14 (5): 681–685.

Clifton, D. and Anderson, E. (2002) *StrengthsQuest: Discover and Develop your Strengths in Academics, Career, and Beyond.* Washington, DC: The Gallup Organization.

Collins, K.M.T., Onwuegbuzie, A.J. and Jiao, Q.G. (2006) 'Prevalence of mixed methods sampling designs in social science research and beyond'. Paper presented at the meeting of the American Educational Research Association, San Francisco, CA.

Creswell, J.W. (2003) *Research Design: Qualitative, Quantitative, and Mixed Methods Approaches,* 2nd edition. Thousand Oaks, CA: Sage.

Creswell, J.W. (2005) *Educational Research: Planning, Conducting, and Evaluating Quantitative and Qualitative Research,* 2nd edition. Upper Saddle River, NJ: Merrill.

Creswell, J.W., Fetters, M.D. and Ivankova, N.V. (2004) 'Designing a mixed methods study in primary care', *Annals of Family Medicine,* 2 (1): 7–12.

Creswell, J.W. and Plano Clark, V.L. (2007) *Designing and Conducting Mixed Methods Research.* Thousand Oaks, CA: Sage.

Creswell, J.W., Shope, R., Plano Clark, V.L. and Green, D.O. (2006) 'How interpretive qualitative research extends mixed methods research', *Research in the Schools,* 13 (1): 1–11.

Crone, L. and Teddlie, C. (1995) 'Further examination of teacher behavior in differentially effective schools: Selection and socialization processes', *Journal of Classroom Interaction*, 30 (1): 1–9.

DeVellis, R.F. (1991) *Scale Development: Theory and Application*. Newbury Park, CA: Sage.

Donovan, J., Mills, N., Lucy, B., Frankel, S., Smith, M., Jacoby, A., et al. (2002) 'Improving design and conduct of randomised trials by embedding them in qualitative research: Protect (prostate testing for cancer and treatment) study', *British Medical Journal*, 325 (7367): 765–768.

Erzberger, C. and Kelle, U. (2003) 'Making inferences in mixed methods: The rules of integration', in A. Tashakkori and C. Teddlie (eds), *Handbook of Mixed Methods in Social and Behavioral Research*. Thousand Oaks, CA: Sage. pp. 457–490.

Greene, J.C., Caracelli, V.J. and Graham, W.F. (1989) 'Toward a conceptual framework for mixed-method evaluation designs', *Educational Evaluation and Policy Analysis*, 11 (3): 255–274.

Hanson, W.E., Creswell, J.W., Plano Clark, V.L., Petska, K.P. and Creswell, J.D. (2005) 'Mixed methods research designs in counseling psychology', *Journal of Counseling Psychology*, 52 (2): 224–235.

Hendrix, C.C., Fournier, D.G. and Briggs, K. (2001) 'Impact of co-therapy teams on client outcomes and therapist training in marriage and family therapy', *Contemporary Family Therapy*, 23 (1): 63–82.

Hossler, D. and Vesper, N. (1993) 'An exploratory study of the factors associated with parental saving for postsecondary education', *Journal of Higher Education*, 64 (2): 140–165.

Idler, E.L., Hudson, S.V. and Leventhal, H. (1999) 'The meanings of self-ratings of health', *Research on Aging*, 21 (3): 458–476.

Ivankova, N.V., Creswell, J.W. and Stick, S.L. (2006) 'Using mixed-methods sequential explanatory design: From theory to practice', *Field Methods*, 18 (1): 3–20.

Jacob, E. (1988) 'Clarifying qualitative research: A focus on traditions', *Educational Researcher*, 17 (1): 16–24.

Kemper, E., Stringfield. S. and Teddlie, C. (2003) 'Mixed methods sampling strategies in social science research', in A. Tashakkori and C. Teddlie (eds), *Handbook of Mixed Methods in Social and Behavioral Research*. Thousand Oaks, CA: Sage. pp. 273–296.

Knodel, J. and Saengtienchai, C. (2005) 'Older-aged parents: The final safety net for adult sons and daughters with AIDS in Thailand', *Journal of Family Issues*, 26 (5): 665–698.

Kutner, J.S., Steiner, J.F., Corbett, K.K., Jahnigen, D.W. and Barton, P.L. (1999) 'Information needs in terminal illness', *Social Science and Medicine*, 48: 1341–1352.

Leahey, E. (2007) 'Convergence and conwdentiality? Limits to the implementation of mixed methodology', *Social Science Research*, 36: 149–158.

Luzzo, D.A. (1995) 'Gender differences in college students' career maturity and perceived barriers in career development', *Journal of Counseling and Development*, 73: 319–322.

McEntarffer, R. (2003) *Strengths-Based Mentoring in Teacher Education: A Mixed Methods Study*. Unpublished Master's thesis, University of Nebraska, Lincoln.

McVea, K., Crabtree, B.F., Medder, J.D., Susman, J.L., Lukas, L., McIlvain, H.E., et al. (1996) 'An ounce of prevention? Evaluation of the 'put prevention into practice' program', *Journal of Family Practice*, 43 (4): 361–369.

Miall, C.E. and March, K. (2005a) 'Community attitudes toward birth fathers' motives for adoption placement and single parenting', *Family Relations*, 54 (4): 535–546.

Miall, C.E. and March, K. (2005b) 'Open adoption as a family form', *Journal of Family Issues*, 26 (3): 380–410.

Miller, J.W., McKenna, M.C. and McKenna, B.A. (1998) 'A comparison of alternatively and traditionally prepared teachers', *Journal of Teacher Education*, 49: 165–176.

Morse, J.M. (1991) 'Approaches to qualitative-quantitative methodological triangulation', *Nursing Research*, 40: 120–123.

Padgett, D.K. (2004) 'Mixed methods, serendipity, and concatenation', in D.K. Padgett (ed.), *The Qualitative Research Experience*. Belmont, CA: Wadsworth/Thomson Learning. pp. 273–288.

Phinney, J.S. and Devich-Navarro, M. (1997) 'Variations in bicultural identification among African American and Mexican American adolescents', *Journal of Research on Adolescence*, 7 (1): 3–32.

Plano Clark, V.L. (2005) 'Cross-disciplinary analysis of the use of mixed methods in physics education research, counseling psychology, and primary care. Doctoral dissertation, University of Nebraska-Lincoln, 2005', *Dissertation Abstracts International*, 66: 02A.

Plano Clark, V.L., Huddleston-Casas, C.A., Churchill, S.L., Green, D.O. and Garrett, A.L. (in press) *Mixed Methods Approaches Implemented in Family Science Research*. *Journal of Family Issues*.

Rogers, A., Day, J., Randall, F. and Bentall, R.P. (2003) 'Patients' understanding and participation in a trial designed to improve the management of anti-psychotic medication: A qualitative study', *Social Psychiatry & Psychiatric Epidemiology*, 38 (12): 720–727.

Russek, B.E. and Weinberg, S.L. (1993) 'Mixed methods in a study of implementation of technology-based materials in the elementary classroom', *Evaluation and Program Planning*, 16: 131–142.

Shulha, L. and Wilson, R. (2003) 'Collaborative mixed methods research', in A. Tashakkori and C. Teddlie (eds), *Handbook of Mixed Methods in Social and Behavioral Research*. Thousand Oaks, CA: Sage. pp. 639–670.

Tashakkori, A. and Teddlie, C. (eds) (2003) *Handbook of Mixed Methods in Social and Behavioral Research*. Thousand Oaks, CA: Sage.

Tashiro, J. (2002) 'Exploring health promoting lifestyle behaviors of Japanese college women: Perceptions, practices, and issues', *Health Care for Women International*, 23: 59–70.

Teddlie, C. and Yu, F. (2007) 'Mixed methods sampling: A typology with examples', *Journal of Mixed Methods Research*, 1 (1): 77–100.

Teno, J.M., Stevens, M., Spernak, S. and Lynn, J. (1998) 'Role of written advance directives in decision making', *Journal of General Internal Medicine*, 13 (7): 439–446.

Thøgersen-Ntoumani, C. and Fox, K.R. (2005) 'Physical activity and mental well-being typologies in corporate employees: A mixed methods approach', *Work & Stress*, 19 (1): 50–67.

Ting, L., Sanders, S., Jacobson, J.M. and Power, J.R. (2006) 'Dealing with the aftermath: A qualitative analysis of mental health social workers' reactions after a client suicide', *Social Work*, 51 (4): 329–341.

Tolman, D.L. and Szalacha, L.A. (1999) 'Dimensions of desire', *Psychology of Women Quarterly*, 23 (1): 7–39.

Trend, M.G. (1979) 'On the reconciliation of qualitative and quantitative analyses: A case study', in T.D. Cook and C.S. Reichardt (eds), *Qualitative and Quantitative Methods in Program Evaluation*. Thousand Oaks CA: Sage. pp. 68–85.

Umberson, D. (1995) 'Marriage as support or strain? Marital quality following the death of a parent', *Journal of Marriage and Family*, 57: 709–723.

Victor, C.R., Ross, F. and Axford, J. (2004) 'Capturing lay perspectives in a randomized control trial of a health promotion intervention for people with osteoarthritis of the knee', *Journal of Evaluation in Clinical Practice*, 10 (1): 63–70.

Way, N., Stauber, H.Y., Nakkula, M.J. and London, P. (1994) 'Depression and substance use in two divergent high school cultures: A quantitative and qualitative analysis', *Journal of Youth and Adolescence*, 23 (3): 331–357.

Waysman, M. and Savaya, R. (1997) 'Mixed method evaluation: A case study', *Evaluation Practice*, 18 (3): 227–338.

Webb, D.A., Sweet, D. and Pretty, I.A. (2002) 'The emotional and psychological impact of mass casualty incidents on forensic odontologists', *Journal of Forensic Sciences*, 47 (3): 539–541.

Weitzman, P.F. and Levkoff, S.E. (2000) 'Combining qualitative and quantitative methods in health research with minority elders: Lessons from a study of dementia caregiving', *Field Methods*, 12 (3): 195–208.

Whittemore, R., Rankin, S.H., Callahan, C.D., Leder, M.C. and Carroll, D.L. (2000) 'The peer advisor experience providing social support', *Qualitative Health Research*, 10 (2): 260–276.

Witcher, A.E., Onwuegbuzie, A.J. and Minor, L.C. (2001) 'Characteristics of effective teachers: Perceptions of preservice teachers', *Research in the Schools*, 8 (2): 45–57.

Part II

APPLICATIONS IN MIXED METHODS DESIGN

6

Why do Researchers Integrate/Combine/Mesh/Blend/Mix/Merge/Fuse Quantitative and Qualitative Research?

Alan Bryman

This chapter is concerned with the issue of why researchers combine quantitative and qualitative research. This is an issue that has preoccupied me for many years. When I first started writing about integrating quantitative and qualitative approaches 20 years ago, I was very much going against the grain of thinking at the time. The paradigm wars were being waged and, although it was clear to me that a fair number of examples of integration could be found, combining the two approaches was not a significant interest for most writers and researchers. When they did write about it, it was largely in the context of triangulation and often about its limits and limitations. I think I was typically viewed, especially in the context of *Quantity and Quality in Social Research* (Bryman, 1988), as a firm advocate of combining quantitative and qualitative research and to a large extent I was and still am. I saw myself as trying to address some of the epistemological and paradigm issues that I felt were hindering the possibility of combining quantitative and qualitative research. I felt that at the level of *practice*, combining them would be feasible and even desirable in many contexts.

Nowadays, the picture could scarcely be more different. Mixing methods has become a popular way of thinking about how to approach research questions in a variety of fields. Indeed, it has almost become a distinctive approach in its own right, with a growing number of books and articles devoted to outlining its fundamentals, rather than treating it as just a hybrid of quantitative and qualitative approaches (e.g. Creswell, 2003; Johnson and Onwuegbuzie, 2004). However, I have found myself becoming increasingly uneasy about the current wave of enthusiasm for mixed methods research. There is a risk that it is being seen as like an each-way bet – you win if your horse comes in second or third as well as if it comes in first.

I have several concerns about this enthusiasm but I'm going to mention just one for the time being. This concern derives largely from three areas: my reading of the current literature on mixed methods research; reading and evaluating articles before and after they are published in journals; and reading research grant applications for the UK's Economic and Social Research Council, which is the major source of responsive mode funding of the social sciences in the UK.

My main concern is that mixed methods research is often insufficiently justified. To a significant extent, it has become fashionable and is often seen as offering the best of both worlds, so that its use sometimes seems to be regarded as requiring only the barest justification. Also, while authors and applicants are invariably quite detailed in the ways in which they present issues to do with such things as data collection in connection with the quantitative and qualitative components of their research, what is actually involved in mixing, integrating, combining, meshing, etc. is quite often under-explained. I ought to say that I'm not making these comments from a lofty position of personal superiority: when I've looked at some of my past articles which have included quantitative and qualitative components, I've realized how easily I've slipped into not explicating my rationales for doing mixed methods research and not explaining what came out of the supposedly combined approach.

There are, I think, several reasons for this state of affairs. First, as Maxwell and Loomis (2003) have observed, it is sometimes quite difficult to work out from a mixed methods study what the quantitative and qualitative components were and how they were combined or otherwise used in conjunction with one another. This may not be the result of failure on the part of social researchers when writing up their work. It may be that the restrictions journals quite legitimately impose on word length for articles militate against the ability of writers to provide detailed accounts of their reasons for conducting mixed methods research and the nature of the components of the approach.

The second point, which is in part a product of the first one, is that we don't have an agreed-upon language for discussing mixed methods studies. Metaphors and allusions to do with: triangulation, putting flesh on the bones of quantitative findings, macro versus micro, and combining quantitative breadth with qualitative depth and richness are frequently found but their precise meanings and significance are difficult to pin down. In part, this lack of a language for writing about mixed methods research derives from the fact that we are trying to run before we can walk. There has been little systematic investigation of mixed methods studies out of which general principles regarding practice and prescription have been honed. Consequently, when mixed methods terms are used, they are often employed in very different ways by authors – triangulation is a classic example of this – and they may or may not derive from the examination of studies combining quantitative and qualitative research. It was very brave of the editors of the *Handbook of Mixed Methods in Social and Behavioral Research* (Tashakkori and Teddlie, 2003) to include a Glossary of terms because it brings out the subtle and sometimes significant differences in the ways in which their contributors employed key terms. A glance at the entry for 'mixed methods' provides an illustration of this point. Precisely because we have little systematic examination of case studies of mixed methods research, we don't have a clear sense of what principles underlie the different ways in which quantitative and qualitative research can be and have been combined. This has hindered the development of a language for mixed methods research.

Third, it is not entirely clear (or hasn't been until recently) what is involved in bringing quantitative and qualitative research together. What I'm getting at here is what it means to integrate, mix, combine, mesh, and so on. Several writers are beginning to try to unpack the meanings of these terms and their implications for practice (e.g. Mason, 2006; Moran-Ellis et al., 2006). As long as we are unclear about the meanings of these verbs in terms of methodological practice, it will remain difficult – even impossible – to express what has emerged out of a mixed methods project.

A related point is that we are largely unable at the present time to write prescriptively about mixed methods research; in other words, to write about how mixed methods research *should* be done. This means that researchers find it difficult to demonstrate that they are engaging in good practice with regard to mixed methods research or don't have a set of principles to be followed. In large part, this has arisen because we don't have any criteria concerning what is a good or successful mixed methods study. In other words, not only do we not have a great deal of systematic research on mixed methods projects, we have even less that allows us to specify what a successful one is. This makes it almost impossible to be prescriptive about mixed methods research. It is impossible to specify beyond the yawningly banal what should be done and what should be avoided when combining quantitative and qualitative research. It is striking that the critical appraisal criteria for mixed methods studies devised by Sale and Brazil (2004) seems not to include among the criteria the degree to which the quantitative and qualitative elements were integrated. Instead, the emphasis is placed upon the degree to which the components meet quality criteria.

Of course, it may be possible to write prescriptively about *the components* of a mixed methods research project: how a self-administered questionnaire study should be conducted, how participants should be interviewed using a semi-structured guide, and so on. But a mixed methods study is more than the sum of its parts. Mixed methods researchers are likely to be using the approach in order to address distinctive research questions that can only be answered with a mixed methods approach, and that is likely to mean that the investigation will aim to generate something that is over and above its individual quantitative and qualitative components.

A research project on mixed methods research

I've tried to make a small contribution to these kinds of issues through a research project on integrating quantitative and qualitative research that I conducted as part of the ESRC's Research Methods Programme. The findings reported in this chapter derive from two components of this project: a content analysis of articles based on mixed methods research and interviews with researchers who have used this approach.

I conducted the content analysis because I wanted to get a sense of the general characteristics of published mixed methods articles in terms of such features as: the main research methods used, the rationales for combining quantitative and qualitative research, and whether one approach appeared to have priority over the other. But in addition, I wanted to understand from the perspective of practitioners how they thought about mixed methods research, the contingencies involved in doing such research, their impressions of the state of mixed methods work, and so on. The two approaches to data collection represented different types of understanding: one was to do with the public face of mixed methods research; the other to do with trying to get inside the heads of mixed methods researchers.

Content analysis

I will first discuss the analysis of articles. Journal articles don't encapsulate all possible contexts in which projects reporting mixed methods research might be found.

However, journal articles are a major form of reporting findings and have the advantage that in most cases, the peer review process provides a quality control mechanism.

The approach to gleaning a sample was to search the Social Sciences Citation Index (SSCI) for articles in which relevant key words or phrases such as 'quantitative' and 'qualitative', or 'multi(-)method', or 'mixed method', or 'triangulation' appeared in the title, key words, or abstract. This means that the sample comprises articles which to some degree foreground the fact that the study is based on both quantitative and qualitative research. Searches using other kinds of key words, such as 'survey' and 'ethnography/ic', produce a far larger sample of articles than could be dealt with within the purview of this investigation. In conducting the search, the emphasis was on uncovering articles in five fields: sociology; social psychology; human, social and cultural geography; management and organizational behaviour; and media and cultural studies. The analysis was restricted to a 10-year period of 1994–2003. The fact that the findings are based on a large corpus of articles suggests that the sample is unlikely to be overly atypical, although claims of representativeness would be impossible to sustain. Judgements about whether articles fell within the purview of the investigation, in terms of whether they could be regarded as deriving from the five fields, were made on the basis of the journal title or information supplied in abstracts. In this way, a total of 232 articles were generated and content analyzed.

The sample is likely to be biased in the sense that by no means all authors of articles reporting mixed methods research foreground the fact that the findings reported derive from a combination of quantitative and qualitative research or do not do so in terms of the key words that drove the online search strategy. However, foregrounding that a study is based on mixed methods research is interesting because it implies that the fact that the different sources of data were employed is important and significant to the author(s) concerned. Since a major focus of the research was the kinds of purposes to which mixed methods research is put, the online search strategy that was used for the study reported here was very relevant, because it might be anticipated that researchers who choose to emphasize this aspect of their studies will have given greater consideration to the issues involved in combining quantitative and qualitative research. In this sense, the articles from which the findings derive constitute a purposive sample. A further issue that suggests some advantages to the sampling approach taken for this chapter is that it allows articles in a wide variety of journals to be uncovered.

Several writers have pointed out that quantitative and qualitative research can be combined at different stages of the research process: formulation of research questions; sampling; data collection; and data analysis. Articles for this study were chosen in terms of data collection and data analysis and then content analyzed in relation to these aspects of the research process. Issues of sampling did materialize in the study, as the findings below will indicate. Data collection and analysis were emphasized because these are arguably defining features of quantitative and qualitative research. Moreover, mixed methods research articles nearly always entail the collection and analysis of both quantitative and qualitative data (Niglas, 2004).

A major focus of the content analysis was on the rationales proffered for combining quantitative and qualitative research. This aspect of the investigation was approached in several ways. First, the rationale given by authors for combining the two approaches to data collection and/or analysis was coded. For this exercise, the reasons that were given *before* the findings were presented, were typically examined. Then, the ways in which quantitative and qualitative research were *actually* combined were coded. In doing so, the coding reflected authors' reflections on what they felt had been gleaned from combining quantitative and qualitative research and any ways in which the two were combined which were not reflected in authors' accounts. The purpose of discriminating between these two ways of thinking about the justification for mixed methods research was that authors' accounts of why they intended to combine quantitative and qualitative research might differ from how they actually combined them in practice.

In coding the justifications for combining quantitative and qualitative research two different schemes were employed. First, the influential scheme devised in the context of evaluation research by Greene et al. (1989) was used. This scheme isolates five justifications for combining quantitative and qualitative research: triangulation; complementarity; development; initiation; and expansion.

An advantage of the Greene et al. scheme is its parsimony, in that it boils down the possible reasons for conducting mixed methods research to just five reasons, although the authors' analysis revealed that one of these – initiation – was uncommon. A disadvantage is that it only allows two rationales to be coded (primary and secondary). In response to these limitations, a more detailed but considerably less parsimonious scheme was devised and it is the findings from this exercise that will be reported today. The scheme was based on an extensive review of the kinds of arguments that are frequently levelled in both methodological writings and research articles. The scheme provided for the following rationales:

a. *Triangulation* or greater validity – refers to the traditional view that quantitative and qualitative research might be combined to triangulate findings in order that they may be mutually corroborated. If the term was used as a synonym for integrating quantitative and qualitative research, it was not coded as triangulation.

b. *Offset* – refers to the suggestion that the research methods associated with both quantitative and qualitative research have their own strengths and weaknesses so that combining them allows the researcher to offset their weaknesses to draw on the strengths of both.

c. *Completeness* – refers to the notion that the researcher can bring together a more comprehensive account of the area of enquiry in which he or she is interested if both quantitative and qualitative research are employed.

d. *Process* – quantitative research provides an account of structures in social life but qualitative research provides sense of process.

e. *Different research questions* – this is the argument that quantitative and qualitative research can each answer different research questions but this item was coded only if authors explicitly stated that they were doing this.

f. *Explanation* – one is used to help explain findings generated by the other.

g. *Unexpected results* – refers to the suggestion that quantitative and qualitative research can be fruitfully combined when one generates surprising results that can be understood by employing the other.

h. *Instrument development* – refers to contexts in which qualitative research is employed to develop questionnaire and scale items, for example, so that better wording or more comprehensive closed answers can be generated.

i.   *Sampling* – refers to situations in which one approach is used to facilitate the sampling of respondents or cases.

j.   *Credibility* – refers to suggestions that employing both approaches enhances the integrity of findings.

k.   *Context* – refers to cases in which the combination is rationalized in terms of qualitative research providing contextual understanding coupled with either generalizable, externally valid findings or broad relationships among variables uncovered through a survey.

l.   *Illustration* – refers to the use of qualitative data to illustrate quantitative findings, often referred to as putting 'meat on the bones' of 'dry' quantitative findings.

m.   *Utility* or improving the usefulness of findings – refers to a suggestion, which is more likely to be prominent among articles with an applied focus, that suggests that combining the two approaches will be more useful to practitioners and others.

n.   *Confirm and discover* – this entails using qualitative data to generate hypotheses and using quantitative research to test them within a single project.

o.   *Diversity of views* – this includes two slightly different rationales, namely, combining researchers' and participants' perspectives through quantitative and qualitative research, respectively, and uncovering relationships between variables through quantitative research while also revealing meanings among research participants through qualitative research.

p.   *Enhancement* or building upon quantitative/qualitative findings – this entails a reference to making more of or augmenting either quantitative or qualitative findings by gathering data using a qualitative or quantitative research approach.

q.   *Other/Unclear.*

r.   *Not stated.*

The rationale for nearly one-third of all articles was coded in terms of 'enhancement' (see Table 6.1). Quite large numbers of articles appeared under the categories: 'completeness' (13%), 'triangulation' (12.5%), and 'sampling' (13.4%). Just over

TABLE 6.1   *Uses of mixed methods research – rationales*

Category	Rationale
	Number of articles (% of all 232 cases)
Triangulation	29 (12.5)
Offset	7 (3)
Completeness	31 (13)
Process	5 (2.2)
Different research questions	13 (5.6)
Explanation	13 (5.6)
Unexpected results	0
Instrument development	18 (7.8)
Sampling	31 (13.4)
Credibility	2 (0.9)
Context	8 (3.4)
Illustration	4 (1.7)
Utility	2 (0.9)
Confirm & discover	9 (3.9)
Diversity of views	26 (11.2)
Enhancement	73 (31.5)
Other/unclear	8 (3.4)
Not stated	62 (26.7)

TABLE 6.2 *Uses of mixed methods research – rationales and practice*

Category	Rationale	Practice
	Number of articles (% of all 232 cases)	
Triangulation	29 (12.5)	80 (34.5)
Offset	7 (3)	4 (1.7)
Completeness	31 (13)	67 (28.9)
Process	5 (2.2)	6 (2.6)
Different research questions	13 (5.6)	10 (4.3)
Explanation	13 (5.6)	32 (13.8)
Unexpected results	0	2 (0.9)
Instrument development	18 (7.8)	21 (9.1)
Sampling	31 (13.4)	43 (18.5)
Credibility	2 (0.9)	5 (2.2)
Context	8 (3.4)	10 (4.3)
Illustration	4 (1.7)	53 (22.8)
Utility	2 (0.9)	2 (0.9)
Confirm & discover	9 (3.9)	15 (6.5)
Diversity of views	26 (11.2)	35 (15.1)
Enhancement	73 (31.5)	121 (52.2)
Other/unclear	8 (3.4)	14 (6.1)
Not stated	62 (26.7)	1 (0.4)

a quarter of all articles couldn't be coded in terms of any category because no rationale could be discerned. In the context of this chapter, this finding is itself interesting.

When the articles are examined in terms of practice and compared with rationales, there are some fairly striking differences (see Table 6.2). For example, 'triangulation' and 'illustration' are considerably more likely to occur as practices than as rationales.

Comparing the rationale and practice columns in Table 6.2 suggests an interesting possibility, namely, that when mixed methods research is employed, practice does not always tally with the reasons given for using the approach, if indeed reasons are given at all. Nor should it be assumed that all articles that appear in terms of a rationale will also be subsumed in that category in terms of use. For example, we should not assume that all of the 26 articles coded in terms of 'diversity of views' will necessarily be included in the 35 articles that were coded in terms of this category when practice was the focus of attention.

In order to explore this issue, a contingency table analysis was undertaken relating rationale and practice following the creation of a multiple response variable for each of these. The resulting table is extremely ungainly, so only highlights will be mentioned. Of the 29 articles that cited triangulation as a rationale, 19 used it in this way. In other words, one-third of all articles intending to use mixed methods research for triangulation did not actually use mixed methods research in this way or at least did not report doing so. Just as interestingly, we can look at this the other way around. Thus, 80 articles employed a triangulation approach, but for just 19 of these articles was triangulation a rationale. In other words, three-quarters of all articles reporting the triangulation of research findings provided other rationales for the use of mixed methods research. What this seems to suggest is that although triangulation may not always be a rationale for combining quantitative and qualitative research, when faced with the two (or in a small number of cases more than two) sets of data, some researchers find it hard to resist making allusions to the consistency or otherwise between their findings. This was in fact the case with an article that I co-wrote some years ago, but which wasn't included in the sample (Deacon et al., 1998).

Taking another example, 'completeness' was a rationale for 31 articles and most (83.9%) used it in this way. However, when practice is examined, completeness could be ascribed to 67 articles. Thus, 71.1% of all articles using completeness did not specify it as a rationale at the outset.

'Enhancement' provides a further example. Seventy-three articles specified this as a rationale although over one-quarter of articles citing it as a rationale did not employ it in this way. More striking is that 121 articles employed the approach meaning that over one half (56.2%) of articles using enhancement in practice had not specified it as a rationale.

'Diversity of views' was a rationale for 26 articles though quite a large percentage (30.8%) did not use it this way. Thirty-five articles employed a diversity of views approach to integrating quantitative and qualitative research but nearly half (48.6%) did not specify this as a rationale.

Among the 62 articles that appear in Table 6.1 as 'not stated', the most common uses were: enhancement (45 articles), triangulation (14), illustration (15), and completeness (10).

What these findings suggest is that there is quite often a mismatch between the rationale for the combined use of quantitative and qualitative research and how it is used in practice. Mixed methods research is something of a moveable feast. For several of the rationales, there is no evidence from the articles that quantitative and qualitative research are combined in the way that the rationale would lead one to suspect. This is not always the case. In particular, when 'instrument development' and 'sampling' are the rationales, they are nearly always used in this way. Only one article was found claiming 'instrument development' as a rationale and only one article claiming 'sampling' as a rationale, but did not report combining quantitative and qualitative research in these ways.

One strategy that the content analysis also showed up is that a small number of articles employ a Gatling gun approach to rationale and practice. When we look at rationale, 6 articles were found to employ 4 or more rationales; in terms of practice, 33 articles (14.2% of the sample) mentioned 4 or more rationales. The record is 7 in terms of both rationale and practice. The Gatling gun approach allows a justification for the use of mixed methods research that entails a listing of a variety of possible reasons for adopting the approach. It may well reflect the reality of writers' justification for their approach but it may also in some cases reflect uncertainty about how to express the reasons for using both quantitative and qualitative research. Researchers simply adopt a 'more is better' approach to justifying what they have done. It is also striking that over five times as many articles employ the Gatling gun approach at the level of practice, as against rationale. What seems to happen is that researchers find a wider range of outcomes resulting from combining quantitative and qualitative research than they initially envisaged.

An interesting explicit discussion of this issue can be found in Hammond (2005). She discusses research concerned with the wider benefits of lifelong learning. The research comprised a qualitative project that was followed by a quantitative one and says that the 'design and implementation of the two projects were not integrated to any great degree' (Hammond, 2005: 240). However, using the Greene et al. (1989) fivefold classification, she is able to show how, although the two projects were not explicitly integrated, together they reflect all five purposes for doing mixed methods research. In other words, although the overall research wasn't explicitly envisaged as an exercise in integrating quantitative and qualitative research, when the two sets of findings were interpreted in tandem, they could be thought of in this way.

This experience is in tune with the suggestion from my content analysis findings that typically mixed methods researchers derive a wider range of outcomes from combining quantitative and qualitative research than the findings concerned with rationales would lead one to expect. To a very large extent, this arises because the outcomes of mixed methods research are not always predictable. In fact, it may be more accurate to say that they are *rarely* predictable. Thus, when the two sets of data are juxtaposed, new possible ways of thinking about the connections between them come to mind. To a certain extent, this is a consequence of the fact that, as is well known, the outcomes of qualitative research are unpredictable, not least because of the less structured research methods that are employed and the tendency for research questions to be less specific than in quantitative research (Bryman, 2008). It is likely, therefore, that mixed methods research outcomes will be similarly affected. However, it is likely that it also reflects the fact that when the quantitative and qualitative components are viewed together, interesting but unanticipated insights are thrown up.

Interviews with mixed methods researchers

Many interesting themes came out of the semi-structured interviews I conducted with mixed methods researchers. Several of these themes are relevant to this chapter and I'd like to mention these.

First and unsurprisingly, my 20 interviewees spoke about their reasons for doing mixed methods research in similar terms to the ones that were coded for the content analysis. Thus, they spoke in terms of: qualitative research as providing preparation for their quantitative work; qualitative findings providing explanations for quantitative findings; qualitative research providing meaning with quantitative findings providing breadth; and so on. No rationales came out of the interviews that weren't covered by my coding scheme.

A second theme is that several interviewees felt that increasingly mixed methods research was expected in various quarters (funding bodies, journal editors, etc.) and by and large they felt this was not a good development. While they themselves were often enthusiastic about mixed methods research, an issue to which I will return, the notion that it was being employed because it was felt to be more likely to be favoured was a concern for them. Examples of comments along these lines are:

> Yes, I think it's becoming much more common, almost to – I mean it's almost becoming obligatory. I actually think that's probably a bad thing. (Respondent 1).
>
> And also, I mean, and I don't know how true this is, but I think there's been a general perception, and certainly I've heard it said several times over that the ESRC had – and certainly in the recent past have undergone quite a quantitative turn and that there was a great – you know, there was a concern about the lack of quantitative research, lack of – concern about lack of quantitative skills and that they particularly kind of favoured projects that used mixed methods or had a strong quantitative component. (Respondent 16)

This last respondent went on to say:

But I also have some reservations that it's becoming a kind of, what's the word? When people - you know, just doing it for the sake of it, and it's not necessarily thought through, you know, and I think there is a tendency to do, what I own up myself, I've said I've been guilty of sometimes and it is that, you know, in name you appear to be doing mixing methods but in practise - in terms of the analysis and writing up that, mixing doesn't always come through in the way the data is analyzed.

A similar view can be discerned in the following statement:

Yeah, yeah. I think it comes back to what I said previous, about there's now expectation that, to have a - a research design which is gonna be robust, which is going to stand up to critique and which is representative - of whatever, whatever that may be, you need to adopt a mixed method approach. And that isn't necessarily the right way to approach a particular research problem because it might not be the right approach at all. (Respondent 6)

Another said that 'people are talking about it as a good thing more than they used to' and 'it feels like there's more emphasis on mixed method approaches being a good thing nowadays'.

What is striking and interesting about these comments from the point of view of the focus of this chapter is that they imply that some researchers are perceived to be doing mixed methods research not so much because of the goodness of fit between the approach and the research questions being asked but because it is seen as more attractive in certain quarters. Certainly many interviewees expressed the need for mixed methods research to be tailored to research questions and were concerned that mixed methods research might be being employed for reasons other than their significance for answering such questions. For example, Respondent 1 discussing the use of mixed methods research, took the view:

...so its [mixed methods research's] use depends upon what your research questions are what sorts of methods you should choose – that's always the first step, but I think there's actually become a bit of a fetishism about using mixed methods...

This comment is also striking for the remark about fetishism which has affinity with the points made earlier regarding a belief among some of the interviewees that mixed methods research was being conducted because it is often seen as a generally superior approach. However, his point about the use of mixed methods research depending on the research questions is very much in tune with the textbook account of the research process. It is also in tune with the philosophy of pragmatism that underpins much mixed methods research thinking and which runs through many of the contributions to the *Handbook of Mixed Methods in Social and Behavioral Research* (Tashakkori and Teddlie, 2003).

However, it is also interesting that many of the interviewees also expressed a belief suggesting that they felt that mixed methods research in itself was a superior approach. In other words, several of them were what might be termed 'mixed methods fans'. Thus, some interviewees saw mixed methods research as only appropriate if it was suited to specific research questions; others saw it as having a more general appropriateness if not superiority. I've portrayed these as competing discourses: one I've called a *particularistic discourse* that maintains that mixed methods research has to be looked at in terms of, and tailored to, the research questions it seeks to answer; the other, a *universalistic discourse* that portrays mixed methods research as having a general superiority.

As an example of the latter (i.e. the universalistic) discourse, Respondent 12 said of mixed methods research: 'Well, I suppose I think that everyone should be doing it' and repeated a few moments later 'I suppose I think everyone should be doing both and be, you know, less moralistic about right and wrong'. She also indicated a universalistic stance when she suggested: 'but if I was designing the ideal project, I would always say combine the different approaches because you'll get a more interesting story but you've got to draw that story out, that's not easy'.

Respondent 5 put it this way:

Well I think, I think you - with that combination, ideally you should get an optimal mix of validity, which might actually mean a certain amount of reproduceability without getting too locked into a kind of a fully positivist agenda, but I mean I think there's a lot there that - that's valuable. You get that with a - a close engagement with the processes of meaning making as well, as far as the media are concerned. So it ideally promises a - a mix of a - an overview of a process that has a - that makes statistical sense in terms of tendencies and probabilities but with an exploration of what's inside the process too...

Equally interesting is that several interviewees shuttled between the two discourses, on one occasion depicting the suitability of mixed methods research in terms of its appropriateness in relation to research questions and on another occasion expressing the view that the approach actually has a general superiority.

For example, Respondent 4 took the view that research questions were key to whether mixed methods research should be employed when he suggested that the decision to use it is 'task driven'. However, he then went on to propose: 'Yeah, I can't imagine many - I cannot imagine there are many research topics that wouldn't benefit from having both elements'. He also proposed that: 'As long as we're talking about that kind of quantitative material, I would be unhappy for any of my PhD students not to include some kind of survey, questionnaire, if you like quantitative material, as part of their work'. This respondent thus shifted from a particularistic discourse to one that is far more redolent of a universalistic discourse that portrays mixed methods research as having a general superiority when he says that he couldn't think of many research topics that wouldn't benefit from including both quantitative and qualitative research.

A superficial way of looking at these data is to suggest that some of my interviewees were confused about these issues. I definitely don't think this is the case. If there is confusion anywhere, it lies in the fact that, as I suggested earlier, we still don't understand mixed methods research as much as we'd like to think we do. For example, there are no guidelines with which I'm familiar that would allow researchers to seek guidance about the generic kinds of research questions that are most suited to mixed methods research. Indeed, it could be argued that the textbook maxim that research questions somehow steer decisions and choices regarding matters of research design and research methods is itself a gross over-simplification. There is frequently custom-and-practice guidance about how research questions and practical research decisions should be allied but it is seldom more than general and is rarely decisive in its implications for such decisions.

A further and related point is that, as one of the referees pointed out in relation to the article in which some of these interview findings will appear, it may also be that researchers are deeply ambivalent about the whole issue of connecting research questions to research practices. In part, this is because experienced researchers know that research questions can often provide only limited guidance in connection with research design and methods issues and because, as I've suggested, the kinds of research questions that mixed methods research is uniquely adept at handling have not been determined.

Yet another point that bears on this issue of ambivalence takes us back to the issue of language for expressing mixed methods research. I've tried to argue that we don't have such a language and there is very little in the way of prescriptive writing on doing mixed methods research. Consequently, I suspect that researchers exhibit some uncertainty about how to portray their positions in relation to mixed methods research. It must have been quite difficult for them when I asked them these questions because doing so places them in a position of feeling they have to display methodological certainty in the face of uncertainty.

None of my questions revealed this uncertainty more than one I asked which invited them to nominate an exemplar of mixed methods research. Virtually all of the interviewees struggled with the question, invariably turning the question on me, asking me to suggest one! They typically agreed, once they'd got over the shock of the question, that the fact that they struggled so much was itself interesting, and this produced some enjoyable conversations about why it was difficult to identify one. Here we may detect yet another factor that contributes to ambivalence and uncertainty about mixed methods research in relation to research questions – there are few if any recognized exemplars of mixed methods research. Interviewees generally agreed that they could find fairly easily exemplary surveys, ethnographies, and experiments, but few could call exemplary mixed methods studies to mind.

The issue of mixing

One final issue that I want to address that in part derives from my findings is the issue that I raised previously about what it means to mix, integrate, combine, etc. As we all know, conducting both quantitative and qualitative research doesn't mean that they are being integrated or mixed. To what extent is mixing genuinely taking place and what are we looking for anyway when we talk about mixing? In the content analysis of published articles, an assessment was also made of whether the findings of the research were truly integrated. I don't feel as confident about the data from this exercise as I do about my other data, because whether integration appears to have occurred is a very subjective judgement. Nonetheless, the issue is worth pursuing and I present my findings tentatively. In only 18% of articles were the two sets of findings genuinely integrated and in 47% the findings were presented in parallel. In the remaining 35% of articles, there was a small amount of integration of the findings but this did not go very far. The main and most striking feature of these findings is that nearly one half of all articles using both quantitative and qualitative research do not in fact integrate the findings. The quantitative and the qualitative findings are largely presented side by side or more or less totally separately. In coding whether integration takes place, I was looking for evidence that the quantitative and qualitative findings are presented in such a way that they are brought together to provide a comprehensive picture that *interweaves* the two sets of data. Standard triangulation exercises were almost always coded in terms of an intermediate level of integration.

A reflexive discussion

I want finally to do a bit of reflexivity! My research after all entails both quantitative and qualitative research! I think I've done a reasonable job of justifying my use of both a content analysis and semi-structured interviews. I think I've also done a reasonable job of specifying how using a mixed methods approach worked out in practice. In fact, in terms of practice, I've ended up with outcomes that are quite consistent with the rationales. But have I integrated my data? Like many of my interviewees, I found this difficult to achieve because the quantitative and the qualitative components do feel as though they are either like different levels of reality or are answering somewhat different research questions. In fact, when I look back at the application for funding, the quantitative and the qualitative elements were indeed largely designed to answer somewhat different research questions. It is this issue of blending that represents the key difficulty and in my view represents the next big issue we need to surmount in mixed methods thinking. However, so long as the language of mixed methods research is limited (as implied by my title), so long as we don't have prescriptive accounts of mixed methods research, and so long as we have so few exemplars, this aspect of mixed methods research practice will be held back.

Summary of key findings

To summarize the main findings that emerge from my research, as they relate to the topic of this chapter:

1. A wide range of rationales for using mixed methods research can be identified in terms of my scheme, but, as with other classifications, some rationales are more common than others.
2. Typically, mixed methods researchers identify more outcomes of the approach than rationales. In other words, when confronted with their findings, they seem to find more uses or advantages of combining quantitative and qualitative research than they had anticipated.
3. While several practitioners pay lip service to the notion that mixed methods research should be conducted only when it is appropriate to research questions, it is also clear that many of them are also enthusiastic about the approach and see it as having general applicability.
4. There is uncertainty about the circumstances in which mixed methods research should be used. This uncertainty derives from the relative absence of a fund of understanding of how mixed methods research should be done as well as from the perceived absence of exemplars.
5. Integration in mixed methods studies is often not achieved and is difficult to do. This may relate to the problems identified under item 4.

Acknowledgements

I wish to thank the Economic and Social Research Council for funding the research project 'Integrating quantitative and qualitative research: prospects and limits' (Award number H333250003) which made possible the research on which this chapter is based. Parts of this chapter are based on Bryman (2006a; 2006b; 2007) and I wish to thank the two journals concerned – *Qualitative Research* and *International Journal of Social Research Methodology* – for permission to use the work in these publications. I also wish to thank Max Bergmann for the invitation to present an earlier version of this chapter in Basel.

References

Bryman, A. (1988) *Quantity and Quality in Social Research*. London: Unwin Hyman.

Bryman, A. (2006a) 'Integrating quantitative and qualitative research: how is it done?' *Qualitative Research*, 6: 97–113.

Bryman, A. (2006b) 'Paradigm peace and the implications for quality', *International Journal of Social Research Methodology*, 9: 111–126.

Bryman, A. (2007) 'The research question in social research: what is its role?', *International Journal of Social Research Methodology*, 10: 5–20.

Bryman, A. (2008) *Social Research Methods*, 3rd edition. Oxford: Oxford University Press.

Creswell, J.W. (2003) *Research Design: Qualitative, Quantitative, and Mixed Methods Approaches*, 2nd edition. Thousand Oaks, CA: Sage.

Deacon, D., Bryman, A. and Fenton, N. (1998) 'Collision or collusion? A discussion of the unplanned triangulation of quantitative and qualitative research methods', *International Journal of Social Research Methodology*, 1: 47–63.

Greene, J.C., Caracelli, V.J. and Graham, W.F. (1989) 'Toward a conceptual framework for mixed-method evaluation designs', *Educational Evaluation and Policy Analysis*, 11: 255–274.

Hammond, C. (2005) 'The wider benefits of adult learning: an illustration of the advantages of mixed-methods research', *International Journal of Social Research Methodology*, 8: 239–255.

Johnson, R.B. and Onwuegbuzie, A.J. (2004) 'Mixed methods research: a research paradigm whose time has come', *Educational Researcher*, 33: 14–26.

Mason, J. (2006) 'Mixing methods in a qualitatively driven way', *Qualitative Research*, 6: 9–26.

Maxwell, J.A. and Loomis, D.M. (2003) 'Mixed methods design: an alternative approach', in A. Tashakkori and C. Teddlie (eds), *Handbook of Mixed Methods in Social and Behavioral Research*. Thousand Oaks, CA: Sage.

Moran-Ellis, J., Alexander, V.D., Cronin, A., Dickinson, M., Fielding, J., Sleney, J. and Thomas, H. (2006) 'Triangulation and integration: processes, claims and implications', *Qualitative Research*, 6: 45–60.

Niglas, K. (2004) *The Combined Use of Qualitative and Quantitative Methods in Educational Research*. Tallinn, Estonia: Tallinn Pedagogical University Dissertation on Social Sciences.

Sale, J.E.M. and Brazil, K. (2004) 'A strategy to identify critical appraisal criteria for primary mixed-methods studies', *Quality and Quantity*, 38: 351–365.

Tashakkori, A. and Teddlie, C. (2003) *Handbook of Mixed Methods in Social and Behavioral Research*. Thousand Oaks, CA: Sage.

7

Quality of Inferences in Mixed Methods Research: Calling for an Integrative Framework[1]

Abbas Tashakkori and Charles Teddlie

Introduction

This chapter presents arguments for generating and expanding an integrative frame-work for assessing the quality of inferences in mixed methods research. The term inference quality is introduced as an umbrella term for evaluating the quality of con-clusions that are made on the basis of the findings in a study. Characteristics of good inferences in quantitative, qualitative, and mixed methods research are described and compared. Finally, the integrative framework is introduced along with two broad aspects of quality (design quality and interpretive rigor) and nine more specific criteria for judging the quality of mixed methods research.

For the past several years there has been a growing recognition that mixed meth-ods research has become the third methodological movement in the social and behavioral sciences, joining the quantitative and qualitative research alternatives. The evidence for this conclusion comes from a variety of sources: several texts have now been written in the area (e.g. Brewer and Hunter, 1989; 2006; Creswell, 2003; Creswell and Plano-Clark, 2007; Greene and Caracelli, 1997; Tashakkori and Teddlie, 1998; 2003a); there are a number of dynamic ongoing debates within the field over issues such as basic definitions, research designs, and how to draw inferences[2] in mixed methods research; there are literally thousands of references to mixed meth-ods research on the internet; and there is now a new Special Interest Group in the American Educational Research Association on mixed methods and a new journal devoted to the field (*Journal of Mixed Methods Research*). In a recent issue of *Educational Researcher*, Johnson and Onwuegbuzie (2004: 14) referred to mixed methods research as a 'research paradigm whose time has come'.

With this rapid growth in the field, concerns have arisen about whether mixed methods is just a 'fad' or whether this methodological orientation has something to offer that goes beyond what quantitative and qualitative methods can offer independ-ently. Those advocating for the uniqueness of the mixed methods approach contend that such research can simultaneously address both exploratory and confirmatory questions, thereby gathering information that can result in 'meta-inferences' about the phenomenon under study that neither the quantitative nor qualitative perspectives could do alone.[3] A meta-inference is an overall conclusion, explanation, or under-standing developed through an integration of the inferences obtained from the qual-itative and quantitative strands of a mixed methods study.[4] The issue of the validity of research findings is an essential one in the debate over the value of mixed methods as a distinct methodological orientation. Theorists in both quantitative research (e.g. Shadish et al., 2002) and qualitative research (e.g. Hammersley, 1992; Lincoln and Guba, 1985; Maxwell, 1992; 2004) have written extensively about the 'validity' of their findings, although the latter group appropriately prefers alternative terms such as 'trustworthiness', 'authenticity', and 'plausibility'. In this chapter, we explore methods whereby mixed methodologists can determine the veracity of the meta-inferences that emerge from their research projects, which have combined both qualitative and quantitative methods, in order to answer questions that would not be answerable using either approach alone.

We seek an *integrative framework* for making validity claims for mixed methods research, but we prefer to use the term 'inference quality' in this discussion rather than design/conclusion validity for reasons to be elaborated upon later in this chapter. Among these reasons is the fact that the term validity is predominantly used by quantitative researchers; it does not differentiate the quality of data from the quality of conclusions, and that it has lost its usefulness due to too many (and sometimes conflicting) subtypes or definitions.

We also distinguish between inference quality (an attribute of the process of meaning making and/or its outcomes) from 'data quality' (an attribute of the inputs to the process of meaning making). Inherent in this distinction is the fact that the process of understanding in research consists of three distinct and inter-connected (recursive) components: data/information, the 'results' that emerge from a systematic analysis of such data/information, and the interpretation of these results to gain an understanding of the phenomenon under study.

The next two sections of this chapter discuss the reasons for utilizing mixed methods and then introduce the reader to the issue of inferences in mixed methods research. Sections after that discuss first the need for an integrative framework and then in turn the characteristics of good inferences in quantitative research, qualitative research, and mixed methods research. The final section of the chapter presents an integrative model of inference quality mixed methods research.

Reasons for utilizing mixed methods

The quality of a mixed methods study is directly dependent on the purpose for which the mixing of approaches was deemed necessary in that study. For example, if the main purpose for utilizing mixed methods is for completeness, a good mixed methods study must provide a more complete understanding of the phenomenon under study than its qualitative and quantitative strands did alone. If the purpose is for corroboration/confirmation, then one strand must be used to assess the credibility of the inferences from the other strand.[5]

This aspect of quality is also dependent on the design of the mixed methods study. For parallel mixed methods, the purpose for mixing must be known from the start. For sequential mixed methods, the purpose might be known from the start, or it might emerge from the inferences of the first strand (i.e. the questions of the second strand may emerge at the end of the first strand). For example, unexpected or ambiguous results from a quantitative study might necessitate the collection and

TABLE 7.1   *Purposes for mixed methods based on several sources*

Purpose	Description
Complementarity	Mixed methods are utilized in order to gain complementary views about the same phenomenon or relationship. Research questions for the two strands of the mixed study address related aspects of the same phenomenon.
Completeness	Mixed methods designs are utilized in order to make sure a complete picture of the phenomenon is obtained. The full picture is more meaningful than each of the components.
Developmental	Questions for one strand emerge from the inferences of a previous one (sequential mixed methods), or one strand provides hypotheses to be tested in the next one.
Expansion	Mixed methods are used in order to expand or explain the understanding obtained in a previous strand of a study.
Corroboration/ Confirmation	Mixed methods are used in order to assess the credibility of inferences obtained from one approach (strand). There usually are exploratory AND explanatory/confirmatory questions.
Compensation	Mixed methods enable the researcher to compensate for the weaknesses of one approach by utilizing the other. For example, errors in one type of data would be reduced by the other (Johnson and Turner, 2003).
Diversity	Mixed methods are used with the hope of obtaining divergent pictures of the same phenomenon. These divergent findings would ideally be compared and contrasted.

Note. This table was constructed on the basis of several sources including Greene et al. (1989), Patton (2002), Tashakkori and Teddlie (2003a), Creswell (2003), and Rossman and Wilson (1985).

analysis of in-depth qualitative data in a new strand of the study (see Creswell and Plano-Clark, 2007 for examples).

Unfortunately, the reasons for using mixed methods are not always explicitly delineated and/or recognized by authors. Some of the reasons that have been identified by scholars (beginning with Greene et al., 1989) are summarized in Table 7.1 together with their definitions. These reasons include complementarity, completeness, developmental, expansion, corroboration/confirmation, compensation, and diversity.

Research inference as a process and an outcome

Consistent with other scholars (Erzberger and Kelle, 2003; King et al., 1994; Miller, 2003), Tashakkori and Teddlie (1998) have suggested using the term 'inference' to denote the last and most important stage of any research project: answering the research questions by making interpretations. We have used the term *inference* to specifically connote both the process of interpreting the findings AND the outcome of this interpretation (i.e. the process of interpreting, as well as the emerging conclusions) to provide answers to the original research questions. We have also suggested using *inference quality* as an umbrella term for evaluating the quality of conclusions that are made on the basis of the findings and *inference transferability* to indicate the degree to which these conclusions may be applied to other *specific* settings, people, time periods, contexts, and so forth.

Inferences are conclusions and interpretations that are made on the basis of collected data in a study. As such, they must be distinguished from the data from which they are derived. Unfortunately, few scholars (e.g. King et al., 1994; Newman and Benz, 1998; Tashakkori and Teddlie, 1998) have distinguished between quality of data (e.g. data validity, reliability, stability, credibility) and quality of inference (e.g. internal validity, credibility of the conclusions, etc.). An implicit distinction may be found in Lancy's (1993) discussion of publishing qualitative research results:

> One can write up a mostly descriptive piece devoid of analysis and conclusions; these are extremely hard to get published. One can write a piece that is long on conclusions and short on description. This is most commonly done but it is a practice that throws away what is most valuable about qualitative research –the "believability" that comes from obviously thorough familiarity with the phenomenon. Or, and I think this is the preferred route, one can, like a gem cutter, fracture one's study along natural division lines and provide several complete accounts of these separate pieces. (Lancy, 1993: 23)

Tashakkori and Teddlie (2003b) tried to make this distinction clear by discussing three general stages of the research process: the sphere of concepts, the experiential sphere, and the sphere of inferences. We placed the data in the 'experiential sphere', while the conclusions and inferences were placed in the 'sphere of inferences' (Tashakkori and Teddlie, 2003b: 681). This distinction, however, does not apply to situations (most probably in qualitative studies) where inferences are continuously made on the basis of available information, which in turn impact the data gathering process. In such studies, there is a continuous feedback loop between the data and inferences, with each impacting the other.

The term inference has been used to denote both a process and an outcome (see Miller, 2003 for a full discussion). As a process, making inferences consists of a series of steps that a researcher follows in order to create meaning out of a relatively large amount of collected information. As an outcome, inference is a conclusion made on the basis of obtained data. Such a conclusion may or may not be acceptable to other scholars, and is subject to evaluation by the community of scholars and/or consumers of research. For example, an inference may be evaluated in terms of the degree to which it is consistent with the theories and the state of knowledge, or with the constructions of the participants in the study. Or, on the other hand, one might ask how good the conclusion is in terms of its relevance and usefulness to policymakers.

King et al. (1994) define inference as:

> ... the process of using the facts we know to learn about facts we do not know. The facts we do not know are the subject of our research questions, theories, and hypotheses. The facts we do know form our (quantitative or qualitative) data or observations. (p. 46)

Inferences are a 'researcher's construction of the relationships among people, events, and variables, as well as his or her construction of respondents' perceptions, behaviors, and feelings and how these relate to each other in a coherent and systematic manner' (Tashakkori and Teddlie, 2003b: 692). Our definition is broad and inclusive, involving the quantitative and qualitative components of mixed methods research.

Inferences are not only answers to research questions; they go beyond such answers by developing new understandings and new explanations for events, phenomena, and relationships. They create an understanding (e.g. 'Gestalt' or whole) on the basis of all results, a whole that is bigger than a simple collection of the miscellaneous findings from a study.

How does one know if inferences that we make are 'good' or 'bad'? Krathwohl (2004), without distinguishing qualitative from quantitative research, characterizes good inferences ('credible results', p. 148) in terms of four sets of standards: plausibility (explanation credibility), quality of implementation (translation fidelity), congruence of evidence and explanations (demonstrated results), and lack of other plausible explanations (rival explanations eliminated). Each of these four standards is applicable to any qualitative or quantitative research finding, at least to some degree.

Before we discuss the need for an integrative framework for the concept of inference quality, we present the following three basic assumptions pertaining to these issues in mixed methods. It is necessary to situate inference quality issues in mixed methods in the context of the research purposes and research questions (i.e. mixed methods inferences exhibit quality to the extent that they address the purpose for the mixing of the methods in the study, such as completion or corroboration/confirmation).

- High quality qualitative and quantitative strands are necessary but not sufficient for a high quality mixed methods study.
- The quality of meta-inferences is dependent on the quality of inferences from both the qualitative and quantitative strands of any mixed methods study.
- Both within and across the strands of a mixed methods study, quality of data is a necessary but not a sufficient condition for inference quality. Evaluations of data quality must be kept separate from those of inference quality.

Building on these fundamental assumptions, we explore various issues that have direct relevance to inference quality in mixed methods in the rest of this chapter.

The Need for an Integrative Framework

There are at least three reasons that we need an integrative framework for determining the inference quality of mixed methods research:

1. An integrative framework might help us make some sense out of the myriad of terms that are used to connote validity or credibility issues in the quantitative and qualitative research strands of mixed methods research.
2. Mixed methodologists need to reconcile two sets of standards (quantitative, qualitative) for assessing the validity/credibility of results. An integrative framework may provide some criteria for reconciling these two sets of standards.
3. An integrative framework is required for making meta-inferences about the phenomenon under study that goes beyond what the quantitative or qualitative strands can explain alone. A set of standards is necessary for making these meta-inferences.

With regard to the first reason for having an integrative framework, the level of confusion that surrounds the use of the term 'validity' has led us and others to conclude that the term has lost its meaning or become obsolete. Elsewhere, we have presented a list of 35 different types of 'validity' and that list is not exhaustive

(Teddlie and Tashakkori, 2003: 13). All these terms refer to some aspect of quality in a research project, be it the quality of collected information, research question, methods of data analysis, or the utilization of findings for policy. Investigators have used research validity, design validity, legitimacy, trustworthiness, credibility, and their numerous (and often inconsistent or conflicting) sub-types in both qualitative and quantitative research. There have been clear pleas by qualitative, quantitative, and mixed methodologists, asking for clarification about what 'validity/quality' issues actually involve (i.e. quality of purpose? data? method of analysis, design, or inferences that are made on the basis of the results?). We think it is crucial for us to develop an integrative framework for mixed methods research in order to help address this controversy over the misuse of terms such as validity/trustworthiness credibility.

With regard to the second reason for developing an integrative framework, mixed methods researchers must address and reconcile two distinct sets of standards (qualitative, quantitative) for assessing the credibility or validity of their inferences. While there are overlapping standards between the two sets, there are also aspects of quality that are unique to each orientation. The next two sections of this chapter present characteristics of good inferences first in quantitative research and then in qualitative research. The presentations of these sets of standards should hopefully provide some ideas for reconciling them in mixed methods research.

The third reason for developing an integrative framework is the most important: to allow us to evaluate the quality of meta-inferences. In mixed methods, meta-inferences integrate the understandings gleaned from the qualitative and quantitative strands of the study. They go beyond what the quantitative and qualitative strands can explain alone. The standards of quality for these meta-inferences also go beyond the standards of quality for their qualitative and quantitative strands. Our integrative framework is an attempt to initiate the development of standards for evaluating these meta-inferences.

Complexities of Assessing the Quality of Inferences

Responding to a question regarding what constitutes 'good' science, Paul (2005: 11–16) summarizes three recent 'markers' in research that demonstrate the complexity of answering that question. The first is the publication of *Scientific Research in Education* (2002) sponsored by the National Academy of Sciences in the United States. Although the report intended to span across both 'scientifically based' qualitative and quantitative approaches, it has been considered to be more applicable to quantitative research (e.g. Maxwell, 2004). Among the concerns expressed in the report was the 'lack of standards for evaluating educational research' (Paul, 2005: 12). The report presents six criteria for good research:

> (1) pose significant questions that can be investigated empirically; (2) link research to relevant theory; (3) use methods that permit direct investigation of the question; (4) provide a coherent and explicit chain of reasoning; (5) replicate and generalize across studies; and (6) disclose research to encourage professional scrutiny and critique (Paul, 2005: 13)

The second 'marker' identified by Paul is the *No Child Left Behind Act* of 2001 in the United States, providing another view of quality as 'research that applies rigorous, systematic, and objective procedures to obtain valid knowledge' (p. 13). This type of research:

1. Employs systematic, empirical methods that draw on observation or experiment;
2. Involves rigorous data analysis that are adequate to test the stated hypotheses and justify the general conclusions drawn;
3. Relies on measurement or observation methods that provide valid data across evaluators and observers and across multiple measurement and observations;
4. Has been accepted by a peer-reviewed journal or approved by a panel of independent experts through a comparably rigorous, objective, and scientific review (Paul, 2005: 13–14).

The third 'marker' identified by Paul (2005) for demonstrating quality in research is the intense political and academic discourse over the publication of a paper in *Psychological Bulletin* in 1998. The paper was based on a meta-analysis of data collected from college students. The main focus of controversy was the study's conclusion that child sexual abuse did not cause pervasive harm to the victims. Despite seemingly solid methodology, the inferences were clearly objectionable to the public, policymakers, and some members of the research community. Paul (2005: 16) summarizes the controversy by raising a general question: 'Does a finding that something is true trump a social value that declares that finding to be harmful?'

We have discussed Paul's three 'markers' in some detail in order to demonstrate that answers to the question 'what are the attributes of good inferences' are quite complex, and sometimes go beyond the quality of the data, method, and design of a study. This complexity is also compounded by the disparity of standards of quality between quantitative and qualitative traditions.

Characteristics of good inferences in quantitative research

Much discussion about inference quality in quantitative research has centered on the issue of internal validity. The term internal validity emerged from Campbell (1957), but did not gain widespread recognition until Campbell and Stanley's well-known monograph in 1963, which was followed by Cook and Campbell's (1979) extended discussion of inference in experimental and quasi-experimental research. The third major iteration of the quantitative position toward validity issues was presented in Shadish et al. (2002) and involved four major validity categories: internal validity (lack of alternative explanations for the findings), statistical conclusion validity (appropriateness of statistical tests, and their adequacy for detecting relationships/differences), construct validity (adequacy of procedures for measuring the constructs under investigation), and external validity (generalizability of the findings to the population).

The initial (and some of the revised) conceptualization of internal validity was focused solely on causal relationships in experimental designs. However, since much of today's quantitative social and behavioral research is non-experimental, internal validity has been used in a less restrictive manner by scholars to denote an inference that rules out alternative plausible explanations for obtained results (see Krathwohl, 2004: 139). As such, it also includes components of statistical conclusion validity. A good inference in quantitative research establishes relations between variables and provides reasonable certainty that such relationships did not happen by chance. This is often achieved by using tests of statistical significance. A good inference also has the intensity that is consistent with the demonstrated magnitude of the relationship between variables (and/or differences between groups). Finally, a good inference is free of systematic bias in interpretation of the results.

We have incorporated most of the indicators/standards of inference quality in quantitative research in our integrative framework that is presented later in this chapter.

Characteristics of good inferences in qualitative research

In qualitative research, a good inference is expected to capture the meaning of the phenomenon under consideration from the perspective of the participants in the study. Druckman (2005: 331) uses the term 'authenticity' to characterize this important component of good inferences in qualitative research in the following quotation:

> ... issues of internal and external validity framed in a positivistic tradition are supplemented by the concerns of authenticity in the constructivist tradition .... Validity is evaluated from the standpoint of the participants in the research process or in terms of the joint vantage points of researcher and participant. This kind of subjective validity reflects an attempt to capture the meanings of experiences or interactions (Druckman, 2005: 331, 341–342)

Guba and Lincoln (1989) consider an inference good if it is *credible*. An inference is credible if 'there is a correspondence between the way the respondents actually perceive social constructs and the way the researcher portrays their viewpoints' (Mertens, 2005: 254).

Bryman (2004: 284) uses *transparency* as one of the indicators of quality, both for quantitative and qualitative studies. Transparency refers to the researcher's clarity of explanation regarding all stages of the study (e.g. who the participants were, how they were selected, how the data were analyzed, and how the conclusions were derived).

Tobin and Begley (2004) echo Arminio and Hultgren's (2002) recommendation to use *goodness* as an indicator of the quality of qualitative research. Aspects of goodness, as summarized by Tobin and Begley (2004: 391) include:

- Foundation (epistemology and theory) – this provides the philosophical stance and gives context to and informs the study.
- Approach (methodology) – specific grounding of the study's logic and criteria.
- Collection of data (method) – explicitness about data collection and management.
- Representation of voice (researcher and participant as multicultural subjects) – researchers reflect on their relationship with participants and the phenomena under exploration.
- The art of meaning making (interpretation and presentation) – the process of presenting new insights through the data and chosen methodology.
- Implication for professional practice (recommendations).

Lincoln and Guba (1985) denied the relevance of quantitative terms such as internal and external validity to qualitative research and introduced a new set of terms.

Using the term trustworthiness as an umbrella term, Lincoln and Guba defined quality in broad terms that included both the data and the investigator's conclusions:

> The basic issue in relation to trustworthiness is simple: How can an inquirer persuade his or her audiences (including self) that the findings of an inquiry are worth paying attention to, worth taking account of? What arguments can be mounted, what criteria invoked, what questions asked, that would be persuasive on this issue? (1985: 290).

Lincoln and Guba (1985: 300–331) presented a variety of techniques for evaluating and enhancing the quality of inferences in qualitative research. Of particular interest here are the dependability audit, the conformability audit, member checks, peer debriefing, negative case analysis, referential adequacy, thick description, reflexive journals, and triangulation techniques. These are often seen as strategies for improving the credibility of the data and findings, rather than standards of quality. Our integrative framework incorporates them more in the latter sense (as standards rather than strategies).

The *dependability audit* concerns the *process* of the inquiry, including the appropriateness of inquiry decisions and methodological shifts. The *conformability audit*, on the other hand, is an examination of the *product* of the inquiry, in order to gain confidence that the interpretations are supported by the results and are internally coherent.

Member checking is a particularly powerful technique for determining the trustworthiness of interpretations that involves asking informants and other members of the social scene to check on the accuracy of the themes, interpretations, and conclusions. If the informants and other members of the social scene agree with the interpretations of the investigators, then this provides evidence for the trustworthiness of the results. *Peer debriefing* introduces another type of individual to the qualitative data gathering and analysis procedure: the 'disinterested' peer. Having a dialog with a disinterested peer, such as a professionally trained researcher working in another area of study, allows the researcher to clarify interpretations and identify possible sources of bias.

Referential adequacy is another strategy for assessing and improving the quality of inferences. It consists of setting aside a part of the raw data, and re-analyzing it to assess the quality of inferences drawn from the first set. *Negative case analysis* consists of an examination of instances and cases that do not fit within the overall pattern of results that have emerged from the analysis.

Thick description and *reflexive journals* provide the tools necessary for assuring data quality, and also for assessing the adequacy and quality of inferences. Thick descriptions are highly detailed accounts of the phenomenon under study including extensive information regarding the context surrounding it. *A reflexive journal* is a diary (daily or as needed) regarding information about the investigator, his/her possible biases, and the methodological decisions that he or she makes. It can be used later in conducting dependability and confirmability audits, and in writing reports with thick descriptions.

These strategies strengthen *credibility*, which is comparable to *internal validity* in quantitative research. Credibility is based on the degree of fit between the participants' realities and the investigator's constructions and representations of these realities.

Characteristics of good inferences in mixed methods research

Despite the increasing utilization of mixed methods in social and behavioral research, there is a dearth of systematic literature on the quality of inferences in such studies. From one point of view, scholars have considered mixed methods as a vehicle for improving the quality of inferences that are potentially obtainable from either the qualitative or quantitative strands of a study. From another point of view, some scholars have expressed concern that mixed methods are potentially susceptible to weak inferences, given the difficulty of implementing two diverse types of designs/procedures for answering the same research question (or two closely related aspects of a single question). Onwuegbuzie and Johnson (2006) have recently called this 'the *problem of legitimation in mixed methods*', which refers to: 'the difficulty in obtaining findings and/or making inferences that are credible, trustworthy, dependable, transferable, and/or confirmable'. Expanding on this concern, they conclude that 'these problems are exacerbated in mixed research because both the quantitative and qualitative components of studies bring into the setting their own problems of representation and legitimation, likely yielding either an additive or a multiplicative threat' (p. 52). Finally, a third view about the quality of inferences in mixed methods is that given the assumed inconsistency between the standards for assessing the quality of inferences derived from quantitative and qualitative designs, assessing the quality of inferences in mixed methods research is impossible.

An important obstacle for mixed methods researchers is that they have to employ three sets of standards for assessing the quality of inferences made in their studies: (a) evaluating the inferences derived from the analysis of quantitative data using quantitative standards; (b) evaluating the inferences made on the basis of qualitative data using qualitative standards; and (c) assessing the degree to which the meta-inferences that are made on the basis of these two sets of inferences are credible. This is especially difficult when the two sets of inferences are not consistent with each other.

One possible strategy for reducing the gap between the two sets of standards is to create an integrative model of inference quality that potentially incorporates both. We agree with Maxwell (2004) in his discussion of the need for more mixed methods research and for better understanding between individuals in the qualitative and quantitative 'camps': Maxwell (2004) concluded that '... practitioners of both approaches will need to develop a better understanding of the logic and practice of the other's approach, and a greater respect for the value of the other's perspective' (p. 9).

Our approach to generating inferences in mixed methods research values equally the quantitative and qualitative inferential processes, yet adds a new dimension associated with meta-inferences across the separate research strands. Figure 7.1 illustrates a popular mixed methods design, the Parallel Mixed Design (Teddlie and Tashakkori, 2006) and may be used as a starting point for introducing our model of inference quality in mixed methods research. The boxes along the left hand side of the figure could represent a qualitative strand of a mixed methods study, while the ovals on the right hand aide of the figure could represent a quantitative strand of the same study. The box at the bottom of the diagram represents the

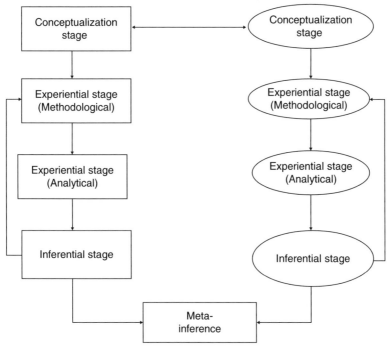

FIGURE 7.1 *Concurrent mixed methods design*

meta-inferences that occur as the researcher makes conclusions that go across the two strands.

There are three inferential processes ongoing in this illustration:

- The qualitative strand employs the various techniques listed in the fourth column of Table 7.2 (e.g., confirmability audit, credibility) in assessing the quality of conclusions that emerge from the analysis of narrative data generated in that part of the study.
- The quantitative strand assesses threats to the validity (again see column 4 of Table 7.2) of the conclusions that are generated from the analysis of numeric data from that part of the study.
- For a mixed methods researcher, the crucial stage of the study is to integrate (e.g. compare and contrast, infuse, modify one on the basis of another) the two sets of inferences that are generated by the two strands of the study. The quality of the meta-inferences that are generated from such an integration is assessed through the process described in the next section of the chapter ('integrative model of inference quality').

Since the integrative model incorporates many of the standards of quality from the qualitative and quantitative research approaches, it is also applicable to the two strands, and might assist the mixed methods researcher by providing at least a 'partial common set' of standards. Table 7.2 elaborates on the three inferential processes that occur in mixed methods studies (qualitative inferences, quantitative inferences, and integrated meta-inferences).

TABLE 7.2   *Quality issues in mixed methods studies*

Stage of study	Approach	Quality issues	Indicators of quality	Integrative framework
Data Collection Stage	QUAL	QUAL Data Quality Issues	Credibility; Dependability	Data Quality
	QUAN	QUAN Data Quality Issues	Reliability; Validity	Data Quality
Data Analysis Stage	QUAL	Within QUAL Strand: Issues Related to Appropriate and Adequate Analytic Strategies	Confirmability	Analytic Adequacy
	QUAN	Within QUAN Strand: Issues Related to Appropriate and Adequate Analytic Strategies	Statistical Conclusion Validity	Analytic Adequacy
Inference Stage	QUAL	Within QUAL Strand: Issues Related to Making Conclusions on the Basis of QUAL Data Analysis Results	Some Aspects of Credibility and Confirmability Transferability	Interpretive Rigor Inference Transferability
	QUAN	Within QUAN Strand: Issues Related to Making Conclusions on the Basis of QUAN Data Analysis Results	Internal Validity; Statistical Conclusion Validity External Validity	Interpretive Rigor Inference Transferability
Integration Stage (Meta-Inferences)	Mixed Methods	Across Strands: Meta-Inferential Issues Related to Integration of QUAL and QUAN Findings and Inferences	Design Quality; Interpretive Rigor Inference Transferability	Design Quality; Interpretive Rigor Inference Transferability

Note: This table does not include quality issues pertinent to conceptualization stage of the qualitative (QUAL) and quantitative (QUAN) strands or the overall mixed methods design.

An integrative model of inference quality in mixed methods research

A strong inference is only possible if there is a strong and appropriate design that is implemented with quality. In such a study, research questions dictate which research design and procedures are needed for answering them. If the procedures are not implemented with quality and rigor, the quality of obtained inferences will be uncertain. On the other hand, even with strong and well-implemented procedures, one might make inferences that are not defensible. Based on these two considerations (quality of the design, quality of interpretations), Tashakkori and Teddlie (2003b) have proposed two broad criteria for evaluating the quality of inferences: Design Quality and Interpretive Rigor. Table 7.3 presents various attributes and components of these two criteria.

TABLE 7.3   *Components or criteria for design quality and interpretive rigor*

Aspects of Inference Quality	Research Criterion	Indicator or Audit
Design Quality	1. Design Suitability	Are the methods of study appropriate for answering the research question(s)? Does the design match the research questions?
	2. Design Adequacy/Fidelity	2a) Are the procedures implemented with quality and rigor?
		2b) Are the methods capable of capturing the meanings, effects, or relationships?
		2c) Are the components of the design (e.g. sampling, data collection procedures, data analysis procedures) implemented adequately?
	3. Within Design Consistency	Do the components of the design fit together in a seamless manner? Io there 'within design consistency' across all aspects of the study?
	4. Analytic Adequacy	Are the data analysis procedures/strategies appropriate and adequate to provide possible answers to research questions?
Interpretive Rigor	5. Interpretive Consistency	5a) Do the inferences closely follow the relevant findings in terms of type, scope, and intensity?
		5b) Are multiple inferences made on the basis of the same findings consistent with each other?
	6. Theoretical Consistency	Are the inferences consistent with theory and state of knowledge in the field?
	7. Interpretive Agreement	7a) Do other scholars reach the same conclusions on the basis of the same results (i.e. is there peer agreement?)?
		7b) Do the investigator's inferences match participants' constructions (i.e. is there researcher-participant agreement?)?
	8. Interpretive Distinctiveness	Is each inference distinctively more plausible than other possible conclusions that can be made on the basis of the same results?
	9. Integrative Efficacy (mixed and multiple methods)	Does the meta-inference adequately incorporate the inferences made from QUAL and QUAN strands of the study?

Design quality

As the name indicates, design quality refers to the degree to which the investigators have utilized the most appropriate procedures for answering the research question(s), and implemented them effectively. This is equally applicable to both qualitative and quantitative research, and directly determines the quality of inferences (both as a process and as an outcome) in both traditions. Design quality is a necessary but not sufficient condition for the quality of inferences. Four basic standards for quality of research design and its implementation are as follows:

• *Design suitability* (also known as translation fidelity, Krathwohl, 2004): Was the method of study appropriate for answering the research question(s)? In other words, were the research questions of the study adequately and appropriately translated into elements of the design (e.g. sampling, data collection) that could potentially answer the research questions? Obviously, different research designs are needed depending on the type of questions and research purposes that any given study has (see Newman et al., 2003).

- *Design Adequacy/Fidelity:* Were the components of the design (e.g. sampling, data collection) implemented adequately? In experimental designs, implementation fidelity refers to the degree to which experimental procedures were strong enough (and were credible to the participants) to create the expected effect.
- *Within Design Consistency:* Did the components of the design fit together in a seamless and cohesive manner? Inconsistencies might happen if the data collection procedures (e.g. interview, focus group questions) are not compatible with the sampling process (e.g. do not match respondents' level of education, or language ability, etc.). This type of problem has been reported in cross-cultural studies in which instruments or instructions are translated from one language or dialect to another.
- *Analytic Adequacy:* Are the data analysis techniques appropriate and adequate for answering the research questions?

Interpretive rigor

Interpretive rigor is the degree to which credible interpretations have been made on the basis of obtained results (Lincoln and Guba, 2000: Tashakkori and Teddlie, 2003b). In order to assess such rigor, and improve the quality of inferences, one has to meet five criteria or standards described in the following section.

Interpretive Consistency: This criterion is based on the consistency of inferences with each other and with the results of data analysis. In other words, does each conclusion closely follow the findings? Also, do multiple conclusions based on the same results agree with each other? There are at least two indicators of this. First, is the type of inference consistent with the type of evidence? An example of inconsistency would be if causal inferences are made on the basis of correlational data in some quantitative research.

Second, is the level of intensity that is reported consistent with the magnitude of the events or the effects that were found? An example from qualitative research is making strong conclusions and recommendations on the basis of limited evidence. In Lancy's (1993) words:

> Then there is the 'soapbox' problem which occurs when the data are not commensurate with the analysis, that is either there simply isn't enough data presented to carry the elaborate analyses and conclusions or the data seem to have been selectively arranged to support what appears to be a preexisting thesis (p. 28).

Theoretical Consistency (also known as explanation credibility, Krathwohl, 2004): Is each inference (explanation for the results or for relationships) consistent with current theories in the academic field and/or with empirical finding of other studies?

Interpretive Agreement: This criterion is based on the agreement of the individuals who are making the conclusions. Would other scholars reach the same conclusions on the basis of the results from the study? If the research approach or purpose places value on the perceptions or interpretations of participants (e.g. in participatory or transformative research), do the researchers' inferences agree with their interpretations? Both in quantitative and qualitative research, one standard of quality has been the degree to which peers, and other scholars in the scientific community, agree with the manner in which conclusions are drawn. A formal demonstration of this process is reflected in the peer-reviewed journals and dissertation committees. In qualitative research, peer debriefing is considered to be one of the mechanisms to ensure this, as noted in a previous section.

In most qualitative and quantitative research, disagreement between scholars is usually an indication of the fact that other plausible interpretations of the same results exist. Bogdan and Biklen (2003: 33) concluded that 'What qualitative researchers attempt to do, however, is to objectively study the subjective states of their subjects'. Bogdan and Biklen consider inconsistency a problem, only if incompatible or contradictory conclusions are made by two researchers (p. 36). Other qualitative researchers feel comfortable about such disagreements, since they do not believe that reaching a single explanation of a set of findings is impossible or disvalued.

Interpretive Distinctiveness: This criterion is based on the necessity of making the strongest and most plausible conclusions from the results of a study. Is each conclusion distinctively different from other plausible conclusions regarding the same results? In other words, is each conclusion clearly different and more defensible than other plausible conclusions that were eliminated by the investigator? In order to meet this condition, the investigator must be clearly able to refute or eliminate the other possible interpretations of the results. Refuting (or at least discussing) the alternative plausible explanations of the results are not unique to quantitative research. Although qualitative researchers are expected to utilize an 'emic' perspective in their interpretations, one of the criticisms of qualitative research has revolved around the gap between the investigator's construction of reality and meaning, and that of their informants. In ethnography, reflective analysis is used as a process of identifying and analyzing one's biases, to make sure the interpretations reflect the 'truth' rather than purely emerge as a result of one's personal biases (Creswell, 2005).

Integrative Efficacy: This is the degree to which inferences made in each strand of mixed methods study are effectively integrated into a theoretically consistent meta-inference. The four previous criteria related to interpretative rigor (i.e. interpretive and theoretical consistency, interpretive agreement and distinctiveness) were applicable both to each strand (qualitative, quantitative) *and* to the meta-inferences that emerge when the inferences of the two or more strands are integrated. Integrative efficacy, in contrast, is unique to meta-inferences in mixed methods (i.e. it does not apply to qualitative or quantitative strands separately). It addresses the degree to which a mixed methods researcher adequately integrates the findings, conclusions, and policy recommendations gleaned from each of the two strands.

Integration does not necessarily mean creating a single understanding on the basis of the results. We are using the term integration as a mixed methods term that denotes making meaningful conclusions on the basis of consistent or inconsistent results. The term incorporates elaboration, completeness, contrast, comparison, and the like. For mixed methods research, the consistency between two sets of inferences derived from qualitative and quantitative strands has been widely considered as an indicator of quality. However, some scholars have cautioned against such a simple interpretation of consistency. Inconsistency, or divergence, may in fact be considered an advantage of mixed methods.[6] One of the major values of mixed methods research might lie in specific instances in which the two sets of inferences do not agree with each other.

Erzberger and Kelle (2003) have argued that consistency might reflect common errors in both sets of results or interpretations. According to them, a mixed methods researcher may discover such a consistency in at least the following ways:

1. The two sets of inferences made agree with each other, increasing the investigator's confidence in his/her conclusions.
2. The two sets might be dissimilar, but provide insights into different aspects of the same phenomenon. Therefore, when combined, they provide a more complete meaning, a Gestalt that is bigger than the sum of its parts. Greene and Caracelli (1997) have called these complementary inferences. Lancy (1993: 11) offers another example in which case studies utilize qualitative and quantitative evidence in a complementary manner: '... qualitative and quantitative research has the potential to contribute vital information bearing on a question or a problem'. Lancy (1993: 11) also indicates that one type of research could be encapsulated within the other as follows: 'Embedded in a large-scale quantitative study, a few in-depth case studies are done to provide added context for and checks on the validity of the quantitative procedures'.
3. The two sets are not the same, but one reveals the conditions under which the other might or might not apply (elaboration, see Brannen, 2005: 176). Once again, by virtue of setting the expected limits of applicability, the meta-inference is stronger than either of the two component inferences. As noted above, the discovery of specific instances in which the two sets of inferences do not agree with each other might be considered a unique benefit from conducting mixed methods research.
4. The two sets are contradictory or dissonant. According to Erzberger and Kelle (2003), consistency between two types of inferences is of less consequence than the consistency between these inferences and a theoretical framework that explains both sets. If the two sets do not seem consistent, the first course of action for the researcher would be to go back and evaluate the quality of both sets of data and inferences.

Inconsistency might be a diagnostic tool for detecting possible problems in data collection and analysis, or the inferences derived from the results of one strand or the other. If this refocusing does not reveal any problems in the two sets of inferences, then the next step would be to evaluate the degree to which lack of consistency might indicate that the two sets are revealing two different aspects of the same phenomenon (complementarity). Not reaching a plausible explanation for the inconsistency, the next step would be to explore the possibility that one set of inferences provides the conditions for the applicability of the other (elaboration, conditionality).

If none of these steps provide a meaningful justification for the apparent inconsistency, the inconsistency might be an indicator of the fact that there are two plausible but different answers to the question (i.e. two different but equally plausible realities exist).

Summary and conclusions

Given the increasing acceptability of mixed methods research, there is a need for developing and expanding a set of standards of quality that transcend the standards of quantitative and qualitative approaches. Our 'integrative framework' is one possible strategy for developing such standards. Until a formal set of standards are developed by scholars to cover all three components/aspects of mixed methods studies (qualitative, quantitative, and integrated), the integrative framework here provides a general set of audits for quality assessment. The integrative framework presented here is based on the assumption that many of the standards/audits from qualitative and quantitative literature are based on similar rationales or principles. Our framework incorporates these general concepts, audits, and standards of quality from the two approaches, and adds new ones that are applicable to mixed studies. Given the narrow scope of the chapter, we did not make an effort to expand the framework to all aspects of quality assessment in mixed methods. For example, we did not discuss specific quality issues for mixed methods questions, data, and data analysis. These remain to be developed.

Notes

1 Parts of this chapter were presented at the 2006 annual meeting of the American Educational Research Association, San Francisco, CA. We would like to express our appreciation to the two anonymous reviewers who provided constructive feedback on an earlier version of this manuscript.
2 Some readers may associate the term 'inference' with the quantitative tradition. We believe this point of view is too narrow, however, and prefer a broader definition of inference that allows for the inclusion of conclusions, understandings, and explanations from both the qualitative and the quantitative components of a mixed methods research study. We present a formal definition of inference later in this chapter.
3 It should be noted that mixed methods researchers advocate for the position that there are many areas of research where a quantitative or qualitative research orientation alone is better suited to answer the research questions, and that mixed methods should be employed only in situations where a combination of the approaches would yield a better understanding of the phenomenon under study.
4 A strand refers to a phase of a mixed methods study in which a qualitative or a quantitative approach is used. Each strand is divided into three stages: the conceptualization stage, the experiential stage (methodological/analytical), and the inferential stage.
5 This might be called the *utilization quality* (or *pragmatic quality*) of mixed methods inferences; that is, inferences that are made at the end of a study are good only if they address the intended purpose for mixing. We propose these terms tentatively, for possible expansion by other scholars, if they deem them useful.
6 An issue for future development is the determination of inconsistency. It is possible to have some differences between the two sets, without calling them inconsistent (i.e. 'different but without a considerable degree of stress'). How much difference is acceptable before two sets of inferences are considered inconsistent?

References

Arminio, J.L. and Hultgren F.H. (2002) 'Breaking out from the shadow: The question of criteria in qualitative research', *Journal of College Student Development,* 43 (4): 446–456.

Bogdan, R.C. and Biklen, S.K. (2003) *Qualitative Research for Education: An Introduction to Theory and Methods,* 4th edition. Boston: Allyn & Bacon.

Brannen, J. (2005) 'Mixed methods: The entry of qualitative and quantitative approaches into the research process', *International Journal of Social Research Methodology,* 8 (3), 173–184.

Brewer, J. and Hunter, A. (1989) *Multimethod Research: A Synthesis of Styles.* Newbury Park, CA: Sage Publications, Inc.

Brewer, J. and Hunter, A. (2006) *Foundations of Multimethod Research: Synthesizing Styles*, 2nd edition. Thousand Oaks, CA: Sage Publications, Inc.

Bryman, A. (2004) *Social Research Methods*, 2nd ed. Oxford, UK: Oxford University Press.

Campbell, D.T. (1957) 'Factors relevant to the validity of experiments in social settings', *Psychological Bulletin*, 54: 297–312.

Campbell, D.T. and Stanley, J. (1963) 'Experimental and quasi-experimental designs for research on teaching', in N.L. Gage (ed.), *Handbook of Research on Teaching*. Chicago: Rand McNally. (Also published as *Experimental and Quasi-Experimental Designs for Research*. Chicago: Rand McNally, 1966).

Cook, T.D. and Campbell, D.T. (1979) *Quasi-Experimentation: Design and Analysis Issues for Field Settings*. Boston: Houghton Mifflin Company.

Creswell, J. and Plano-Clark, V.G. (2007) *Designing and Conducting Mixed Methods Research*. Thousand Oaks, CA: Sage Publications, Inc.

Creswell, J.W. (2003) *Research Design: Qualitative, Quantitative, and Mixed Methods Approaches Set*, 2nd edition. Thousand Oaks, CA: Sage Publications, Inc.

Creswell, J.W. (2005) *Research Design: Qualitative, Quantitative, and Mixed Methods Approaches*, 2nd edition. Thousand Oaks, CA: Sage Publications, Inc.

Druckman, D. (2005) *Doing Research: Methods of Inquiry for Conflict Analysis*. Thousand Oaks: Sage Publications, Inc.

Erzberger, C. and Kelle, U. (2003) 'Making inferences in mixed methods: The rules of integration', in A. Tashakkori and C. Teddlie (eds), *Handbook of Mixed Methods in Social and Behavioral Research*. Thousand Oaks, CA: Sage Publications, Inc. pp. 457–490.

Greene, J.C. and Caracelli, V.J. (1997) 'Defining and describing the paradigm issue in mixed-method evaluation', in J.C. Greene and V.J. Caracelli (eds), *Advances in Mixed-Method Evaluation: The Challenges and Benefits of Integrating Diverse Paradigms. New Directions for Evaluation no. 74*. San Francisco: Jossey-Bass. pp. 5–17.

Greene, J.C., Caracelli, V.J. and Graham, W.F. (1989) 'Toward a conceptual framework for mixed-method evaluation designs', *Educational Evaluation and Policy Analysis,* 11: 255–274.

Guba, E.G. and Lincoln, Y.S. (1989) *Fourth Generation Evaluation*. Newbury Park, CA: Sage Publications, Inc.

Hammersley, M. (1992) 'Ethnography and realism', in M. Hammersley (ed.), *What's Wrong with Ethnography: Methodological Explorations*, London: Routledge. pp. 43–56.

Johnson, B. and Onwuegbuzie, A. (2004) 'Mixed methods research: A research paradigm whose time has come', *Educational Researcher*, 33 (7): 14–26.

Johnson, B. and Turner, L.A. (2003) 'Data collection strategies in mixed methods research', in A. Tashakkori and C. Teddlie (eds), *Handbook of Mixed Methods in Social and Behavioral Research*. Thousand Oaks, CA: Sage Publications, Inc. pp. 297–319.

King, G., Keohane, R.O. and Verba, S. (1994) *Designing Social Inquiry: Scientific Inference in Qualitative Research*. Princeton: Princeton University Press.

Krathwohl, D.R. (2004) *Methods of Educational and Social Science Research: An Integrated Approach*, 2nd edition. Long Grove, IL: Waveland Press.

Lancy, D.F. (1993) *Qualitative Research in Education: An Introduction to the Major Traditions*. New York: Longman.

Lincoln, Y.S. and Guba, E.G. (1985) *Naturalistic Inquiry*. Beverly Hills: Sage Publications, Inc.

Lincoln, Y.S. and Guba, E.G. (2000) 'Paradigmatic controversies, contradictions, and emerging confluences', in N.K. Denzin and Y.S. Lincoln (eds), *Handbook of Qualitative Research*, 2nd edition. Thousand Oaks, CA: Sage Publications, Inc. pp. 163–188.

Maxwell, J.A. (1992) 'Understanding and validity in qualitative research', *Harvard Educational Review,* 62: 279–299.

Maxwell, J.A. (2004) 'Causal explanation, qualitative research, and scientific inquiry in education', *Educational Researcher*, 33 (2): 3–11.

Mertens, D.M. (2005) *Research Methods in Education and Psychology: Integrating Diversity with Quantitative, Qualitative, and Mixed Methods*, 2nd edition. Thousand Oaks, CA: Sage Publications, Inc.

Miller, S. (2003) 'Impact of mixed methods and design on inference quality', in A. Tashakkori and C. Teddlie (eds), *Handbook of Mixed Methods in Social and Behavioral Research*. Thousand Oaks, CA: Sage Publications, Inc. pp. 423–455.

Newman, I. and Benz, C.R. (1998) *Qualitative-Quantitative Research Methodology: Exploring the Interactive Continuum*. Carbondale, Il: University of Illinois Press.

Newman, I., Ridenour, C., Newman, C. and DeMarco, Jr., G.M.P. (2003) 'A typology of research purposes and its relationship to mixed methods research', in A. Tashakkori and C. Teddlie (eds), *Handbook of Mixed Methods in Social and Behavioral Research*. Thousand Oaks, CA: Sage Publications, Inc.

No Child Left Behind Act of 2001, Pub. L. No. 107-110, 115 Stat. 1425 (2002).

Onwuegbuzie, A.J. and Johnson, R.B. (2006) 'The validity issue in mixed research', *Research in Schools,* 13 (1): 48–63.

Patton, M.Q. (2002) *Qualitative Research and Evaluation Methods,* 3rd edition. Thousand Oaks, CA: Sage Publications, Inc.

Paul, J.L. (2005) *Introduction to the Philosophical Foundations of Research and Criticism in Education and the Social Sciences*. Upper Saddle River, NJ: Pearson Education, Inc.

Rossman, G. and Wilson, B. (1985) 'Numbers and words: Combining quantitative and qualitative methods in a single large scale evaluation study', *Evaluation Review,* 9: 627–643.

Shadish, W., Cook, T. and Campbell, D. (2002) *Experimental and Quasi-Experimental Designs for General Causal Inference*. Boston: Houghton Mifflin.

Shavelson, R.J. and Towne, L. (eds) (2002). *Scientific Research in Education*. Washington, DC: National Academy Press.

Tashakkori, A and Teddlie, C. (1998) *Mixed Methodology: Combining Qualitative and Quantitative Approaches*. Thousand, CA: Sage Publications, Inc.

Tashakkori, A. and Teddlie, C. (eds) (2003a) *Handbook of Mixed Methods in Social and Behavioral Research*. Thousand Oaks, CA: Sage Publications, Inc.

Tashakkori, A. and Teddlie, C. (2003b) 'The past and future of mixed methods research: From data triangulation to mixed model designs', in A. Tashakkori and C. Teddlie (eds), *Handbook of Mixed Methods in Social and Behavioral Research*. Thousand Oaks, CA: Sage Publications, Inc. pp. 671–702.

Teddlie, C. and Tashakkori, A. (2003) 'Major issues and controversies in the use of mixed methods in the social and behavioral sciences', in A. Tashakkori and C. Teddlie (eds), *Handbook of Mixed Methods in Social and Behavioral Research*. Thousand Oaks, CA: Sage Publications, Inc. pp. 3–50.

Teddlie, C. and Tashakkori, A. (2006) 'A general typology of research designs featuring mixed methods', *Research in the Schools,* 13 (1): 12–28.

Tobin, G.A. and Begley, C.M. (2004) 'Methodological rigour within a qualitative framework', *Journal of Advanced Nursing*, 48 (8): 388–396.

8

Method Mix, Technical Hex, and Theory Fix

Ray Pawson

Introduction: three jaunty theses and one daunting challenge

Thesis one: 'Method mix' is the new methodological Holy Grail. After years in their paradigmatic silos, social researchers have woken up to the discovery that society is multi-faceted, multi-layered and multi-perspectival. And, in order to begin to tame this hydra-headed beast, forms of inquiry are required capable of fusing the wayward forms of available evidence and uniting the current diversity of research perspectives.

Thesis two: 'Technical hex' is the attempt to do so by way of the development of new methods of analysis. A new breed of multi-method technocrats has appeared devising auxiliary methods with which to weave and weft the disorderly threads of social inquiry. These technical solutions always end up in witchcraft. Because they are procedural solutions they always carry the signature of a primary methodological orientation. They do not resolve the perspectival schisms; rather they dissolve them temporarily by creating fresh sets of practical rules for research. The result is hybridity of method rather than cumulation in understanding.

Thesis three: 'Theory fix' is rainbow's end – the resolution to mixed method analysis. It is, and always has been, the job of theory to beckon, order and explain empirical evidence. The welcome call to get to grips with a more complex vision of social reality is thus actually a summons to deploy well-rounded and better-grounded theory. The puzzle about how to combine 'qualitative' and 'quantitative' data is solved the moment we begin to theorize about how 'processes' lead to 'outcomes'. More complex explanatory propositions in social science will recognize conceptual roles for 'context', 'time' and 'change' and testing such theory will automatically call on 'comparative' and 'historical' and 'longitudinal' data. Thinking more clearly about how to interrogate theory with data is the path to methodological pluralism.

These three brief (and somewhat polemical!) paragraphs express the broad thesis to be pursued in this chapter and next in this prologue I introduce the arena in which I will attempt to substantiate these propositions. My case study takes this volume into the domain of evidence-based policy. Research here takes the form of empirical evaluations of social interventions – in order to determine which of them work best – in order to inform policymakers where expenditure is wise. Evaluation research has become industrial in proportion in recent years. Similar social programmes have been tried and tried again, and researched and researched again.

Accordingly, there has been some rethinking of the basic quest and the strategy of 'systematic review' has become the perspective of choice for evidence-based policy. Evaluation research is field research in the raw, often rough and ready, sometimes quick and dirty. Single studies are therefore deemed unsafe. The race is on to find a method that will most adequately synthesize all of the bygone research in order to root evaluative judgements even more firmly and cumulatively in the *weight of evidence* (Petticrew and Roberts, 2006).

It is useful to acquaint non-specialist readers with a brief history and a basic logic of this change of emphasis – for these pathways lead, arguably, to the most daunting challenge for the venture of mixed method research. Systematic review, in its original incarnation was unequivocally and proudly quantitative in outlook. On this model, what were sought from the various trials of a given intervention were solid outcome measures (namely, 'net effects'). What gave that evidence solidity was the requirement that it should be extracted from only those primary studies that followed rigorous experimental procedures (namely, 'randomized controlled trials'). What constituted the synthesis of the evidence was a statistical procedure (namely, 'meta-analysis') that pooled together the totality of evidence thus providing a 'mean effect' calculation. That statistic constituted the numerical verdict with which to judge the overall efficacy of the family of interventions. This measured approach still constitutes the mainstream, with levels of sophistication being added over the years in moving from simple 'vote-counting' estimates of programmes success to more recent models that seek to account for 'mediator and moderator variables' as well as the main programme effects (Lipsey and Wilson, 1993).

But then came a challenge. The meta-analytic approach, so goes the prevailing critique, is fine for drawing together evidence on clinical research in which the interventions are singular and discrete and the intended effects are simple and agreed. Social programmes, by contrast, are made in long and contested implementation chains; they depend for their efficacy on the vagaries of human volition; their effects are enormously sensitive to context; they throw up a range of intended and unintended consequence; and, if all that was not enough, they even tend to change the conditions that make them work in the first place.

Because this medley of difficulties has been apparent for some time, evaluation research (in its primary form) evolved a portfolio of research strategies in order to penetrate more deeply into the inner workings (the fabled 'black-box') of interventions. Thus, alongside experimental and quasi-experimental trials, we now have formative evaluation, developmental evaluation, process evaluation, theory-driven evaluation, goal-free evaluations, dialogic evaluation, action research and a whole lot more (Stern, 2004). There is no need for me to supply the multifarious technical details here because readers will already see the almighty predicament lying in wait. If one accepts the stout good sense of attempting to base policy recommendations on an ensemble of previous primary research, we face the ultimate challenge of multi-method inquiry. Not for systematic reviewers the mere tribulation of trying to combine 'qualitative' and 'quantitative' data: rather the task at hand is to find some way of synthesizing the entire methodological repertoire of applied social research.

Luckily, pluckily, a number of research programmes have been prepared to face up to this challenge and the main purpose of this chapter is to consider some fundamental principles lying behind these embryonic approaches. The emerging perspectives go by a number of names: narrative summary, meta-ethnography, meta-study, Bayesian meta-analysis, critical interpretative synthesis, EPPI-analysis, realist synthesis and so on. They have been supported by a number of different collaborations and funding bodies, some of which are identified in the references. I will not attempt to map the family tree here. Readers interested in the full lineage might consult Dixon-Woods et al. (2004). The point to re-emphasize for this volume is that this whole area of research synthesis constitutes a perfect laboratory for understanding the problems of mixed method social research.

The chapter now returns to its three core theses. The first is done and dusted. I have accepted wholeheartedly the case for the primary proposition. Both in general terms and in the specific case of systematic review, it is evident that social inquiry will prosper if we discover more adequate strategies for combining idiosyncratic methods and synthesizing ideographic data.

Some approaches to mixed method systematic review have accepted this challenge, as per the second proposition, as a technical cause. According to thesis two, this tactic always ends in tears and technical slight of hand. The charge of wizardry is pursued in the next section of the chapter via a cross-examination of two technical tactics that have come to the fore in the attempt to cut through the evidence jungle. The methods in question are: (i) Bayesian synthesis, which works by converting delicate qualitative reportage into muscular quantitative data; and (ii) standard setting, the attempt to create formal appraisal tools for the unruly qualitative realm, which parallel their strict judicial function in quantitative synthesis.

The final section of the chapter considers the third and positive thesis. The approach to systematic review championed here is one of 'theory-driven synthesis' (Pawson, 2006). Social interventions are themselves theories. They begin in the heads of policymakers who reason (i.e. theorize) – 'if we provide these resources to these subjects they will rethink so producing the desired change in behaviour'. The best way to investigate such hypotheses is to draw together evidence on 'for whom', 'in what circumstances', 'in what respects', 'with what staying power', and above all 'why' such programme theories work. This comprehensive explanatory quest automatically calls on the collection and analysis of a wide range of data in a wide range of forms.

But this is merely the starting point. The various incarnations of programme will meet with mixed success and this needs explaining. Qualitative information on poor management of a particular programme may explain quantitative evidence on a poor outcome. One type of evidence makes sense of another. This learning about how best to implement the programme may then provide a lesson about its differential reach. If we are beginning to understand why the programme works we can take in evidence from a particular trial about the uneven success rates of different subgroups of subjects. The explanation can be further consolidated drawing in wider comparative evidence from programmes in different locations and contexts. Knowing about the mechanisms of programme success may also allow us to interpret longitudinal data on the bloom and fade of positive outcomes. Before too long, whole suites of evidence are in place being absorbed into and reconciled with the developing explanation. Over time, as this core explanation becomes more secure it becomes the tool to test the credibility of new information. In short, research synthesis provides for the refinement of theory, which in time becomes the test bed for the authenticity of new data.

This thesis is pursued in the final section of the chapter, which ends with an illustration of this process of explanation building. It examines how evidence with quite different methodological provenance and power can be brought together in a theory-driven synthesis of the research on a well-known criminal justice intervention.

Technical hybrids – transmogrification and parallel universes

As already noted, and as with many other forms of investigation, research synthesis began life under the heavy influence of one particular paradigm. I illustrate this in Figure 8.1, which spells out the familiar sequence of steps involved in conducting research synthesis in the preferred manner, namely the 'meta-analytic' mode. As can be seen, each step calls upon standard techniques associated with quantitative inquiry

Leaving aside all matters concerning the internal conduct, effectiveness and limitations of this conventional approach, we come to the sixty-four-thousand-dollar question. What happens if one tries to accommodate other types of primary studies into this formula? Given that experimental studies may only constitute a tiny fraction of the available evidence, how should the remainder be incorporated into a review?

Before revealing my preferred solution, I dwell on two technical misadventures. Although I will criticize quite specific examples and forms of data manipulation in

---

1. *Formulating the review question.* Identifying the exact causal hypothesis connecting the independent variable (the programme) to the dependent variable (a particular outcome)

2. *Identifying and collecting the evidence.* Searching for and retrieving all the relevant primary studies of the effectiveness of that family of interventions. Building a complete census of studies via data-banks, bibliographies and websites.

3. *Appraising the quality of the evidence.* Deciding which of the foregathered studies is serviceable for further analysis by distinguishing rigorous from flawed primary studies. Creating a hierarchy of evidence favouring randomised controlled trials.

4. *Extracting and processing the data.* Presenting the raw evidence from the preferred studies on a data matrix, gathering the same information on the same variables from all primary inquiries.

5. *Synthesising the data.* Collating and summarising the evidence in order to gauge the efficacy of the family of programmes. Each primary study generates a measure of the effect size of the intervention. Meta-analysis pools these to provide an estimate of the mean effect of that class of interventions.

6. *Disseminating the findings.* Reporting the results to the wider policy community in order to influence new programming decisions. Identifying best practice and eliminating dangerous interventions.

FIGURE 8.1 *The basic systematic review template (meta-analysis version)*

what follows, the real reason for highlighting this pair is that they represent two broader impulses in the brave new world of multi-method research:

- The first approach carries the urge to deal with different forms of evidence by transforming, translating and converting from one to another. In the archetypal case, qualitative information is examined for its quantitative implications, which are then folded into the statistical synthesis.
- The second approach is more likely to assume the integrity of the different types of data – qualitative remains qualitative and quantitative remains quantitative. Instead, this strategy favours creating parallel technical systems for research synthesis. Qualitative evidence is assessed and analyzed in its own right – but in a way that shadows the quantitative imprimatur.

I. Bayesian synthesis

The Bayesian perspective treats systematic review as an aid to decision-making and the core concern lies with estimating the probability of success of a given intervention. In coming to real policy choices, it is assumed (wisely) that real decision-makers always contemplate the available evidence in the context of existing beliefs, experiences, hunches and so on. The goal of Bayesian synthesis is thus to simulate this process by establishing a 'prior' benchmark of expectations about an intervention before inspecting the outcome data from a range of quantitative studies and then combining the two in a 'posterior' estimate of the likelihood of programme success (Sutton and Abrams, 2001). This process is depicted in Figure 8.2, which recasts the familiar forest plots of meta-analysis in a pocket illustration of how qualitative information is used to provide the prior estimate, which is then overlaid into the quantitative analysis.

So much for first principles, let us now confront the devil by looking at the details. The best-known study of the ilk is Roberts et al.'s (2002) review of factors affecting the uptake of childhood immunization. Qualitative evidence played its part in building up the precursor – the prior estimates of the probability distribution of factors influencing vaccination programme usage.

This 'prior' was manufactured in two stages. First in a preliminary exercise in which a small team of reviewers listed their 'subjective opinions on key factors likely to affect the uptake childhood immunisation'. Their combined musings were transcribed and subjected to a content analysis, which revealed that 10 different factors were in play in their considerations. The same judges then reviewed the evidence from 11 primary qualitative studies (focus groups studies and open-ended interviews, etc.) on the said topic. Their task was to read the studies in detail and to provide a ranking of factors which they thought the studies identified as crucial in families coming to the decision to immunize their children. The overall rankings were then pooled and calibrated to unity – thus manufacturing a list of prior probability estimates.

The quantitative analysis was then performed somewhat more straightforwardly. The quantitative studies (32) were selected by dint of their original purpose, namely the explicit task of identifying factors that had played a part in the decision to have children immunized. Data on the relative influence of different variables was thus

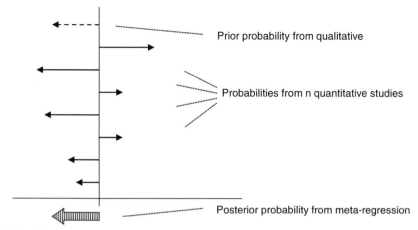

FIGURE 8.2 *Prior and posterior estimates in Bayesian analysis*

extracted and encoded into the same framework devised for the prior investigation. Meta-regression methods were then used to combine the two sets of probabilities. Details of the statistical techniques are not central to the case here, though the results are of considerable interest:

- The factors deemed important in the 'qualitative' and 'quantitative' perspective are not coterminous (only 6 of the 10 qualitative priors fetched up in the quantitative work; 2 factors identified in the quantitative work had not been previously identified).
- Close agreement between the two sources of evidence is rare and so the synthetic estimate often shifts markedly (e.g. the prior for the factor 'child's health' is 0.177, the posterior becomes 0.219).

This was a pioneering study and so, as the authors acknowledge, a cortege of innovative technical decisions is made en route. Nevertheless, the core strategic assumptions are worthy of careful scrutiny and I select out two that are closest to the concerns of this volume:

1. What is the source of the prior estimate – what exactly do the qualitative studies contribute?
2. What is the nature of qualitative evidence as understood in these manipulations?

On the first question (from whence the prior?) my answer is that, unmistakably and unequivocally, the genesis of data lies in the heads of the judges and in the technical procedures for combining their judgements. Indubitably and indisputably, the data in question do not reside in the original field encounters, nor in focus-group talk, nor in qualitative analytic strategies. In short, it is not the primary research but various readings and reconsiderations of the studies that are made to count. Let me quote directly the judges' modus operandi: 'the reviewers read the qualitative studies in randomised order, extracted the factors from each study *that they thought* the research had identified, and indicated their relative importance' (Roberts et al., 2002:

1598, *my italics*). Recall, furthermore that the judges were already pre-sensitized to think of the issue in terms of 'factors' before they even began to inspect the qualitative research. So whether the original studies were built to articulate such factors or indeed whether the original research subjects pondered them in such a formal and orderly manner was not at issue. The reviewers' task was to impose them within their readings of the qualitative materials.

Now, if the reasoning under review is really that of the reviewers, we are of course entitled to enquire of their identity. Roberts et al. make it quite clear that the research team (i.e. Roberts et al.) were responsible for making the prior judgements. Indeed, the five authors/judges are introduced explicitly – 'some of them were parents as well as having knowledge of statistical, sociological and psychological methods'. The purpose of this little passage is difficult to determine but it is hard not to perceive it as an own goal. The pivotal role of the judges as creating the data is acknowledged but is the statement an attempt to claim coverage of a broad representation of real stakeholder interests in immunization? Or is it a claim to great expertise in the ability to deconstruct qualitative inquiry? Neither assertion looks convincing but, whichever way it is viewed, this is most certainly not the customary qualitative call to heed the untainted and unmediated voice of research subjects.

This brings us to the second matter – what is the nature of qualitative evidence by the lights of this strategy for mixing methods? What are the qualitative studies supposed to uncover? The answer is again quite clear and again perplexing. Throughout the chapter, we are told that the qualitative studies allow the reviewers to uncover the potential 'factors', or 'considerations', or 'variables', or 'determinants' that underlie the choice to vaccinate. Indeed, the substantive gain of the synthesis is its revelation that the qualitative and quantitative studies discern a different range of influences being brought to that decision.

The methodological point, however, is that factors, influences, variables, whatever one wants to call them, are not really the stuff of qualitative research. Qualitative research rarely proceeds by making analytic distinctions between causes and effects. Rather explanations build holistically and informally though narrative devices such as 'thick description' and more formally through the use of 'pattern explanation', analytic induction', 'respondent validation' etc. Becker and Geer (1957: 29) described this rich explanatory texture many, many years ago and little has happened to gainsay it:

> The most complete form of the sociological datum … is the form in which the participant observer gathers it: an observation of some event, the events which precede and follow, and explanations of its meaning by participants and spectators, before during and after its occurrence.'

Thus even if qualitative research uncovers a particular 'factor' in a family's thinking about immunization (though it would more likely be termed a 'meaning structure', 'word-view', 'rule of thumb', 'mindset', 'habitus' etc.) this would merely be the starting point of analysis. One would expect fieldwork and analysis to go on to describe the legacy, support, rivalry, culture, norms, payoffs and values that sustain that reasoning. This is the very purpose of qualitative inquiry. And it is a purpose that is stripped away in this form of multi-method synthesis. The methodological mix affected in this strategy is best described as transmogrification. Qualitative studies are in attendance, but a quantitative reading is superimposed on them and then overlaid into the metrics of factor and regression models.

II. Appraising qualitative studies

In the mid-nineties, a group of qualitative researchers looked across at the protocols for meta-analytic review (Figure 8.1) and simultaneously liked and disliked what they saw. They loathed the fact that there was no room at the inn for qualitative research – it is relegated to an also-ran in research appraisal (step 3). But they did admire the close inspection and the stringent demands for rigour involved in admitting studies into the review process. If one has spent a lifetime on the receiving end of criticism of qualitative research for being wishy-washy tittle-tattle, then the thing to do is to make a claim for clear thinking and attention to detail back on one's own side of the fence.

For my second critical foray, I turn to attempts to create a technical apparatus for appraising qualitative research in readiness for synthesis. The core ambition remains – namely, raising the profile of qualitative studies in systematic review. In this instance, there is no sleight of hand involved in passing off qualitative evidence as something else. It is championed in its own right. The broad impulse is to create entirely fresh machinery for gathering, extracting, appraising and synthesizing qualitative data.

The love/hate relationship with meta-analysis manifested itself in the creation of a parallel universe of qualitative tools to be used in qualitative synthesis. Each formal step of the review sequence has been recreated for the contrasting terrain. I have no space here to look at all six stages, so I light upon on point 3 – perhaps the sore point. Meta-analysis sees qualitative research as little more than mere opinion. Qualitative researchers gritted teeth and chose to differ, but did so rather subtly. Just as there are better and worse experiments, so qualitative research also has its standards. And in respect of critical appraisal tools, the consequence is that there are by now several dozen attempts to set frameworks to assess the quality of qualitative research. I focus on, arguably, the biggest and best of these, namely *Quality in Qualitative Evaluation* a report produced for the UK Cabinet Office (Spencer et al., 2003).

What hits one in the eye about this particular appraisal tool is the enormity of its reach. The key reform is to inculcate standards for a much greater range of investigatory activities. In classic meta-analytic reviews the assessment criteria stray little beyond a *design* issue (i.e. is it a double-blinded randomized controlled trial (RCT)?) as the telling feature of the original studies. The new standards police, by contrast, aim to cover all phases of the research cycle. And in many ways this is an entirely reasonable expectation. There is no pronounced emphasis in qualitative research on design. In these circles it is no disgrace to be 'unstructured', 'flexible' and 'adaptive'.

Accordingly, good qualitative research is widely recognized as multi-faceted (or 'organic' or 'holistic') and the Cabinet Office framework responds by having something to say under eight major headings on the following aspects of research: 'findings', 'sample', 'data collection', 'analysis', 'reporting', 'reflexivity and neutrality', 'ethics' and 'auditability'. Each of these features is then subdivided so that, for instance, in considering the quality of 'findings' the reviewer is expected to gauge their 'credibility', their 'knowledge extension', their 'delivery on objectives', their 'wider inferences' and the 'basis of evaluative appraisal'.

The original subdivision into the 8 research stages thus jumps to 18 major themes or 'appraisal questions'. I will not list them all here because for each of these questions there are then 'quality indicators', usually running to 4 to 5 per indicator. This leaves us with a final set of 75 indicators with which to judge the quality of qualitative research. Again, I refrain from attempting a listing, though it is worth reproducing a couple of items (below) for they illustrate the intended mode of application. That is to say, the indicators are not *decision points* (is it an RCT or not?). Rather they invite the appraiser to examine rather more complex propositions as 'possible features for consideration', as for example:

- Is there discussion of access and methods of approach and how these might have affected participation/coverage? (a 'sampling' indicator)
- Is there a clear conceptual link between analytic commentary and presentation of original data? (a 'reporting' indicator)

To cap it all Spencer et al.'s report concludes, with some self-reflection on possible *omissions* from the framework (such as insufficient coverage of ethics and the failure to different sub-types of qualitative research such as discourse analysis). Hopefully, this miniature description gives a flavour of a massively painstaking undertaking. But now the point is reached for critical appraisal of the appraisal tool. I begin by assessing the framework in its own terms. Does it work? Can such a tool be used to support systematic review? Does it fill the Government Chief Social Researcher's ambition of 'providing a useful and useable guide for assessing the credibility, rigour and relevance of individual research studies' (Spencer et al., 2003: preface). I begin the critique by briefly rehearsing five practical impediments to using such an instrument as a quality threshold:

I. Boundless standards. Broadening the domain of quality standards creates quality registers that are dinosaurian in proportion. Spencer et al.'s assessment grid looks rather more like a scholarly overview of methodological requirements than a practicable checklist. A reviewer might well have to put hundreds of primary studies to the microscope. It takes little imagination to see that wading through the totality of evidence in the light of seventy-five general queries (rather than a pointed one on the design employed) can render the exercise unmanageable.

II. Abstract standards. Broadening the domain of quality standards results in the usage of 'essentially contested concepts' to describe the requisite rules. Amongst the imponderables that find their way into the Cabinet Office criteria are the requirements that the research should have 'clarity', 'coherence' and 'thoughtfulness', that it should be 'structured' and 'illuminating' and so forth. Again, it is easy to decipher whether a study has or has not utilized an RCT and thus deliver a verdict on its quality. But a concern for rigour, clarity, sensitivity and so forth generates far, far tougher calls.

III. Imperceptible standards. Broadening the domain of quality standards exacerbates one of the standards predicaments of systematic review, namely the foreshortening of research reportage caused by publishing and reporting conventions. Inevitably, the first victim of 'word-length' syndrome, especially in journal formats, is the technical detail on access, design, collection, analysis and so forth. The consequence, sadly, is that an appraisal of research standards cast in terms of 75 wide-ranging yardsticks will frequently have no material whatsoever with which to work.

IV. Composite standards. Broadening the domain of quality standards also raises novel questions about their balance. Should 'careful exposition of a research hypotheses' be prized more than 'discussion of fieldwork setting'? And how do these weigh up alongside 'clarity and coherence of reporting'? The permutations, of course, increase exponentially when one is faced with quality indicators by the score. By and large the new standards regime has resisted formulating an algorithm to calculate the relative importance of different criteria, as do Spencer and colleagues (2003: 82).

V. Permissive standards. With the above problems in mind, qualitative assessment tools usually come with the proviso that their application requires 'judgement'. In this case: 'We recognise that there will be debate and disagreement about the decisions we have made in shaping to the structure, focus and content of the framework. The importance of judgement and discretion in the assessment of quality is strongly emphasised by authors of other frameworks, and it was underlined by participants in our interviews and workshops. We think it is critical that the framework is applied flexibly, and not rigidly or prescriptively: judgement will remain at the heart of assessments of quality' (Spencer et al., 2003: 91).

One would be hard put to find a more sensible statement on the sensitivity needed in quality appraisal in this domain. The point, however, is to question why the processes ended in the production of an instrument that is too big, too abstract, too general, too indeterminate and so brings us full circle in calling on judgement as the ultimate arbiter in the qualitative realm. And my explanation for the muddle on qualitative quality assurance is that it has been reduced to a technical exercise. The culprit here is that the ambition to create a quality appraisal tool (and one, moreover, that matches the muscularity of the quantitative hierarchies) has run ahead of consideration of its function. The funders of the report saw this framework as 'an important step forward in ensuring that Government Policy is informed by robust, valid and appropriate research evidence' (Spencer et al., preface). They were hoping for some quick, slick checklist that would allow them reliable access to the real gems of qualitative evidence. Instead, Spencer's team served them with the methodological equivalent of realpolitik. The more rigorous the exploration of conduct of qualitative inquiry, the more unwieldy becomes the appraisal apparatus. The moral of the tale is that one cannot estimate the quality of qualitative evidence without prior consideration of how it might be used in research synthesis. Not for the first time, government analysts commissioned the cart before the horse.

So how can we get qualitative quality appraisal to work? The answer resides in neither technical trick nor quick fix; there is no point in marching down to the foot of the hill via the production of an abridged instrument reducing, say, the 75 key issues to a neat and tidy 7. One needs to go back to square one to identify the analytic problem. Despite the methodological despotism of the RCT-or-bust approach, it does produce a batch of primary studies up and ready to deliver a consignment of net effects that can be synthesized readily into an overall mean effect. Form fits function.

The qualitative quality appraisal tools, by contrast, are functionless; they are generic. Accordingly, the prior question regarding qualitative assessment is this – what do we expect the synthesis of qualitative inquiries to deliver? Tougher still, what is the expected product of the synthesis of an array of multi-method studies? An initial temptation might be to remain true to the 'additive' vision of meta-analysis – but a moment's thought tells us there is no equivalent of adding and taking the mean in qualitative inquiry. Any single qualitative inquiry, any one-off case study, produces a mass of evidence. As we have seen, one of the marks of good research of this ilk is the ability to fill out the pattern, to capture the totality of stakeholders' views, to produce thick description. But these are not the qualities that we aspire to in synthesis. We do not want an endless narrative; we do not seek a babel of viewpoints; we do not crave thicker description! In general, a model of synthesis-as-agglomeration is doomed to failure. We need a new master principle for research synthesis.

A theory-driven approach to research synthesis

And here it is. Research synthesis is the process of building, testing and refining theories. Mixing method is the matter of drawing together the evidence to enable this process.

A good starting point for grasping this thesis is to reconsider some elementary rules of explanation building in social science. Quite often our attention is stirred by empirical uniformities. As we navigate through life we note that it has its patterns and trends: some countries are more warlike than others; some institutions have greater longevity than others; some groups grab more resources than others; some social interventions are more successful than others. To establish such regularities, we have to engage in one way or another in quantitative research. We have to estimate or measure or count or calculate what we mean by state warfare, by organizational endurance, by social capital, by programme success and so on.

These rhythms and associations of social life are constant enough. However, there is nothing immutable about them. Something brings them about. And inquiry needs to be deepened to find out what. Thus the next step is to investigate the propensities of those states, organizations, groups and interventions, from which advantage stems. This may involve discoveries about the proclivity to violence of dictatorships, about staying power of bureaucracies, about social closure in professional groups, about the targeting of interventions to aspirational subjects. These lessons may spring from historical documents or institutional records or face-to-face inquiries or first-hand observation. But whichever way they emerge, they cover modes of inquiry that, in one way or another, are qualitative.

Because empirical uniformities are not laws, we are never particularly surprised when the associations don't work out as expected. We are not surprised if things change. Occasionally other countries, different institutions, rival groups and fresh interventions make the running. Social science, in other words, has to cope with a little paradox with which we are all able to live, namely when the 'exception proves the rule'. And, in understanding change, explanations need to be further deepened. In terms of the standing examples, we may go in search of reasons for why constant warfare saps resources, why traditional organizations fail to innovate, why power corrupts, and why programmes lead to the displacement of problems. Whichever the issue, these explanations require the support of some form of comparative, historical or longitudinal data.

At the risk of rehearsing Sociology 101, what I am trying to point out here is that routine explanation building in social science automatically calls on diverse study types. If we want to fully investigate an apparent uniformity, we need to measure it, we need to explain what brings it about, we need to discover its scope conditions, we need to track its staying power and so on. In this sense multi-method inquiry is nothing new. A good investigation will develop hypotheses on all these matters and more. A good investigation will collect data to interrogate all such propositions and more. And what is more, most of the theories in play during such an investigation will have had a previous life in empirical research. So what is under inquiry are further refinements to theories that have met with some previous success, and progress is made on the back of a broad sweep of earlier evidence. In short, cumulative social inquiry is multi-method inquiry.

Although, I am supremely confident about this proposition, the notion that mixed method investigation happens anyway or should happen anyway is probably not what this collection aspires to demonstrate. And indeed it is possible to devise more constructive guidance by locating the general insight about explanation building in the context of specific research strategies and designs. So, as the final act of the chapter, I return to the business of systematic review in evidence-based policy and see how this core logic can be applied.

In this respect, one needs to go back to basics and ask − what is synthesized in research synthesis? The new first principle I have in mind centres the idea of building explanations of how programmes work. In evaluation jargon this is all matter of refining the 'programme theory'. All social interventions are created out of the ideas, hopes, inspirations, convictions, beliefs and plans that what is delivered will change behaviour. With these 'theories' as the unit of analysis, systematic review becomes a different exercise with the function of testing and refining intervention hypotheses. Primary data are inspected not just for outcomes but for what they reveal about the programme theory. The core task of the review transforms from that of trying delivering a numerical verdict on whole families of programmes to that of building explanations of why, for whom, in what circumstances and in what respects they work. And this is multi-method inquiry incarnate.

To practicalities. Carrying out such a programme of work, as with any method of systematic review, is a long and labour-intensive business. Hundreds, potentially thousands, of primary inquiries have to be spotted, captured, digested, dredged and then sewn back together to deliver policy recommendations. I have no space here to describe the precise technical sequence and readers are referred to Pawson (2006) for details for the full strategy of 'realist synthesis'. Figure 8.3 represents a highly compressed summary, presented in such a way as to draw a deliberate contrast with the orthodox model as in Figure 8.1. As just argued, all of the main practical steps remain − the difference being that they are all now infused with programme theory.

It remains to provide an example of realist synthesis in action. The US sex offender notification and registration programme (know as Megan's Law) forms the case study for this illustration. The law was rushed onto the statute books following the murder of Megan Kanka by a released sex offender living anonymously in her community. Responsibility for implementing the programme lies in many hands (policymakers and police and probation officers and the public), with the result that the programme theory is long and complex (and prone to error). The initiative was driven by public outrage and evidence on its effectiveness has only trickled in as an afterthought.

1. *Theory elicitation.* Preliminary overview of policy documentation to discover the causal process of change assumed in designing and implementing the programme.

2. *Theory selection.* Formulating the review question by selecting out a key subset of mechanisms and process that are deemed crucial in changing behaviour.

3. *Identifying and collecting the evidence.* Searching for and retrieving the relevant primary inquiries with which to test the theory of change. A purposive sample locating studies which interrogate all aspects of the change hypothesis.

4. *Extracting and processing the data.* Extracting the raw evidence from the relevant studies. These will offer a multiplicity of data forms relating to processes, contexts and outcomes.

5. *Appraising the quality of the evidence.* Selecting and appraising primary studies (of all study types) on the basis of their ability to pinpoint and test the various components of the programme theory.

6. *Synthesising the evidence.* Juxtaposing, adjudicating, reconciling and consolidating the multiple sources of evidence to refine the programme theory. Producing a refined understanding of why and when it works.

7. *Disseminating the findings.* Reporting the results to the wider policy community in order to influence new programming decisions. Offering advice on the design, targeting and implementation of programmes.

FIGURE 8.3 *The basic systematic review template (realist version)*

Unsurprisingly, that data is uneven in respect of coverage, inquiry methodology and quality of research.

The full review is presented in Pawson (2002). Here I concentrate on the idea that a theory-driven synthesis will test and refine our understanding of how this programme works and, all importantly, that mixed methods analysis is automatically generated in that learning process. We begin at phase one, with an overview of the causal process of change assumed in design and implementation of the programme as presented in Figure 8.4.

The purpose of the review is to test out these assumptions and in particular to examine their integrity. Does the four-step sequence work out as anticipated? Are there flows or blockages or diversions? For purposes of illustration, I bring to the table just three studies (out of the available hundreds) in order to show how they might lead us to refine our understanding of this theory of change. Each very different nugget of evidence is briefly summarized before moving on to the substantive and methodological consequences.

Study 1: a quasi experiment

Conventional meta-analytic reviews concentrate on outcome studies. A lowering of recidivism rates is the intended outcome of the law and results of such inquires are of obvious interest to our investigation of the intended steps towards that goal. In fact, there are only two studies (Iowa Department of Human Rights, 2000; Schram and Milloy, 1995) that do approximate to the so-called gold standard of the

Step 1 Problem identification	**Step 2** Public disclosure	**Step 3** Sanction instigation	**Step 4** Offender response
Problem: intolerable danger of reoffence by released sex offenders. Solution: identify high-risk offenders and create valid and reliable registers, carrying public and constitutional endorsement.	Problem: ex-offenders reside anonymously in communities, denying potential victims the ability to defend themselves. Solution: issue bulletins and press releases identifying high-risk offenders.	Informed citizens take precautions to minimise threat of victimisation. They become co-producers of community responses with the police and probation. Increasing surveillance provides a capacity to monitor suspicious behaviour	Recidivism reduces with the offender recognising decreased opportunity and higher risk of arrest. The shaming and stigmatising effects of publicity also guard against reoffence.

FIGURE 8.4 *Megan's Law: basic programme theory*

controlled comparison. Both evaluations fail to discover a significant effect on recidivism. However, the small print of their findings provides an interesting refinement to the programme theory, which can be pursued via the former study.

Clearly, this is a field in which the random application of subjects to experimental and control groups is impracticable. The researchers therefore use a quasi-experimental design, to compare the recidivism rates of members of the first group of offenders released under Washington's notification regime (1990–1993) with those of a matched sample selected from those released prior to the enactment of the new law. The key comparison focused on the percentages re-arrested for a sexual offence within four and a half years of release. The headline results from the study are as follows:

- At the end of the 54 months at risk in the community, the notification group had a slightly lower estimated rate of sexual recidivism (19%) than the comparison group (22%) but, because we are dealing with small numbers, this difference was not found to be statistically significant.
- The timing of re-arrest, however, was significantly different for the notification and comparison groups. Offenders subjected to community notification were arrested for new crimes much more rapidly than comparable offenders who were released without notification (Schram and Milloy, 1995: 3).

In theory refinement terms, a first suggestion emerges here that the registration and notification programme might favour detection rather than prevention.

Study 2: a prospective simulation

A second piece of evidence that sheds light on the integrity of our step-by-step model is a simulation by Petrosino and Petrosino (1999). They take on the difficult task of trying to estimate the difference Megan's Law makes to the capacity of the public to defend itself. The inquiry was conducted in Massachusetts, the last of all states to bring Megan's Law to the statute book, and the researchers had no current registrations with which to work. Given these difficulties, their ingenious response was to work forward from a current set of actual offences, seeking to discover how many current offenders *would have been* under surveillance *if* the law had been in place. Their estimate is summarized in Figure 8.5.

Of the 136 offenders, only 36 had a prior conviction that would have triggered the notification process. We do not know how many previous offenders have gone undetected – but these, of course, also fall outside the gaze of the law. Of those with prior convictions, 12 committed a stranger-predatory offence and 24 offended against family, friends or co-workers. It must be supposed that notification has little protective effect on offenders' 'associates' whom, in all likelihood, already knew of the history of convictions. Attention thus focuses on the 12 stranger-predatory offenders. In six of these cases it was deemed very unlikely that the victim could have been forewarned by notification because these offenders were from out of state. The simulated notification chain thus ends with just six victims who might have had a realistic chance of responding to local alerts.

136 Serious sex offences (offenders considered criminal sexual psychopaths)

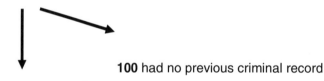

100 had no previous criminal record

36 had a previous offence that would have been eligible for registration

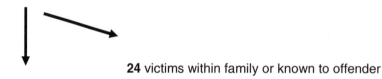

24 victims within family or known to offender

12 committed stranger-predatory offence

6 offenders from out of state

6 cases remain with the potential to respond to community notification

FIGURE 8.5 *The diminishing target of Megan's Law in Massachusetts*

In theory testing terms, we see substantial gaps appearing in the implementation chain and raise a cautionary note here of the perils of a programme theory pinning its main hopes on public surveillance.

Study 3: Narrative responses to open-ended questions

Step three in the programme theory assumes that notification increases opportunities for a community response in partnership with law enforcement and that, in particular, the prospects for surveillance, protective action and preventative strategies are all increased. Among the sources of evidence that shed light on how well these theories correspond to reality is a survey of Wisconsin probation and parole officers with day-to-day responsibility for supervising sex offenders (Zevitz and Farkas, 2000). Here, I extract some of the answers to open-ended questions focusing on how changing duties brought about by Special Bulletin Notification cases (SBNs) altered their caseloads.

Megan's Law, as the probation officers emphasized, is an 'unfunded mandate' and this new obligation diverted the balance of their daily activities towards SBN cases: for example, 'I don't think management understands the huge number of collateral contacts necessary for a sex offender caseload – family of defendant, victim's family, D.A., clinician, employer and so on'. Perhaps the most significant comments on caseload (in respect of both magnitude and implications) refer to the problems of having to manage the community's reactions to offenders. Minor harassment is routine, housing problems commonplace, death threats occasional. Such qualitative research is well placed to capture the tensions present. All of which is rather evocatively summarized in the sardonic observation of one probation officer: 'there is more pressure to baby-sit (spend greater amounts of time) with SBN cases, simply because they are SBN cases'.

In theory development terms, a key assumption – namely that the community will work in partnership with the law enforcement authorities – is called into question. Indeed, it seems that practitioners spend a substantial amount of time protecting offenders from the harsher edge of the community's attention.

Conclusions

I will attempt to wrap up the substantive conclusions to the mini-review before addressing the key concern about mixed method analysis. Inspection of this trio of primary evaluations shows that the theory of change assumed in the Megan's Law legislation may not always run true. There are disappointing end-of-the-line results on recidivism rates. We also have distinctive signs of side effects – the sparse opportunity for surveillance of offences, the increased opportunity for harassment of offenders, and the extended watch of the probation service. Further analysis of the thicket of decision points in Figure 8.4 uncovers many more instances where inconsistency at one point triggers an unanticipated outcome later in the sequence (Pawson, 2002). Vastly superior co-ordination of the programme is needed to make it an effective deterrent.

The true nature of research synthesis also glimmers from the juxtaposition of the three pearls of evidence. Each one makes sense of the other. Study one indicates that Megan's Law may influence the ability to apprehend repeat offenders rather than prevent repeat offences. Study two indicates some reasons why surveillance capacity to intercept sex offences in the making is surprisingly limited. The third study shows that the scrutiny that is engendered is about tracing the released offender's movement in and out of work, housing, family and neighbourhood conflict. This awareness of 'known associates' together with the notification records providing 'offender profiles' including fingerprints, palm prints, blood and saliva samples serves the classic purpose of crime detection, rather than prevention. So whilst the programme itself generates vicious spirals of perverse effects, the synthesis produces a virtuous circle of explanation.

Coming to the matters methodological, it cannot have escaped the reader's attention that the three empirical cases represent quite distinctive research traditions. Because programme theory is unit of analysis, the review automatically calls upon such diverse ingredients. Because explanation building is the crux of the analysis a tincture of quasi-experimentation, a touch of prospective simulation and a hint of narrative data are digested effortlessly. And within this simple example resides a powerful general principle, namely that the process of theory building, testing and refinement is both means and ends in the quest for mixed method research. Whilst it is beyond the scope of this chapter to make the case, I would argue that what is good for research synthesis is equally good for primary research. The tenet about well-rounded explanation generating well-rounded data can be applied to any substantive inquiry. *(Editor – possible references to other chapters here?)*

A brief postscript on research quality is also triggered by this principle. Theory building is not only the guiding light on the need to capture explanatory components from diverse study types; it also provides the vantage point from which to assess their quality. Readers will recall that systematic review is much troubled in devising criteria with which to decide whether primary studies warrant inclusion in a review. Rather than assess studies in the round and against a generic set of requirements, the theory-building axiom creates a different rule – namely, that what should be assessed is the credibility of the contribution to explanation building.

Study one, assessed in its own right, is a mere quasi-experiment and open to all the difficulties of capturing the entire set of variables on which to match experimental and control groups. This is a decisive weakness if the task is to measure precise outcome scores. But our interest in the study concerned the vast difference between effectiveness in terms of recidivism and arrest, and it is almost inconceivable that the method of matching could have made a major difference in this respect. The second study would have raised a different issue when standing before the quality inspectorate in that there are no agreed and rehearsed standards in respect of its rather imaginative design. But the key theory-driven criteria concerns whether its picture of the Megan's Law's limited coverage of the spectrum of serious sex offence is valid and typical. And, once again, the balance of data is so decisive that to deny the inquiry a voice would seem churlish. The third study, read in full, turns out to be a rather partisan account of the steadfastness of the probation service and their ability to minimize sex re-offence rates. The latter claim is probably wrong, the heroics may or may not be true, but there seems good reason to believe the evidence on changing workload patterns and the attendant responsibilities. Our mix of evidence seems secure. A highly standardized approach to research quality assessment might well have missed all three of these pearls of wisdom.

References

Becker, H. and Geer, B. (1957) 'Participant observation and interviewing', *Human Organization*, 16 (3): 28–32.

Dixon-Woods, M., Agarwal, S., Young, B., Jones, D. and Sutton, A. (2004) *Integrative Approaches to Qualitative and Quantitative Evidence*. London: Health Development Agency.

Iowa Department of Human Rights (2000) *The Iowa Sex Offender Registry and Recidivism*. Division of Criminal and Juvenile Justice Planning and Statistical Analysis Centre.

Lipsey, M. and Wilson, D. (1993) 'The efficacy of psychological, educational and behavioral treatment: confirmation from meta-analysis', *American Psychologist*, 48 (12): 1181–1209.

Pawson, R. (2002) 'Does Megan's Law Work: A theory-driven systematic review'. Working Paper No 8, ESRC UK Centre for Evidence Based Policy and Practice.

Pawson, R. (2006) *Evidence-Based Policy: A Realist Perspective*. London: Sage.

Petrosino, A.J. and Petrosino, C. (1999) 'The public safety potential of Megan's Law in Massachusetts: an assessment from a sample of criminal sexual psychopaths', *Crime and Delinquency*, 45 (1): 140–158.

Petticrew, M. and Roberts, H. (2006) *Systematic Reviews in the Social Sciences: A Practical Guide*. Oxford: Blackwell.

Roberts, K., Dixon-Woods, M., Fitzpatrick, R., Abrams, R. and Jones, D. (2002) 'Factors affecting the uptake of childhood immunisation: A Bayesian synthesis of qualitative and quantitative evidence', *The Lancet*, 360 (9345): 1596–1599.

Schram, D. and Milloy, C. (1995) *Community Notification: A Study of Offender Characteristics and Recidivism*. Olympia, WA: Washington State Institute for Public Policy.

Spencer, L., Ritchie, J., Lewis, J. and Dillon, L. (2003) *Assessing Quality in Qualitative Evaluation*. Government Chief Social Research's Office.

Stern, E. (2004) *Evaluation Research Methods*. London: Sage.

Sutton, A. and Abrams, D. (2001) 'Bayesian methods in meta-analysis and evidence synthesis', *Statistical Methods in Medical Research*, 10: 277–303.

Zevitz, R. and Farkas, M. (2000) 'The impact of sex-offender community notification on probation/parole in Wisconsin', *International Journal of Offender Therapy and Comparative Criminology*, 44 (1): 8–21.

Web materials

http://www.evidencenetwork.org/
http://www.leeds.ac.uk/sociology/realistsynthesis/
http://www.campbellcollaboration.org/
http://eppi.ioe.ac.uk/cms/

9

Mixing Data Collection Methods: Lessons from Social Survey Research[1,2]

Edith de Leeuw and Joop Hox

Introduction

The term 'mixed-mode' means different things to different people. Mixed-mode research is often used as an alternative to the better established term 'mixed methods research' (e.g. Nicholls et al., 2001) and refers to studies that combine qualitative and quantitative research in a single or multi-phase study (Tashakkori and Teddlie, 1998). In survey research, the term mixed-mode refers to the use of more than one quantitative data collection method. While this chapter centers on the latter, the issues raised here are directly related to mixed methods research, where different modes are usually employed to collect data for the qualitative and quantitative parts of the research project. In addition, different collection modes may exist within the qualitative and quantitative part of the mixed methods research design. For example, research relating to doctor-patient relations is often conducted within a mixed methods research design but, depending on the preferences, impairment, and abilities of patients, different kinds of data collection methods may be used for the qualitative as well as the quantitative part of the study.

With the notable exception of Kemper et al. (2003) and Teddlie and Yu (2007), few texts exist that explore fundamental issues such as employing different data collection methods and different sampling strategies in relation to mixed methods research designs. But even these texts consist primarily of a review of the main sampling strategies for social science research in general, before connecting sampling design more explicitly to mixed methods designs combining qualitative and quantitative methods, e.g. the combination of probability and purposive sampling techniques. As little empirical research exists in the mixed methods literature on the consequences of combining different data collection methods for data quality and inference, this chapter will attempt to close the gap by employing findings from a different set of literature: an exploration of lessons learned from mixed-mode survey research and its potential applications for mixed methods research designs.

Characteristic for most surveys is that a large sample of the population is studied with a structured questionnaire. Data collection in surveys can be carried out using several data collection methods or modes. Traditionally, social surveys data are collected either by an interviewer visiting a respondent, the face-to-face interview, or through a self-administered questionnaire, usually sent by mail. In the second half of the twentieth century, these practices changed. Telephone surveys became increasingly popular, reaching their zenith in the 1990s. Advances in computer technology in the past 30 years have made computer-assisted survey methods possible. Characteristic of all forms of computer-assisted data collection is that questions are read from the computer screen, and that responses are entered directly into the computer, either by an interviewer or by the respondent. An interactive program presents the questions in an established order. In more advanced forms, questions and question order may be different for different (groups of) respondents. For each paper-and-pen data collection method, there is now a computer-assisted alternative available. Face-to-face interviewers often carry laptops and use computer-assisted personal interviewing (CAPI), telephone interviews are usually conducted in a centralized setting using computer-assisted telephone interviewing (CATI) systems, and there are several forms of computer-assisted self-administered questionnaires (CASI) of which the web or internet survey is by now the most popular (e.g. de Leeuw et al., 2003; Nicholls et al., 1997).

With all these possibilities, the choice for a specific data collection mode is often based on complicated assessments of the strengths and weaknesses of each data collection method, and sometimes the best results are achieved by employing more than one data collection method, i.e. a mixed-mode approach (de Leeuw, 2005). In mixed-mode designs, there is a clear trade-off between cost and errors, i.e. coverage error, nonresponse error and measurement error. Coverage error is concerned with whether the whole population of interest is covered by the sampling frame, in other words, does the sampling frame include all units of the population or does the researcher miss out on some (undercoverage), or do some units appear more than once in the sampling frame (overcoverage)? Nonresponse error focuses on the percentage of the sample that does not respond, as well as the systematic differences between the respondents and nonrespondents on issues relevant to the research focus. Measurement error is error introduced by data collection itself, such as interviewer effects, social desirability, and question wording or question format effects (e.g. Biemer and Lyberg, 2003; Groves, 1989; Foddy, 1993).

Some examples: although an increasing number of people have access to the World Wide Web, internet penetration is far from complete and ranges from 75% coverage for Sweden to less than 1% for 19 African countries (www.internetworldstats.com, data from February 2007). Thus, many countries have a considerable coverage problem when internet-based data collection methods (e.g. online surveys or discussion groups) are used. Furthermore, within these countries, the elderly, lower educated, lower income, and minorities are less likely to be online. To compensate for coverage error in web surveys, mixed-mode strategies are employed, such as telephone-internet and mail-internet surveys, where respondents who cannot be contacted through the internet are approached by phone or postal mail to reduce undercoverage of those who have no web access. A second example relates to nonresponse reduction: following up the nonrespondents in a mail survey by telephone or face-to-face interviews can increase response rates further and reach and convert reluctant respondents more effectively than simply mailing a reminder.

In the above two examples, coverage error and nonresponse error are reduced by using a mixed-mode design, which improves data quality. But there also is a potential risk associated with using multiple data collection methods: the mode itself may have an effect on the respondents and thereby on the data. One may rightly question whether data collected with different data collection methods can be combined and compared. In other words, mixing modes may decrease data quality and increase measurement error (de Leeuw, 2005; Dillman and Christian, 2003).

These problems may be compounded by mixed methods research designs, which not only employ different modes for the qualitative and quantitative parts of the research project, but, within the qualitative or quantitative parts, different data collection modes may also exist. In the remainder of this chapter, we present a systematic overview of different types of mixed-mode strategies in social surveys, discuss their advantages and disadvantages, and offer some tentative suggestions for mixed methods research.

Types of mixed-mode designs

There are many forms of mixed-mode designs for social surveys and many ways of summarizing them. Dillman (2000: 219) focuses on the data collection and its objectives, while Balden (2004) uses time of interacting with respondents (i.e. contact phase, response phase, and follow-up phase) as organizing principles. These overviews can be integrated and expanded by including *data collection mixtures* and *means of communication mixtures*. It is important to realize that researchers communicate with sample members at different points in time and that they may use different modes of communication such as prenotifications in the form of advance letters and reminders.

A very good example of a mixed-mode survey design is the Nielsen media research methodology (e.g. Trussell and Lavrakas, 2004). This mixed-mode survey design uses a random sample (RDD) of household telephone numbers to which addresses are matched. The full mixed-mode data collection design consists of seven steps: first a pre-recruitment postcard is mailed to all homes for which addresses are available; this is followed by a recruitment phone call; the third contact attempt is again by mail and is an advance postcard announcing the diary; next the diary survey packet is mailed to all homes for which an address is now available (regardless of the result of the recruitment call). This diary survey packet includes a cover letter, diaries, a cash incentive, a return envelope, and a brochure. A reminder postcard in step 5, a reminder phone call in step 6, and again a reminder postcard in step 7 follow the survey package. Although the actual data collection uses one single method (diaries), the data collection system is multi-mode with mail and telephone advance notifications and reminders.

In Figure 9.1 we give a systematic representation of different types of mixed-mode systems, the reason to employ them and the potential effect on data quality.[3] This overview is ordered according to the phase of data collection.

Contact phase and multiple modes

During the contact phase, mixed-mode designs can be used for prenotification and recruitment. A classical example is the use of advance letters in telephone surveys. This particular mixed-mode design is chosen, because it is easier to establish legitimacy and trust in an official letter that has a letterhead, contact information and signature, than with a mere voice over the phone. In establishment surveys the opposite

Mixed-mode system	Rationale for implementation	Effect on data quality
Contact phase mode change		
Advance notification in different mode than data collection	• Correct sampling frame • Raise response rate • Enhance credibility/trust	• Reduce coverage and nonresponse error • No threats to measurement if data collection is single-mode
Recruitment/Screening/Selection in different mode than data collection	• Reduce cost • Enhance efficiency • Update/expand contact information for main mode	• Timeliness • If pure screening no threats to measurement • If screening plus first part data collection in other mode risk of potential mode effects on measurement
Response phase mode change		
Different (sample) persons by different modes when collecting data from one sample at one time point	• Reduce costs • Improve coverage • Improve response	• Reduction of coverage and nonresponse error • Mode effects on measurement confounded with subgroups
Different parts of a data collection method (e.g. questionnaire) *by different modes* when studying one sample at one time point	• Improve privacy of measurement • Reduce social desirability	• Improved data quality, especially with very sensitive questions
Same persons with different modes in same sample at multiple time points (panel)	• Reduce costs	• Measurement differences causing confounding of time effects and mode effects
Different (whole) samples by different modes, often at different times with different data collection methods	• Comparative research • Different research traditions • Different coverage • Different cost structure	• Coverage error • Nonresponse error • Measurement error • Incomparability
Follow-up phase mode change		
Reminders in different modes from mode in which all respondents are asked to complete questionnaire.	• Raise response	• Reduce nonresponse error • If pure reminder no threats to measurement • If reminder plus part data collection in other mode risk of potential mode effects on measurement
Partly based on:	Dillman (2000)	Balden (2004)

FIGURE 9.1 *Types of mixed-mode survey systems, rationale, and effect on data quality based on de Leeuw, 2005, Figure 1*

mix – a telephone precontact before a mail or web survey – has been found to be effective. Research on businesses faces different methodological issues than research on households, and a telephone conversation is far more efficient than a letter in getting past gatekeepers and in identifying the targeted most knowledgeable respondent in the establishment (Dillman, 2000, chap 10). As the actual data collection in these cases is using one single data collection mode, this mixed-mode system has no potential negative effect on measurement, but will reduce nonresponse.

A different situation occurs when an advance notification is used to invite sample members to participate in a research project, and leaves it to the respondent to choose a mode. For instance, a paper mail advance letter with an invitation to complete a web survey, but also offering the respondent a paper questionnaire or phone interview instead. An example is the American lung association survey of asthma awareness among school nurses. In this survey, postcards are sent to a random sample of respondents, inviting them to participate online via an indicated website or by telephone via a toll free number. A procedure like this is often used to reduce coverage error, but as the data collection itself now is multi-mode, other errors may arise. First, self-selection may cause systematic variations in socio-demographic characteristics, as respondents choosing the internet as the means of communication may differ from those choosing a telephone conversation. Second, the data collection method itself may cause systematic response differences, as respondents may give different answers to an interviewer over the phone, than when they respond over the web. The researcher has to decide which scenario is the best: multiple mode with reduced coverage error at the price of increased measurement error or a single data collection method approach with a larger coverage error component. In web surveys, where the risk of coverage error is still high, researchers usually opt for the multi-mode approach and accept the risk of method effects.

The above reasoning can also be applied to screening and selection. For reasons of time efficiency and cost, screening for special groups and respondent selection is often done over the telephone. If the telephone conversation is only used for screening and recruitment purposes and the subsequent data collection is done in a different mode, than there is a win–win situation of increased efficiency without added method effects in the main data collection phase. Sometimes a screening procedure is used to get additional (e-mail) address information to facilitate the main study. Again, if the data collection in the main study is using one single method, like in the Nielsen diary study mentioned above, there is a win–win situation. But often, screening and recruitment are part of a longer interview. If a respondent is eligible, an interview takes place and ends with a request for participation in the study. This is quite common in longitudinal studies, but also in recruitment for internet panels and 'access' panels. In those cases, different data collection methods are often used for subsequent waves or data collection periods: a form of sequential multiple mode. Here the danger of mode effects is a serious risk, as it is hard to decide whether a change over time is a real change in the person or if it is caused by a change in mode. Time effects and mode effects in the results are then fully confounded.

Main data collection phase and multiple modes

When two or more methods at the same time are used to collect data, this is called a concurrent mixed-mode design. In a sequential mixed-mode design, different data collection modes are used over time (Balden, 2004). There are several situations in which these designs can be employed.

One sample, one time period, and different data collection methods
The first response phase mode change mentioned in Figure 9.1 is where one mode of data collection is used for some respondents of a sample and another mode for

others in that same sample in order to collect the same data. An example of a concurrent mixed-mode design for this situation is a paper mail survey with a web
option. Another example is the asthma awareness survey among school nurses mentioned earlier, which offers a choice between web and telephone mode. The aim in
these cases is to reduce coverage bias and costs. It is also assumed that giving a sample
member a choice may reduce nonresponse, as certain persons may express certain
mode preferences. However, there is no firm empirical evidence for this. Still, giving
respondents a choice may be a good option, as it may create good will and save costs,
and in establishment surveys it is more usual than in household surveys to allow
respondents to choose their preferred method (e.g. paper, fax, and web).

Far more common and effective are sequential multi-mode designs for reducing
nonresponse. Usually an inexpensive mode is used as the main mode for the whole
sample and a more expensive mode is used for the nonresponse follow-up to
improve response rates. This approach originates from the empirical work of
Hochstim (1967), who compared three strategies of mixed-mode data collection:
starting with the expensive face-to-face interview, starting with the less expensive
telephone survey, and starting with the least expensive mail survey. In two independent studies, Hochstim found that the three mixed-mode strategies were highly comparable regarding final response rate and completeness of questionnaires, and that the
substantive responses did not vary systematically across these modes. The only important difference was costs per interview, which varied considerably by strategy. These
findings were corroborated by Siemiatycky (1979), who concluded that strategies
beginning with mail and telephone, and following them up with other methods,
provided response rates as high as face-to-face interviews for one half of the cost.
Subsequently, various studies used sequential mixed-mode strategies and showed that
switching to a second and even third mode is an effective means of improving
response for household and establishment surveys.

However, there are two sides to a coin, and there is a potential for error as different data collection modes may cause systematic mode-based differences. Hochstim
(1967) reported that substantive findings were virtually interchangeable and this
study had much influence in accepting mixed-mode strategies. Later studies emphasized the differences between data collection methods and the danger of mode
effects. Not only do data collection methods differ in presence versus absence of
interviewers, they also differ in the way information is transmitted, for instance
visual, aural, or auditory, and verbal versus nonverbal communication. This may
indeed influence measurement and data quality (e.g. de Leeuw, 1992; 2005; Dillman
and Christian, 2003; Groves, 1989).

One sample, one time point, and different modes
for different parts of the data collection process
A second form of a mixed-mode design is when different modes are used for a subset
of questions in the data collection process during one single data collection period.
Usually a mix of interviews and self-administered forms is used to exploit the strong
points of both methods. One of the most consistent findings in mode comparisons
is that self-administered forms of data collection perform better than interview
modes when sensitive questions are asked (for an overview, see de Leeuw, 1992).
Therefore, mixed-mode approaches using a self-administered paper form to elicit

sensitive information in face-to-face interviews have been standard good practice for a long time. With the use of computer-assisted interviewing, this same practice was implemented in interview programs and within CAPI. Now a computer-assisted form of self-administered interviews (CASI) is used for sensitive questions. These self-administered forms reduce social desirability and enhance privacy as neither the interviewer nor any other person in the vicinity will know the answers given. This specific mixed-mode situation, in which a subset of sensitive questions is asked using a self-administered mode, while the remainder of the (non-sensitive) questions is administered in an interview, only has positive advantages and is not a case for concern.

One sample, different modes, different time points

The third form of a mixed-mode design for data collection is a longitudinal study or a panel in which data from the same respondents are collected at different time points, and where different data collection modes are used at those different time points. Practical considerations and costs are the main reasons for this multiple mode approach. For instance, the problem may be whether or not a good sampling frame with contact information is available at the first time point. Sometimes addresses are available, but telephone numbers or e-mail addresses are not and these have to be collected.

Sometimes no sampling frame is available at all and area probability sampling is the only option. This means that an initial contact with respondents must be made using a face-to-face method. Together with the greater flexibility of an interviewer to gain cooperation at the doorstep and the opportunities for optimal screening, a face-to-face interview is often the favourite choice for the base-line or initial data collection occasion of a panel. To reduce costs, less expensive methods are used after the first wave whenever possible.

A combination of face-to-face interviews for the first wave and telephone interviews for the next waves is used for Labour Force surveys in several countries. Another example of a mixed-mode panel combines an initial face-to-face interview with mail surveys in the next waves. Sometimes, modes even alternate and after an initial face-to-face survey, data is collected via telephone and mail with an occasional face-to-face survey interspaced at crucial points. For instance, in longitudinal health surveys or in growth studies of infants, it may be necessary to include simple medical tests at regular times, which need a face-to-face contact. Internet panels often are formed after data were collected initially by telephone.

Although there are many practical advantages, there are also problems from a data integrity point of view. In all the sequential mixed-mode studies described above, time effects and data collection mode effects are confounded, and it is difficult to assess whether a change over time is a real change over time or the result of a change of data collection mode.

Different samples, different modes

The fourth and last variation in multiple mode data collection uses different data collection modes for different (sub-)populations. Reasons for using different data collection methods for different populations vary: different countries may have different data collection traditions or different practical constraints. For example, in a densely populated country face-to-face surveys and interviews are feasible, but in sparsely populated areas this may not be the case. Some countries have detailed reg-isters with address information for sampling purposes; while in other countries area probability-based samples may be the only option. Low literacy levels can preclude mail surveys, and in impoverished regions electronic equipment may be difficult to use. Furthermore, different data collection agencies may have different traditions and therefore may differ in the availability of experienced and trained staff that is needed for specific data collection modes. Different agencies may also differ in the availability of other required resources, such as a large centralized telephone unit.

To enhance comparability between the data, design factors should be kept con-stant as far as possible. For example, the International Social Survey Programme (ISSP) operates on the principle of 'keep as much the same as possible' across imple-mentations. At the start of the ISSP the required data collection method was self-completion, but as new members joined in, the self-completion format proved unsuitable for populations with low literacy rates and face-to-face interviews were allowed (Skjåk and Harkness, 2003). A clear example of different data collection modes for different samples is the Behavioural Risk Factor Surveillance System (BRFSS) of the Centers for Disease Control and Prevention (CDC) in the USA. In this study 15 states participate in a monthly data collection. To enhance comparabil-ity of the data across the 15 states, a standard core questionnaire was developed by CDC for all states to use. However, the data collection method itself varies by state, which results in a single-mode approach within a state, but a mixed-mode design for the total study summarizing and comparing data of all 15 states.

Although mode effects may cause differences in results between countries, a single-mode approach is often not feasible in international research. One may even argue that keeping modes the same across countries is inflating the differences between countries, as a mode that is optimal for one country or target population may be a poor choice for another. In planning cross-cultural and international stud-ies a careful consideration should be made of the relative risk of mode effects in a mixed-mode approach compared to differential effects of other error sources in a single-mode approach.

Even when researchers are not collecting the data themselves but use existing data files, mode effects may be a serious source of error too. Different data collection methods may have been used, but other errors also may play a role and pose serious threats to the internal validity of the conclusions. For instance, the studies of which the data are used may suffer from differential nonresponse, non-equivalence of data collection methods, and time differences in data collection. Here the issue is not just mixed-mode data collection, but non-equivalence of the total design. A problem is that the primary data sources used in secondary research often do not report such differences in sufficient detail (Hox and Boeije, 2005).

Follow-up phase and multiple modes

Reminders are an efficient tool to increase response (e.g. Dillman, 2000). Sometimes reminders employ the same mode of contact, for instance a postcard in a mail survey, an e-mail message in an internet survey, or a telephone reminder in a telephone interview. Sometimes a different mode of contact is used for the follow-up contact.

For instance, costs and time restraints may prohibit in-person follow-ups in a face-to-face interview. A different mode for the follow-up may also lead to additional information about the sampling frame or improved contact information (e.g. a telephone reminder to an internet or mail survey), and changing modes may improve the attention or novelty value of the reminder.

Persuasion letters are a specific form of a mixed-mode follow-up contact. Reluctant respondents in face-to-face and telephone interviews are sent a special persuasion letter, emphasizing the importance of participating in a study, before they are re-approached by interviewers. Persuasion letters have to communicate the legitimacy and importance of the study to the reluctant respondent, and if possible, should be tailored to subgroups of reluctant respondents or refusers.

If the mode change only involves the follow-up reminder, potential errors through mode effects are avoided, while the potential benefits of a second mode of communication can be exploited: a win–win situation just as in using prenotifications. However, when the follow-up is also used to collect additional data, a potential mode effect may occur. If the full questionnaire is administered in another mode to reduce nonresponse, a sequential mixed-mode approach is used, and there are risks of data integrity (see section entitled 'Main data collection phase and multiple modes'). A special case of a sequential mixed-mode approach for nonresponse reduction is when a reduced questionnaire is used to decrease the response burden and collect data on hard-to-get nonrespondents. These data may shed some light on selectiveness of nonresponse and can be used for weighting and adjustment. In this case the researcher should again decide which source of error is the most important, and whether mode effects or nonresponse is the worst of two evils.

Implications

There are several types of mixed-mode systems as described above, which may be employed effectively also in mixed methods research. Sequential mixed-mode contacts with a single data collection mode do not pose any problems from a data integrity point of view. When different modes are used for precontact, screening, and reminders only, but not for data collection, mixing modes has only advantages. The main data collection is being done in one mode only with its known characteristics and data quality implications, while the (pre) contacts and follow-ups use different modes that can be used to their special advantages: a win–win situation.

However, when multiple modes are used for the data collection – either in a sequential or concurrent multiple mode design as is often the case in mixed methods research, the situation is far more problematic. In mixed-mode data collection, questions of data integrity play a role, such as whether data that are collected in different modes can be combined or compared with each other. There is only one situation in which a concurrent multiple mode design has well-documented positive effects on data quality. This is the case in which a second, more private mode is used in an interview for a *subset* of special questions to ensure more self-disclosure and less social desirability. Here, an interviewer is available for assistance and to pose solely those less sensitive, but perhaps complicated questions that may benefit from interviewer assistance. The expected mode differences between self-administered and interviewer-administered questions for sensitive behavioural and attitudinal items are precisely the reason why researchers combine these two data collection methods and use one method for one subset of questions and a second method for another subset. Here the combined effect ensures better data. Examples are a paper questionnaire within a face-to-face interview, or (Audio-) CASI within a CAPI interview. In all other cases, be it sequential or concurrent, mixed-mode approaches for data collection can have negative consequences for the resulting data.

Depending on the research context one has to decide about the best design, carefully appraising the potential sources of error (e.g. coverage, sampling, nonresponse, and measurement). Only after careful consideration can one decide if the expected mode effects and the associated measurement errors are serious enough to avoid mixed-mode designs or if the advantages of mixing modes in reducing coverage and nonresponse error outweigh the risks. If a researcher opts for multiple data collection modes there are certain safeguards one can implement in the data collection procedure to reduce potential mode effects. Among these are carefully constructed robust questions and a specially designed questionnaire.

Mixed-mode designs

Whenever a mixed-mode design is used in the data collection phase, one should be aware of potential mode effects and the data collection procedure has to be specially designed to reduce these effects as far as possible. For an optimal design it is important to analyze the original research question and distinguish between *two completely different* situations:

1. There is one main or preferred data collection method plus some additional auxiliary data collection methods. For instance, a longitudinal survey with screening and recruitment done by face-to-face interviews, but the chosen data collection methods in all waves is by telephone interview.
2. There is a truly multiple mode design in which the different methods are equally important. For instance, a web/mail or web/telephone mix, in which respondents are given the choice.

In the first case, a main mode should be chosen that accommodates the research question, population of interest, research context, etc. best. This preferred data collection mode is used to its maximum potential. Other modes are used as auxiliary or complementary modes only. To avoid mode effects these auxiliary data collection methods are adapted to the main and preferred mode of data collection. This may imply that the auxiliary methods are not used to their fullest potential. For instance, because the main mode is a telephone survey and a face-to-face interview is only used for screening and recruitment or nonresponse follow-up, the questionnaire is designed for auditory presentation only and a limited number of response categories are used for each question. This is the mixed-mode situation Biemer and Lyberg (2003: 208–210) describe, where the design is optimized for the main or preferred mode, while the auxiliary mode is adapted to the preferred mode. In a mixed-mode study that uses such a design one presents the same questions in the same layout, optimized for the preferred mode, with the risk of not using the auxiliary modes to their fullest potential. This avoids questions about data integrity when combining the data collected by the preferred and the different auxiliary modes.

In the second case, there is no preferred mode, but all modes are considered equally important. A good example is the study by Pierzchala et al. (2004), who used a mail, web, and CATI mix in a survey of college graduates. In this case, there is no main or auxiliary mode, but all modes are equal. For this specific situation Dillman (2000: 232–240) presents a number of principles for unified or uni-mode design that are helpful in minimizing mode differences between the data collection modes used. The goal of unified-mode or uni-mode design is to construct the questions and the questionnaire in such a way that the survey is not sensitive to mode effects. Examples of uni-mode design principles are to make response options the same across modes; not to use category labels in a visual mode if they cannot be used in the aural mode; not to use a 'check all that apply' format for a set of questions on an internet survey if there is a telephone mode where all these questions are asked as a sequence of yes/no questions. For practical examples of how these principles were used in constructing equivalent questionnaires for different modes, see de Leeuw (1992: 36–38; see also Wilmot and Dewar, 2006).

Finally, designing for multiple modes is important, but even after careful unified (uni-) mode design it is possible that differences between modes still remain. To cope with these, it is useful to collect additional data in the survey on possible mode effects, for instance by planning a mode comparison experiment in the pretest phase or as part of the data collection phase itself. These data give insight in potential remaining mode effects and, if necessary, can be used in the analysis phase to correct for mode differences.

While the main thrust of this chapter was primarily focused on mixed-mode research as it relates to large-scale survey research, similar problems arise in mixed methods research as, first, different modes of data collection are used in the qualitative and quantitative parts of a project and, second, more complex mixed methods research designs are likely to include different data collection modes within the qualitative and quantitative parts. Kemper et al. (2003) have described four studies in which probability and purposive sampling techniques were combined in a mixed methods design. This chapter approached this issue from a different perspective, exploring how lessons learned from survey research with regard to mixed modes could be employed fruitfully for mixed methods research. It is hoped that this chapter has encouraged researchers engaged in mixed methods designs to consider carefully different sampling and data collection issues and their consequences as outlined here. Until a better knowledge base is created by mixed methods researchers, these attempts will have to guide researchers involved in this design. Thus, this chapter is an attempt to summarize selected findings from the survey research literature and to encourage theoretical and empirical work on mixed modes in mixed methods research designs.

Notes

1 This chapter draws with permission on E.D. De Leeuw (2005). To mix or not to mix: Data collection modes in surveys, which appeared in *Journal of Official Statistics*, 21 (2): 1–23.
2 The authors thank Max Bergman for his insightful comments.

3 While this table focuses primarily on surveys, it should be obvious that similar issues are relevant if other types of data collection methods, e.g. qualitative interviews, focus groups, etc. were employed. Thus, issues relating to advance notification, recruitment, screening, and selection of interviewees on the one hand, and response phase mode change according to context and interviewees' characteristics are applicable to these methods as well, and are therefore likely to have different effects on coverage and data quality.

References

Balden, W. (2004) 'Multi-mode data collection: Benefits and downsides'. Paper presented at the 2004 conference of the great lakes chapter of the Marketing Research Association, Cancun, Mexico. Available at: http://glcmra.org/cancun (accessed December 1, 2006) (full paper upon request from the author).

Biemer, P.P. and Lyberg, L.E. (2003) *Introduction to Survey Quality*. New York: Wiley.

de Leeuw, E., Hox, J. and Kef, S. (2003) 'Computer-assisted self-interviewing tailored for special populations and topics', *Field Methods*, 15: 223–251.

de Leeuw, E.D. (1992) *Data Quality in Mail, Telephone, and Face-to-face Surveys*. Amsterdam: TT-Publikaties. Also available at: http://www.xs4all.nl/~edithl/pubs/disseddl.pdf (accessed December 1, 2006).

de Leeuw, E.D. (2005) 'To mix or not to mix: Data collection modes in surveys', *JOS*, 21 (2): 1–23.

Dillman, D.A. (2000) *Mail and Internet Surveys: The Tailored Design Method*. New York: Wiley.

Dillman, D.A. and Christian, L.M. (2003) 'Survey mode as a source of instability in responses across surveys', *Field Methods*, 15: 1–22.

Foddy, W.H. (1993) *Constructing Questions for Interviews and Questionnaires: Theory and Practice in Social Research*. Cambridge: Cambridge University Press.

Groves, R.M. (1989) *Survey Errors and Survey Costs*. New York: Wiley.

Hochstim, J.R. (1967) 'A critical comparison of three strategies of collecting data from households', *Journal of the American Statistical Association*, 62: 76–989.

Hox, J.J. and Boeije, H.R. (2005) 'Data collection, primary versus secondary', in K. Kempf-Leonard (ed.), *Encyclopedia of Social Measurement*. San Diego, CA: Academic Press.

Kemper, E.A., Stringfield, S. and Teddlie, C. (2003) 'Mixed methods sampling strategies in social science research', in A. Tashakkori and C. Teddlie (eds), *Handbook of Mixed Methods in Social and Behavioral Research*. Thousand Oaks, CA: Sage. pp. 273–296.

Nicholls, M.G., Clark, S. and Lehaney, B. (eds) (2001) *Mixed-mode Modeling: Mixing Methodologies for Organizational Intervention*. Dordrecht: Kluwer Academic publishers.

Nicholls, W.L.II, Baker, R.P. and Martin, J. (1997) 'The effect of new data collection technologies on survey data quality', in L. Lyberg, P. Biemer, M. Collins, C. Dippo, E. de Leeuw, N. Schwarz and D. Trewin (eds), *Survey Measurement and Process Quality*. New York: Wiley. pp. 221–248.

Pierzchala, M., Wright, D., Wilson, C. and Guerino, P. (2004) 'Instrument design for a Blaise multimode web, CATI, and paper survey'. Available at: http://www.blaiseusers.org/IBUCPDFS/2004/24.pdf (accessed 20 May 2005).

Siemiatycki, J. (1979) 'A comparison of mail, telephone, and home interview strategies for household health surveys', *American Journal of Public Health*, 68: 238–245.

Skjåk, K.K. and Harkness, J. (2003) 'Data collection methods', in J.A. Harkness, F.J.R. van de Vijver and P.Ph. Mohler (eds), *Cross-cultural Survey Methods*. New York: Wiley.

Tashakkori, A. and Teddlie, C. (1998) *Mixed Methodology: Combining Qualitative and Quantitative Approaches*. Thousand Oaks: Sage.

Teddlie, C. and Yu, F. (2007) 'Mixed methods sampling: A typology with examples', *Journal of Mixed Methods Research*, 1 (1): 77–100.

Trussell, N. and Lavrakas, P.J. (2004) 'The influence of incremental increases in token cash incentives on mail survey response: Is there an optimal amount?', *Public Opinion Quarterly*, 68 (3): 349–367.

Wilmot, A. and Dewar, A. (2006) 'Developing harmonised questions for use in a mixed-mode data collection environment', *Survey Methodology Bulletin*, 58: 75–89. Also available at: http://www.statistics.gov.uk/about/services/dcm/reports_publications.asp (accessed December 1, 2006).

10

Analysis with APES, the Actor Process Event Scheme

*Thomas Widmer, Christian Hirschi,
Uwe Serdült and Chantal Vögeli*

Introduction

Case study research has a long tradition in investigating social processes. This holds true for political science as well as for many other social sciences. The case study approach gives the researcher the possibility to investigate a social process in a detailed way. In addition, a case study can grasp the complexities of social interactions including the inherent dynamic aspects of social behaviour in an appropriate manner. Thus, the case study approach has obvious advantages compared to other analytic approaches.

However, in terms of analytical power, the case study strategy is much weaker than other types of social research. Some strands of case study research do not consider establishing theoretical considerations by intention. Others do rely on social science theory, either in an inductive or deductive way, although they focus on local theories with case-specific explanations in the first place and do not attempt to use case study evidence for broader aims.

The existing methods for comparing empirical data from case study research show some clear weaknesses. Although case studies do deal mainly with dynamic phenomena, the existing comparative strategies do rarely include longitudinal perspectives. Furthermore, case study comparisons usually have to lower the number of variables for analytical reasons and are therefore not in the position to reflect the complexity of case study evidence in a comparative analysis.

This contribution presents an analytical framework called actor process event scheme (APES) with the aim to overcome these shortcomings. This analytical framework aims at increasing the analytical power of comparative case study research by using qualitative information from case studies for standardized analytic procedures. The framework is designed for including diachronic perspectives on the one hand but takes into account structural considerations on the other hand.

The APES approach incorporates mainly qualitative information provided by case study research in a standardized analytical framework. As such, APES establishes a possibility to turn to account the empirical richness of case studies in comparative research by applying standardized quantitative procedures to qualitative evidence from case study research. The goal is to contribute to the mixed-method research toolbox a method that incorporates the dynamic and contextual factors of case study research by applying standardized procedures of graphical and quantitative analyses. The data generated by APES allows for a systematic analysis, using either more interpretative or a standardized method. A rather qualitative analysis of APES data could include a systematic description and comparison of different process variables (such as actor inclusion or time measurements) as they are visualized within the APES graphical display. A more quantitative analysis of APES-generated data can be done by applying standardized social network analysis procedures (such as multidimensional scaling, cluster analysis, centrality measurements) on the actor-event participation matrix that underlies the APES visualization. Thus, APES attempts to bridge the divide between qualitative and quantitative methods and contributes to the growing field of mixed methods research.

The chapter is structured as follows. First, we will discuss the current practices in case study research with a special emphasis on the analytical power of existing comparative methods in terms of their capacities to both reflect the empirical richness of case studies and to incorporate diachronic perspectives. In the next section, the APES approach with its procedural steps will be presented. The following chapter illustrates then the comparative capacities of this procedure. The final section discusses the possibilities of the APES method and emphasizes some areas for further development.

Current practices in case study research

Although the case study method is presumably one of the most widespread analytical concepts in social science methodology, its conceptual foundations are not clear at all. Or, in the words of John Gerring (2004: 342): '... the term "case study" is a definitional morass'. The understanding varies considerably within and between social science disciplines. Usually, but not always, qualitative data collection and data analysis procedures are applied in case study research. A quantification of the qualitative data is usually not intended and not conducted with the exception of simple enumerations in rare cases. Furthermore, case study research can mostly be located in the small-N research tradition, although large-N case studies exist as well. In addition, we can observe that the term case study is widely used but seldom defined. If the term is explicitly defined, this is rarely done in the same way as other scholars have done it before. As we deal here with a nominal definition, arguing about its correctness is obviously meaningless. Therefore, we take a pragmatic perspective and avoid a generic definition of the concept, since our rationale holds for most of the methods within case study research (however defined) applied in social sciences.

Case studies deal with cases as units of analysis. Thereby, the spectrum of possible cases is wide. The entity under investigation can constitute a wide array of units, mainly on a meso-level, as for example organizations, administrative units, social movements, legislations, policies or programmes or some kinds of social processes. We will focus in the following on the latter type, namely case studies dealing with a process defined as a sequence of interrelated events in a given context. Since case studies of this type are investigating a longitudinal phenomenon, they have usually a diachronic perspective by investigating the entity under investigation during a certain period of time.

Case studies research is oftentimes under harsh critiques by scholars emphasizing cumulation of knowledge and herewith arguing that case study research produces no generalizable evidence. Case studies practitioners, on the other hand, argue that in-depth knowledge and understanding of a single entity or of a small number of entities does avoid misleading conclusions and generates relevant evidence of particularities. This discussion reflects the long-standing debate about the primateship of internal or external validity in social science research (see Campbell and Stanley, 1966; Cook, 2000; Cook and Campbell, 1979: 37–94; Cronbach, 1982).

To avoid these critiques concerning the marginal theoretical significance of case study research, various strategies have been developed. The most popular among them are the following (for an overview, see George and Bennett, 2005: especially 205–232):

- *Insisting on the importance of singularities:* Some scholars judge the in-depth knowledge of a single entity as such as a valuable contribution to research. They deny the necessity and/or the feasibility of generalization. In the first place, the argument is put forward that the worth of a research contribution is context-bound and not transferable to other entities. In extremis, researchers have to start from scratch in each case. Theoretical considerations are in general rare in this tradition. Some scholars intend to contribute to social science theory by induction, although they restrict themselves to local theories (in the sense of case-specific explanations) without the ambition to generate transferable theories. Others reject the assumption that the generation of theoretical knowledge should be a goal of social science research. They deny the possibility that comparisons between cases can provide valuable insights. The epistemic perspective in general can be described as phenomenological. It can be argued that the local understanding of phenomena is useful especially in the case of applied research where the audiences are in the first place practitioners concerned with questions in relation with the case under investigation. However, this approach marginalizes itself by denying the possibility to generate or contribute to broader applicable theories of social phenomena.
- *Classical comparative case studies designs:* The classic ways of doing case study comparisons, as systematized by Arend Lijphart (1971; 1975) and Harry Eckstein (1975) – to name just two prominent scholars – could also be described as the mainstream perspective to case study research in political science and other social science disciplines. Scholars adhering to this tradition of research acknowledge the importance of theory beyond case-specific theoretical knowledge. They took a comparative perspective by comparing distinct entities in order to create or test theoretical knowledge (see Mahoney, 2000). This stream of case study research is devoted to theory-oriented research – inductive or deductive. The challenge hereby lies with the procedures to select cases as (usually) the number of cases is restricted to a small number for economy of research reasons. Therefore, the way in which cases are selected becomes crucial. Because the law of large numbers does not hold true for a small number of cases, researcher in this tradition use foremost theoretical sampling strategies (instead of random sampling in the case of large-N research) in order to reach a well-founded empirical basis for their research. Although this stream of research produces rich case descriptions by putting a lot of effort into empirical investigation, the analytical comparison is often quite restricted in means and ends.[1] The most broadly spread approach is the variable-oriented approach, on the one hand to observe regularities in order to

formulate theoretical relationships or, on the other hand, to test a priori formulated hypotheses mainly referring to John Stuart Mill's 'method of difference'. Although, the case studies often deal with longitudinal phenomena, the analysis is to a far extent cross-sectional oriented and therefore static. Furthermore, for the purpose of comparison the richness of the case studies is reduced to a limited number of variables and therefore does not allow to profit fully from the rich empirical data in the case studies.

- *Event-structure analysis:* To incorporate the dynamic components of social processes scholars in the tradition of narrative explanations (Abell 2004) have proposed to convert narratives into an event-structure format to analyze them in a diachronic way. This event-structure analysis (ESA; Heise 1989, 1991) for the analysis of sequences of events reconstructs the narratives from case study research in the form of a decision tree (for examples, see Griffin, 1993 and Stevenson and Greenberg, 2000). This method does acknowledge the time dimension. As a drawback for our purposes, the procedure is designed primarily for in-case exploration and explanation. Since it does not provide a rationale for comparison and is restricted in its theoretical relevance (Abell, 2004: 305–306) it does not solve the problems at hand.

- *Cumulation by meta-analysis:* This line of research is part of the quantitative tradition of social science research. Instead of criticizing (mostly qualitative) case study research for its weaknesses in rigour and external validity, this perspective strives for a better usage of the 'intellectual gold of case study research' (Jensen and Rodgers, 2001). The meta-analytic approach (Glass et al., 1981; Hunter et al., 1983; Light and Pillemer, 1984; Hunter and Schmidt, 2004) is mainly used as a means to cumulate experimental studies in the quantitative domain, but can also be used for cumulating (predominantly qualitative) case study research. To be included, case studies have to have the variable of interest in common. In addition, the variable of interest has to be converted to a common metric scale. These conditions are restrictive and for many cases not suitable at all. Furthermore, the meta-analytic procedure enforces the researcher to simplify and to reduce the information provided by the underlying case studies (Pawson, 2006: 38–72).

- *Qualitative comparative analysis:* In order to overcome these shortcomings, Charles Ragin launched the 'Qualitative Comparative Analysis' method (QCA; Ragin, 1987). Furthermore, an advanced (less restricted) version of the approach was presented with the so-called fuzzy sets (Ragin, 2000). Nowadays, these approaches have been applied to various research questions in distinct fields (see for example Balthasar, 2006; Rihoux and Grimm, 2006). In short, the perspective rejects a variable-oriented approach to social research and, instead, investigates causal configurations by relying on Boolean algebra. Without deepening the discussion of the advantages and disadvantages of the method (see George and Bennett, 2005: 162–164; King et al., 1994: 87–90; Rihoux, 2003: 357–360) we can state that the QCA and fs/QCA approaches are not capable to deal with time issues in a satisfactory way (Rihoux, 2003: 360). First attempts to incorporate the time component into the QCA framework are ongoing (Krook, 2006).

Some of these perspectives can be understood as mixed method research, others are clearly relying on a single methodological orientation. But none of the strategies discussed above do provide an analytical tool to conduct a systematic analysis of social processes which are dynamic by definition and, at the same time, do allow for a theory-oriented comparison of distinct processes without largely diminishing the content of the case studies. In this chapter we try to overcome the difficulties for social scientists in general and political scientists in particular applying a narrative, process-oriented case study strategy to integrate the concept of policy networks as one variable among others to a set of hypotheses (see Adam and Kriesi, 2007). For this purpose, we propose that out of well-documented case studies about the political process one can develop the structural configuration of political actors in the sense of a policy network by applying some rather simple transformations to an APES. In the following section, we outline the basic principles of this procedure.

APES: the Actor-Process-Event-Scheme

Step One: The Actor-Process-Event Scheme (APES)[2]

We assume that it is possible to derive a structure – understood as relations between nodes from process. Every process understood as a sequence of linked events contains the information necessary to derive an underlying structure. In Social Network Analysis (SNA; Jansen, 2003; Scott, 2000; Serdült, 2002; Trezzini, 1998; Wassermann and Faust, 1999), there are many applications based on this idea under the name of affiliation networks or actor-event networks (Jansen, 2003: 102; Wasserman and Faust, 1999: 291–343). For our purposes, we propose that the participation of political actors in an event of the decision-making process on the one hand and process links connecting these events on the other hand are sufficient indicators in order to operationalize the structure of the decision-making process in the sense of a policy network. In fact, as many social network researchers before, we regard event participation to be basic information in order to study affiliation networks (see Wasserman and Faust, 1999: 295–296). In more practical terms, it becomes necessary to systematically extract information on (a) political actors, (b) process links, and (c) events from a case study of a decision-making process.

By agreeing in advance on the events of a decision-making procedure (defined by institutional characteristics and the rules of the political system under study) and the political actors or groups of political actors (such as the president, the executive, public administration, interest organizations, etc.), a descriptive case study can be transformed into an APES in which the political actors interact by (a) event participation and (b) procedural (institutional) linkages.

APES components

The APES is a graphical interface linking the participating actors with the chronological sequences of the decision-making process. It runs within a two-dimensional space, spanned by an axis with the involved governmental and non-governmental actors on the vertical reference line and a timeline in the horizontal that separates the policy process into different stages and events.

In the actor dimension, the scheme's focus is on corporate actors (Coleman, 1974), which are distinguished along political hierarchy levels and organizational distinctive features. According to our data on foreign policy decision-making processes, there are – on the top level – the international actors. On the subordinate levels, there are the domestic actors, subdivided in national governmental agencies, parliament and parliamentary committees, governmental actors from hierarchically subsidiary jurisdictions and domestic non-governmental bodies. However, the arrangement of the actors and the distinction between different groups of actors can be different, according to the process under investigation.

In the process dimension, the scheme is based in principle on the concept of the 'policy cycle' (Howlett and Ramesh, 1995: 9–15; Lasswell, 1956), in that the scheme deals either with the outflow of a complete policy cycle or with one or more specific stages of the policy cycle of a political program or problem.[3] To simplify matters, the scheme used in this chapter is phase focused in that it illustrates the process stages of policy formulation and decision-making (decision-making in the broader sense, in delimitation to implementation). In spite of entitled criticism on this 'stage heuristic' and the limits of its application (Sabatier, 1999: 6–7), the concept serves here a useful purpose by dividing the very complex policy process into discrete stages (see also Parsons, 1995: 79–81). Nevertheless, we have to concretize these stages and adjust them to empirically observable events in order to generate a scheme of the policy process under investigation.

The definition and selection of the crucial events within the policy process depends, on the one hand, on parameters of the political system and, on the other hand, on specific characteristics of the policy process under investigation. Therefore, the definition and containment of the relevant events of the policy process has to be done in accordance with the specific characteristics of the object of investigation and its context. Taking into account the domestic and international dimension of the decision-making processes, the following process events are crucial for our analysis of decision-making processes in Swiss foreign policy[4]:

1. *Inner-administrative preliminary investigations,* defined as preparatory work within the administration, before a first draft of a political program/measure or a statement on a policy problem is available.
2. *Development of preliminary draft,* defined as assessment of results of inner-administrative preliminary investigations, leading to a first draft of a political program/measure or policy statement.
3. *Consultations outside the administration,* defined as inclusion of actors from outside the public administration in the process of discussing/developing an appropriate political program/measure.
4. *Consultations within the administration,* defined as inclusion of other actors from inside the public administration (besides the agency in charge) in the process of discussing/developing an appropriate political program/measure.
5. *International negotiations,* defined as the process in which authorized negotiators bargain with international partners.
6. *Consultations between departments/ministries and proposal to the government,* defined as the submission of an elaborated proposal for a political program/measures from the department/ministry in charge with the dossier to other departments/ministries ('Mitberichtsverfahren') and the deciding governmental authority (in Switzerland normally the Federal Council).
7. *Decision of the government (Federal Council),* defined as the authoritative decision of the responsible governmental body (in Switzerland normally the Federal Council), usually based on a proposal of the department in charge and the results from the consultations

between other departments, on (a) negotiation positions, (b) signing, (c) adoption of a message to the parliament, or (d) ratification.

8. *Initialization of an international treaty*, defined as the event on the international political level on the occasion of the termination of the international negotiations (on a technical level).

9. *Signing of an international treaty,* defined as the event on the international political level on the occasion of the fixation of the subject terms of the international treaty.

10. *Session of the parliamentary committees,* defined as the phase in which the responsible parliamentary committee(s) debate and decide on the proposed program/measure.

11. *Parliamentary session*, defined as debate and decision-making on the proposed program/measure in the parliamentary plenum.

12. *Ratification of an international treaty,* defined as the event on the international political level on the occasion of the proclamation of the definitive volition according to international law.

Information

A more or less 'thick description' (Geertz, 1973) of a policy process, as we generally find in case studies (Stake, 1995; Yin, 2003b; 2003a), is the source material of an APES.[5] The (thick) description is a detailed narration of the incidents within and around the defined crucial events of the policy process, with particular attention to the involvement and non-involvement of governmental and non-governmental actors. Actors participating actively in a specific event of the policy process are indicated in the scheme with a black bullet (●), whereas only passively involved actors are marked with a gray bullet (◌). The distinction between active and passive participation has to be defined by the researcher. In our analysis of decision-making processes in Swiss foreign policy, an actor is actively participating if at least one representative of the actor is directly taking part in the specific event under consideration. An actor's involvement in a specific event is passive if the actor is only informed about the procedure and/or the results of the specific event without being directly involved in that event. Actors participating in the same event are linked (symbolized as: ●—●).

Whether an actor is a participant or not (and if yes, in which way) can only be judged on previously defined criteria. For our analysis, two sources for tracing empirical evidence have been relevant: (1) empirical evidence for actor participation in written documentation about the specific events (such as protocols, negotiation reports or file notes), based on a document analysis of governmental and non-governmental sources (Reh, 1995; Widmer and Binder, 1997: 223–224); (2) information given by the political actors themselves, based on interviews with representatives of participating and non-participating actors (Kvale, 1996; Meuser and Nagel, 1991).

A dashed line (----), finally, symbolizes the course of the policy process. The dashed line links the actors in charge (indicated by a triangle ▲) with the object of the policy process (the political program/measure or the dossier on a specific policy problem, in our example the international treaty that is under consideration) on the occasion of the specific events of the policy process.

Data

For illustrative purposes we present empirical data derived from a research project that has been conducted at the Department of Political Science, University of

Zurich, dealing with domestic decision-making processes on Swiss foreign policy issues (for a full account see Klöti et al., 2005). We illustrate our data in a first step with one case only, the 1992 UN Framework Convention on Climate Change. In a further step, we will expand the empirical basis with three additional cases illustrating the capacities of the approach in comparative analysis (see below).

The United Nations Framework Convention on Climate Change (UNFCCC) was signed at the Earth Summit in Rio de Janeiro in June 1992 and came into force on 21 March 1994, after 50 states (among them Switzerland) had ratified the international agreement. In Switzerland, an intensive inner-administrative negotiation process on the country's position towards international climate policy preceded the ratification of the UNFCCC. The response to climate change was organized through several committees, operating at various levels. An Interdepartmental Working Group (IWG) on the Evolution of the Climate System was set up in 1989 (event 3 in the corresponding APES, see Figure 10.1). The agencies in charge with the dossier

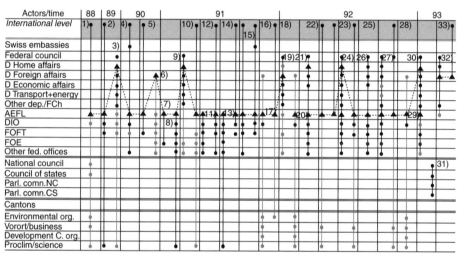

Events:

1) Expert talks IPCC
2) IPCC working group sessions
3) Founding of IWG
4) 1st PrepCom session
5) Preporatory meeting Geneva
6) Coordination meeting IKEH
7) Bilateral talks FOE-AEFL
8) Preparation INC
9) Decision Federal Council: Participation Rio
10) 1st negotiation round INC
11) Session of sub working group 'Climate'
12) 2nd PrepCom session
13) 7th + 8th IWG sessions
14) 2nd negotiation round INC
15) 3rd PrepCom session
16) 3rd negotiation round INC
17) 1st NGO hearing

18) 4th negotiation round INC
19) Decision Federal Council: Participation of NGOs
20) 2nd NGO hearing
21) Decision Federal Council: 4th PrepCom session
22) 5th negotiation round INC/1
23) 4th PrepCom session
24) Decision Federal Council: 5th neg. round INC/2
25) 5th negotiation round INC/2
26) Decision Federal Council: Participation Rio
27) Decision Federal Council: Signing of the treaty
28) Signing of the treaty
29) 3rd NGO hearing
30) Decision Federal Council: Message to parliament
31) Parliamentary decision
32) Decision Federal Council: Ratification
33) Ratification

FIGURE 10.1 *Actor-process-event scheme of the Swiss ratification of the UN Framework Convention on Climate Change 1992* (mainly the Agency for the Environment, Forests and Landscape and the Directorate for International Organizations in the Federal Department of Foreign Affairs) have consulted from time to time representatives from the civil society (especially of environmental organizations and the energy industry; events 1, 17, 20, 28, and 29 in Figure 10.1), but only scientific circles (ProClim) have been incorporated continuously in the decision-making process (events 2, 8, and 13). In general, we can observe a weak inclusion of civil society agents; the process is mainly dominated by public sector actors from the federal executive branch. However, the Federal Council (the Swiss government) has been hardly involved in the preparatory work. Only in the run-up to the international conference, the policy process has shifted from the administrative onto the governmental level (events 19, 21, 24, 26, 27, and 30). Although, the parliament was informed at the beginning of the process (event 1), the legislative branch was only at the very end of the process involved in the process in an active way. Furthermore, the Cantons (the federal states) are not at all involved in the process under investigation.

As demonstrated with Figure 10.1, the visualization of the policy-making process provides a highly illustrative basis for further interpretation. It is especially useful since it does reflect the dynamics of the process in a concise way. In addition, it contains standardized information, which constitutes the point of departure for the following quantitative procedures in the next step.

Step two: from Actor-Process-Event-Scheme to policy network

After having established the visualized policy process out of information of the descriptive case study in a first step, we then convert the qualitative case study data into quantitative data by the means of APES. In terms of SNA, the visualized policy process by APES is nothing else than a data matrix containing data about event participation (a so-called 'two mode actor-event matrix'). By the use of APES, qualitative case study data are displayed as a quantitative data matrix that can be imported into a network analysis application software such as UCINET (Borgatti et al., 2002) or Pajek (Batagelj and Mrvar, 1996) and then be converted to one-mode actor network data. With this procedure, APES becomes an interface between qualitative case study data and quantitative network data, and finally allows a most wanted standardization in the field of comparative case study analysis.

Event participation
Matrix (a) with the predefined actors in the rows and the events in the columns is generated by filling the cells with a value of one (1) in case an actor did actively or passively participate in an event, with a value of zero (0) in case an actor did not participate. We then transform this actor-event matrix into an actor-actor matrix applying the adequate procedure in UCINET 6 for Windows. This transformation creates a matrix containing symmetric relations between all pairs of actors participating in one form or another in the decision-making process. Since reflexive ties do not make sense here, the diagonal of the resulting matrix can be set to zero. As an example: a value of 5 in the cell 6-7 of matrix (a) means that both actors 6 (Department of Transport and Energy) and 7 (Agency for the Environment, Forests and Landscape) jointly participated in five events.

This whole transformation assumes that there was interaction between all actors participating in an event. We are aware that this is a rather problematic assumption given that a distinction could be made between active and passive participation and that event participation does not necessarily lead to interaction with all actors.[6] However, we hold that the resulting matrix (a) serves as a good approximation in order to reflect one important aspect of the policy network concept.

Procedural links

Matrix (b) with the predefined actors in the rows and the columns is generated by filling the cells with the sum of all process links. In case an actor has a process link with another actor we attribute a value of one (1); in case there is no process link a value of zero (0). The resulting matrix can be asymmetric and has the same size as the transformed matrix (a).

Because we regard both dimensions represented in matrices (a) and (b) as important in order to reflect the structure of the decision-making process in the form of a policy network, we suggest not to just sum up the two matrices but to multiply them. Computationally, the multiplication of the matrices gives what we regard an adequate weight to the process link matrix (b), which otherwise would only play a minor role not compatible with our understanding of the importance of process links in a decision-making process. As a result, actors with process links become more weight in the resulting matrix.

The multiplication of matrix (a) and (b) is supposed to represent the policy network derived from procedural data extracted from the original descriptive case studies with the help of APES.

The graphical representation of the policy network regarding the Swiss domestic decision-making process on the UN Framework on Climate Change in Figure 10.2 visualizes the strong interaction between the agency in charge (Agency for the Environment, Forests and Landscape; AEFL) and the two mainly involved Federal Departments (of Foreign and Home Affairs [DFA and DHA]) in the core of the network.[7] The Federal Council (FC) is rather in the periphery of the policy network, as well as the parliament and organizations of the civil society are. The Cantons (the federal states) are isolates, that is, not linked with other nodes in the network. Once the final data matrix is established we can compute standard SNA measures such as the density of the network or degree centralities for all actors.

Software tool

In order to provide an easier way to handle the operations described above, a software programme is developed that conducts these procedures automatically. The programme provides an interface to feed in the case study information into the system. Currently the programme does automatically generate the APES and provides the data matrices for the SNA. At the current state, the SNA itself has to be executed in a separate software programme such as UCINET.[8] The APES software programme gives the researcher not very familiar with standardized techniques (not an unusual phenomenon in the case study community) the possibility to apply the procedures described in an easy way. The software is accessible for free (Serdült et al., 2005).

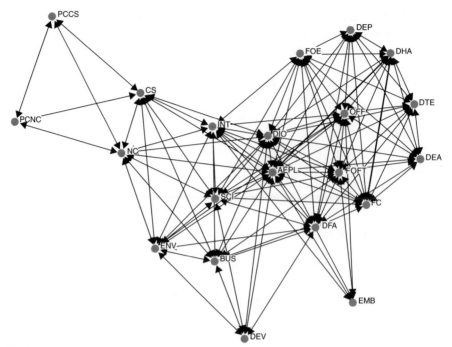

FIGURE 10.2 *Network for the Swiss ratification process of the UN Framework Convention on Climate Change 1992 (valued graphs)*

Comparative analyses with APES

As emphasized above, our intention by developing the APES framework was not only a systematization of the within case analysis. Instead, the main aim of the procedure is the comparative analyses of several cases. Therefore, we include three additional cases in order to illustrate some of the capacities of the APES framework. The three additional cases are analyzed in case studies following the same systematic as the first case discussed before. In addition to the UN Framework Convention on Climate Change (1992), the three additional case studies deal with three other domestic policymaking processes with respect to international treaties:

- Unemployment Insurance Treaty with Germany (1982)
- Investment Protection Treaty with Ghana (1991)
- Transit Traffic Agreement with the European Community (1992)

APES

In a first step we demonstrate the possibilities for comparative analyses by the graphical tools, namely the APES and the SNA graphs only. In Figure 10.3, the four APES are presented.

This is not the place to discuss the four policymaking processes in detail. However, the four APES visualizations demonstrate at a first glance that the processes under investigation do differ in various respects:

- The processes have different sizes in terms of duration and number of events and interactions.

- The inclusion of sub-national public actors varies between the processes. The Cantons (federal states) have a strong say in the case of the Unemployment Insurance Treaty with Germany (Figure 10.3a), but they are not represented in the other three processes.
- On the other hand, the Unemployment Treaty process does not involve civil society actors at all. In the case of the UN Climate Convention (Figure 10.3d) the involvement of civil society actors is stronger than in the other three processes.
- The participation by the parliament varies considerably as well. In the two cases of the Figure (Figures 10.3b and 10.3d), we can observe a passive inclusion of the parliament; in the two cases at the top (Figures 10.3a and 10.3c), there is no such involvement in the beginning of the processes. However, the parliament is involved at the end of the processes in all four cases. Nevertheless, only in the policymaking process regarding the Transit Traffic Agreement with the European Community (Figure 10.3c), a deliberation took place in the parliament.
- The process dynamic of the four cases is distinct. The policymaking process regarding the Investment Protection Treaty with Ghana (Figure 10.3b) shows a clear break in the middle of the process whereas the other three cases show a more continuous pattern.

These are just some selected observations that could be easily made based on the APES visualization. A more in-depth analysis of the graphs could reveal more detailed knowledge about the design of the policymaking processes at hand. In a next, quantitative step, we will explore the possibilities for comparison provided by a Social Network Analysis.

SNA

SNA provides in a first stage graphical representations of the structural components of the policymaking processes based on quantitative data. The graphs corresponding to the four cases under investigation are presented in Figure 10.4.

As already demonstrated with the APES graphs in Figure 10.3, the SNA graphs allow a graphical comparison of the four cases. Without going into detail, we can observe, based on a comparison of the four graphs, the following characteristics of the respective policy networks:

- Obviously, the first two processes (Figures 10.4a and 10.4b), namely the Unemployment Insurance Treaty with Germany and the Investment Protection Treaty with Ghana, involve a smaller number of actors than the other processes.
- Furthermore, these two processes have one single central actor; whereas the other two processes (Figures 10.4c and 10.4d) show a more dispersed pattern. Both central actors in the network graphs on the left (10.4a and 10.4b) have a crucial position in the network because they maintain the connectedness of the other actors in the network.
- Comparing the Transit Traffic Agreement with the European Commission (Figure 10.4c) with the UN Framework Convention on Climate Change (Figure 10.4d), we can observe a distinct structure of the network. In the first case, there is a tendency of the network to split up in two parts. The second in contrast is more integrated since nearly every actor interacts with all the other actors in the network.

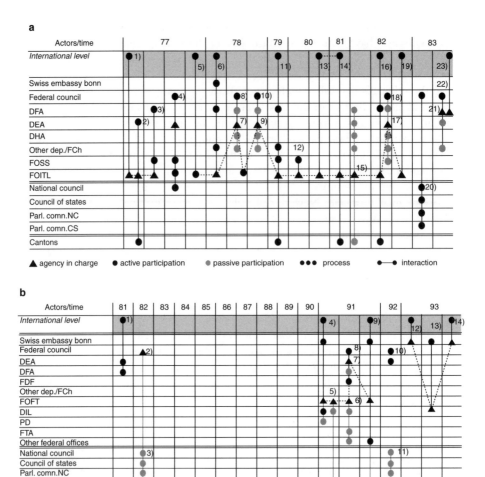

FIGURE 10.3 *APES of four domestic decision-making processes on international treaties.**
a, Unemployment insurance Germany (1982). b, Investment protection Ghana (1991)
**The APESs in this figure are abbreviated as the legend explaining each event is omitted.*

These are just some of the observations that can be made based on a quick graph-ical analysis of the respective policy network which relies on quantitative analysis. However, the graphical analysis is only one component of the SNA. In addition, the approach is offering quantitative measures for various characteristics of the networks. In Table 10.1, some examples for measures to characterize a network are presented.

The measures vary considerably between the four cases. The *number of actors* lies between 14 and 25. The *federal actors* are dominant in all four cases; in the case of the Investment Protection Treaty with Ghana there is only one non-federal actor involved. The participation of non-federal actors is comparatively high in the policymaking process regarding the UN Framework Agreement on Climate Change.

c

d

FIGURE 10.3 c, *Transit traffic EC (1992)*. d, *UN climate convention (1992)*

In the case of the UN Framework Agreement on Climate Change, the *network density* is high – compared to the other three networks. The respective values for the policymaking processes regarding the Investment Protection Treaty with Ghana and the Transit Traffic Agreement with the European Community are relatively low. This reflects the degree of integration of the network. Because the network integration is higher in the case of UN Framework Agreement on Climate Change, the connections among the actors involved are more frequent. The *relative contact frequency* is high for the Investment Protection Treaty with Ghana and to a lesser extent for the Unemployment Insurance Treaty with Germany, because in these networks all the contact frequencies are relatively low. The contrast case is the policymaking process concerning the UN Framework Agreement on Climate Change, where some of the relations show a higher contact frequency whereas others do not.

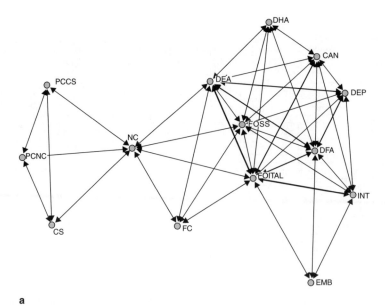

a

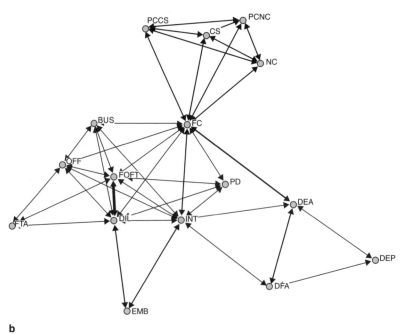

b

FIGURE 10.4 *SNA of four domestic decision-making processes on international treaties*
a, *Unemployment insurance Germany (1982)* b, *Investment protection Ghana (1991).*

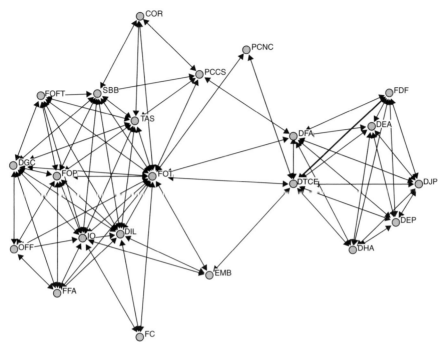

c

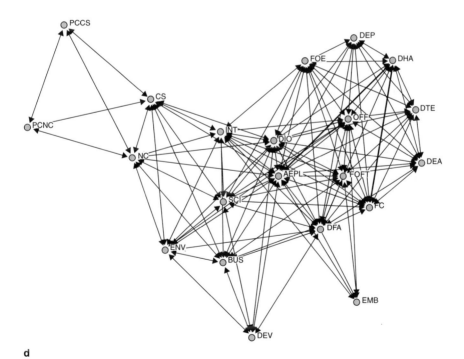

d

FIGURE 10.4 c, *Transit traffic EC (1992)* d, *UN climate convention (1992)*

TABLE 10.1   *Network analytic measures of four domestic decision-making processes on international treaties*

	Unemployment Germany	Investment Ghana	Climate Change UN	Transit Traffic EC
Number of actors	14	16	21	25
Proportion of federal actors[10]	86%	94%	76%	82%
Network density[11]	46%	33%	53%	34%
Relative contact frequency[12]	9.2%	14.8%	0.2%	4.3%
Degree centralization[13]	36%	46%	41%	46%

Finally, the *degree centralizations* for the four cases do not vary very much. It is slightly higher for the Investment Protection Treaty with Ghana and the Transit Traffic Agreement with the European Community.

Visualization of the process with APES supports the qualitative interpretation of the process in terms of actor involvement over time, inclusion of different actor levels, duration of individual process phases, etc. Underlying actor-event-affiliations matrix can be exported to statistical software packages and then be analyzed using formal methods. As this selection of network measures demonstrates, SNA provides a good quantitative basis for a thorough investigation of the interaction patterns in the framework of a policymaking process.

Discussion

The APES framework's main aim is to enrich the analytical capacities of case study research. In contrast to other strategies developed for comparative analyses emphasis lies on an adequate analytical representation of diachronic social phenomena as social processes. However, APES does not have the intention to substitute pre-existing analytical procedures; rather, APES should complement established comparative methods to approach case study research.

APES is a graphical interface, which (1) displays qualitative case study data by linking the participation actors with the chronological sequences of a policy process, and (2) converts the qualitative data into quantitative network data, that can be used for further calculations within SNA. The transformation from qualitative into quantitative data is performed while displaying the actor's event participation within the two-dimensional space of APES. The visualized policy process by the means of APES namely corresponds, in the terminology of SNA, to a two-mode-network data matrix. Once the user has read in the data, he obtains not only a visualization of the qualitative data but also the possibility to import the displayed data matrix into another application software for further quantitative analyses. The advantage of this combination of qualitative with quantitative procedures lies in the increased profit one drains from qualitative data. Finally qualitative case studies can be standardized and compared with each other so that an expedient gain in terms of a generalization of findings can be extracted. As such, APES is a mixed method research procedure for a qualitative and quantitative analysis of social processes.

We illustrated the capacities of APES by presenting empirical data on foreign policymaking processes in Switzerland. The potential field of application is much wider, since the method is suitable not only for policymaking processes in general but also for other types of social processes. Therefore, the approach could contribute to mixed method research in social science research in various disciplines. Furthermore, APES offers the opportunity to the interested social researcher to take advantage of the huge amount of case study research already existing in secondary analysis, without neglecting the diachronic characteristics of social phenomena.

In the political science domain, various research questions deal with political processes, for example in respect to policy formulation and implementation. Whereas political science scholars have focused in the last decades more on system-wide, macro-level analyses, recently the focus of research is again increasingly on meso-level phenomena. This can be illustrated by the increasing interest by scholars in the quality of democracy and democratization research for the quality of political processes (see for example Orenstein, 2002; Schmitter, 2005). Furthermore, the debate about governance can be enriched by providing systematically gathered empirical evidence on the inclusiveness of public policy processes.

The analytical capacities of APES go beyond the content of this contribution. The network measures presented in the chapter represent only a selection of available measures. Besides other measures for networks, various measures regarding the single network actors do exist as well. Furthermore, we have restricted the presentation in this chapter to static network analysis. The methodological progress in dynamic network analysis (see Snijders 2005; Widmer and Troeger, 2004; 2005) provides not only the possibility to analyze a cross-sectional process network structure in a stage-by-stage manner but also to model the dynamic evolution of a network over time.

Notes

1 This does not mean that the comparative case study tradition has not contributed to scientific knowledge in the past. Many highly respected and influential contributions to social science research are conducted in this framework, see for example Allison, 1971; Heclo, 1974; Katzenstein, 1977; Kingdon, 1984; Martin, 1992; Pressman and Wildavsky, 1984; Putnam, 1993; Stake, 1986 and many more.

2 The APES (see also Serdült and Hirschi 2004) was developed within the National Research Programme 'Swiss Foreign Policy' (NRP42; see Goetschel et al., 2002) funded by the Swiss National Science Foundation (for a full account see Klöti et al., 2005) and is also based on work of the late Ulrich Klöti (see Klöti, 1984) as well as previous research within other projects, especially see Buser (1984).

3 In this model, agenda-setting refers to the process by which problems come to the attention of governments; policy formulation refers to the process by which policy options are formulated within the government; decision-making refers to the process by which the governments adopt a particular course of action or non-action; policy implementation refers to a process by which governments put policies into effect; policy evaluation refers to the processes by which the results of policies are monitored by both state and societal actors, the result of which may be re-conceptualization of policy problems and solutions (Howlett and Ramesh, 1995: 11).

4 In Switzerland, usually an expert group from the federal administration prepares draft legislation which is then presented to the different federal departments for comment. The text is passed to the Federal Council, which in turn engages in a consultation process with

the public, including political parties and cantonal authorities. Every proposition or bill destined to become federal law has to be approved by a simple majority in both chambers of parliament. In general, laws may be challenged by the people if 50,000 signatures to this effect are collected (mandatory referendum in the case of an amendment to the Constitution); the question is then settled through a national referendum (see Klöti, 1984; Linder, 1994). Analyzing decision-making processes on foreign policy issues, specific events on the international political level have to be taken into account, too (Spinner, 1977).

5 The epistemological views followed by the formulation of the case studies are not discussed here in detail. The APES framework is open for (post-) positivist as well as (radical) constructivist positions. In both cases, the same procedures can be applied, no matter if they attempt to represent objectively existing reality or socially constructed realities. The paradigmatic orientation is nevertheless crucial in the way the APES products are interpreted.

6 Currently, we are working on an improved version of the procedure that will give the flexibility to define all interactions within a single event. See www.apes-tool.ch for current developments.

7 For the sake of convenience and as a graphical illustration only, we display a slightly rearranged MDS solution of the geodesic distances as provided in network drawing program NetDraw (Borgatti, 2002).

8 A research team is currently working on a further improvement of the programme in order to give the users greater definitional flexibility and in order to improve the analytical (esp. comparative) and graphical capacities of the programme. This research is funded by a grant of the Swiss National Science Foundation (grant Nr. 100012-112061/1).

9 The software programme as well as further information about the APES framework is accessible online under the following URL: www.apes-tool.ch

10 Federal actors are defined as all governmental actors on the federal level, i.e. federal administration, federal government, federal parliament and federal courts. Civil society actors and sub-national governmental actors (Cantons and communes) are therefore not included.

11 Defined as proportion of observed relations in relation to all possible relations based on a binary matrix (existence or non-existence of a relation), or, in other words, the network density is the total number of ties divided by the total number of possible ties in a binary network; see Borgatti et al. (2002).

12 The relative contact frequency is defined as proportion of observed contact frequencies in relation to the maximal observed contact frequency in a given network; see Borgatti et al. (2002).

13 This is a measure for the concentration of the network to one or a small number of actors. A degree centralization of 100 per cent can be reached with a star graph, where every actor is linked with one central actor and the non-central actors are not linked with each other; see Borgatti et al. (2002); Freeman (1979).

References

Abell, P. (2004) 'Narrative explanations: An alternative to variable-centered explanation?' *Annual Review of Sociology*, 30: 287–310.

Adam, S. and Kriesi, H. (2007) 'The network approach', in Sabatier, Paul A. (ed.), *Theories of the Policy Process*, 2nd ed. Boulder: Westview Press. pp. 129–154.

Allison, G.T. (1971) *The Essence of Decision. Explaining the Cuban Missile Crisis*. Boston: Little Brown.

Batagelj, V. and Mrvar, A. (1996) Pajek. Available at: http://vlado.fmf.uni-lj.si/pub/networks/pajek/default.htm (accessed May 2, 2007).

Balthasar, A. (2006) 'The effects of institutional design on the utilization of evaluation: Evidenced using Qualitative Comparative Analysis (QCA)', *Evaluation*, 12 (3): 353–371.

Borgatti, S.P. (2002) *NetDraw: Graph Visualization Software*. Needham, MA: Analytic Technologies.

Borgatti, Steve P., Everett, M.G. and Freeman, L.C. (2002) *Ucinet for Windows: Software for Social Network Analysis*. Needham: Analytic Technologies.

Buser, M. (1984) 'Umweltschutzgesetzgebung und Wirtschaftsverbände', *Wirtschaft und Recht*, 36 (4): 245–302.

Campbell, D.T. and Stanley, J.C. (1966) *Experimental and Quasi-Experimental Designs for Research*. Chicago: Rand McNally.

Coleman, J.S. (1974) *Power and the Structure of Society*. New York: Norton.

Cook, T.D. (2000) 'Toward a practical theory of external validity', in Bickman, L. (ed.), *Validity & Social Experimentation*. Thousand Oaks: Sage. pp. 3–43.

Cook, T. D. and Campbell, D.T. (1979) *Quasi-experimentation. Design and Analysis for Field Settings*. Boston: Houghton Mufflin.

Cronbach, L.J. (1982) *Designing Evaluations of Educational and Social Programs*. San Francisco: Jossey-Bass.

Eckstein, H. (1975) 'Case study and theory in political science', in Greenstein, F.I. and Polsby, N.W. (eds), *Strategies of Inquiry. Handbook of Political Science*, volume 7. Reading: Addison-Wesley. pp. 79–137.

Freeman, L.C. (1979) 'Centrality in social networks: Conceptual clarification', *Social Networks*, 1: 215–239.

Geertz, C. (1973) 'Thick description: Toward an interpretive theory of culture', in Geertz, C. (ed.), *The Interpretation of Cultures*. New York: Basic Books. pp. 3–30.

George, A.L. and Bennett, A. (2005) *Case Studies and Theory Development in the Social Sciences*. Cambridge: MIT Press.

Gerring, J. (2004) 'What is a case study and what is it good for?' *American Political Science Review*, 98 (2): 341–354.

Glass, G.V., McGaw, B. and Smith, M.L. (1981) *Meta-Analysis in Social Research*. Beverly Hills: Sage.

Goetschel, L., Bernath, M. and Schwarz, D. (2002) *Schweizerische Aussenpolitik: Grundlagen und Möglichkeiten*. Zürich: Verlag NZZ.

Griffin, L.J. (1993) 'Narrative, event-structure analysis, and causal interpretation in historical sociology', *American Journal of Sociology*, 98 (5): 1094–1133.

Heclo, H. (1974) *Modern Social Politics in Britain and Sweden*. New Haven: Yale University Press.

Heise, D.R. (1989) 'Modeling event structures', *Journal of Mathematical Sociology*, 14: 139–169.

Heise, D.R. (1991) 'Event structure analysis: a qualitative model of quantitative research', in Fielding, N.G. and Lee, R.M. (eds), *Using Computers in Qualitative Research*. London: Sage. pp. 136–163.

Howlett, M. and Ramesh, M. (1995) *Studying Public Policy: Policy Cycles and Policy Subsystems*. Toronto: Oxford University Press.

Hunter, J.E. and Schmidt, F.L. (2004): *Methods of Meta-Analysis: Correcting Error and Bias in Research Findings, 2nd ed.* London: Sage.

Hunter, J.E., Schmidt, F.L. and Jackson, G.B. (1983) *Meta-Analysis: Cumulating Research Findings Across Studies*. Thousand Oaks: Sage.

Jansen, D. (2003) *Einführung in die Netzwerkanalyse: Grundlagen, Methoden, Forschungsbeispiele. 2. Aufl.* Opladen: Leske + Budrich.

Jensen, J.L. and Rodgers, R. (2001) 'Cumulating the intellectual gold of case study research', *Public Administration Review*, 61 (2): 235–246.

Katzenstein, P.J. (ed.) (1977) 'Between power and plenty: Foreign economic policies of advanced industrial states', *International Organization*, 31 (4).

King, G., Keohane, R.O. and Verba, S. (1994) *Designing Social Inquiry: Scientific Inference in Qualitative Research*. Princeton: Princeton University Press.

Kingdon, J.W. (1984) *Agendas, Alternatives, and Public Policies*. Boston: Little Brown.

Klöti, U. (1984) 'Politikformulierung', in Klöti, U. (Hrsg.), *Handbuch Politisches System der Schweiz, Band 2: Strukturen und Prozesse*. Bern: Haupt. pp. 313–339.

Klöti, U., Hirschi, C., Serdült, U. and Widmer, T. (2005) *Verkannte Aussenpolitik: Entscheidungsprozesse in der Schweiz*. Zürich: Verlag Rüegger.

Krook, M.L. (2006) 'Temporality and Causal Configurations: Combining Sequence Analysis and Fuzzy Set/Qualitative Comparative Analysis'. Paper presented at the Annual Meeting of the American Political Science Association, Philadelphia, PA, August 31–September 3, 2006.

Kvale, S. (1996) *InterViews: An Introduction to Qualitative Research Interviewing*. Thousand Oaks: Sage.

Lasswell, H.D. (1956) *The Decision Process. Seven Categories of Function Analysis*. College Park: University of Maryland.

Light, R.J. and Pillemer, D.B. (1984) *Summing Up: The Science of Reviewing Research*. Cambridge: Harvard University Press.

Lijphart, A. (1971) 'Comparative politics and the comparative method', *American Political Science Review*, 65 (3): 682–693.

Lijphart, A. (1975) 'The comparable-cases strategy in comparative research', *Comparative Political Studies*, 8 (2): 158–177.

Linder, W. (1994) *Swiss Democracy: Possible Solutions to Conflict in Multicultural Societies*. London: Macmillan Press.

Mahoney, J. (2000) 'Strategies of causal inference in small-N analysis', *Sociological Methods & Research*, 28 (4): 387–424.

Martin, L. (1992) *Coercive Cooperation: Explaining Multilateral Economic Sanctions*. Princeton: Princeton University Press.

Meuser, M. and Nagel, U. (1991) 'Experteninterviews viel erprobt, wenig bedacht', in Garz, D. and Krainer, K. (Hrsg.), *Qualitativ-empirische Sozialforschung*. Opladen: Westdeutscher Verlag. pp. 441–471.

Orenstein, M.A. (2002) 'Quality of democratic policy processes: In central and eastern Europe and the former Soviet Union'. Paper presented at the American Political Science Meeting, Boston, August 29–September 2, 2002.

Parsons, W. (1995) *Public Policy: An Introduction to the Theory and Practice of Policy Analysis*. Cheltenham: Edward Elgar.

Pawson, R. (2006) *Evidence-based Policy. A Realist Perspective*. London: Sage.

Pressman, J.L. and Wildavsky, A. (1984) *Implementation*, 3rd ed. Berkeley: University of California Press.

Putnam, R.D. (1993) *Making Democracy Work: Civic Traditions in Modern Italy*. Princeton: Princeton University Press.

Ragin, C.C. (1987) *The Comparative Method. Moving Beyond Qualitative and Quantitative Strategies*. Berkeley: University of California Press.

Ragin, C.C. (2000) *Fuzzy-set Social Science*. Chicago: University of Chicago Press.

Reh, W. (1995) 'Quellen- und Dokumentenanalyse in der Politikforschung: Wer steuert die Verkehrspolitik?', in Ulrich von Alemann (Hrsg.), *Politikwissenschaftliche Methoden*. Opladen: Westdeutscher Verlag. pp. 201–259.

Rihoux, B. (2003) 'Bridging the gap between the qualitative and quantitative worlds? A retrospective and prospective view on Qualitative Comparative Analysis', *Field Methods*, 15 (4): 351–365.

Rihoux, B. and Grimm, H. (2006) *Innovative Comparative Methods for Policy Analysis*. New York: Springer.

Sabatier, P.A. (1999) 'The need for better theories', in Paul A. Sabatier (ed.), *Theories of the Policy Process*. Boulder: Westview Press. pp. 3–17.

Schmitter, P.C. (2005) 'The ambiguous virtues of accountability', in L. Diamond and L. Morlino (eds), *Assessing the Quality of Democracy*. Baltimore: Johns Hopkins University Press. pp. 18–31.

Scott, J. (2000) *Social Network Analysis. A Handbook*. London: Sage.

Serdült, U. (2002) 'Die Soziale Netzwerkanalyse: eine Methode zur Untersuchung von Beziehungen zwischen sozialen Akteuren', *Österreichische Zeitschrift für Politikwissenschaft*, 31 (2): 127–142.

Serdült, U. and Hirschi, C. (2004) 'From process to structure: developing a reliable and valid tool for policy network comparison', *Swiss Political Science Review*, 10 (2): 137–155.

Serdült, U., Vögeli, C., Hirschi, C. and Widmer, T. (2005) *APES – Actor-Process-Event Scheme. Software*. Zurich: IPZ, University of Zurich. Available at www.apes-tool.ch (accessed May 2, 2007).

Snijders, T.A.B. (2005) 'Models for Longitudinal Network Data', in Carrington, P.J., Scott, J. and Wassermann, S. (eds), *Models and Methods in Social Network Analysis*. Cambridge: Cambridge University Press. pp. 215-247.

Spinner, B. (1977) *Die Kompetenzdelegation beim Abschluss völkerrechtlicher Verträge in der Schweiz*. Zürich: Polygraphischer Verlag.

Stake, R.E. (1986) *Quieting Reform*. Urbana: University of Illinois Press.

Stake, R.E. (1995) The Art of Case Study Research. Thousand Oaks: Sage.

Stevenson, W.B. and Greenberg, D. (2000) 'Agency and social networks: Strategies of action in a social structure of position, opposition, and opportunity', *Administrative Science Quarterly*, 45 (4): 651–678.

Trezzini, B. (1998) 'Konzepte und Methoden der sozialwissenschaftlichen Netzwerkanalyse: Eine aktuelle Übersicht', *Zeitschrift für Soziologie*, 27 (5): 378–394.

Wasserman, S. and Faust, K. (1999) *Social Network Analysis: Methods and Applications*. Cambridge: Cambridge University Press.

Widmer, T. and Binder, H.-M. (1997) 'Forschungsmethoden', in Bussmann, W., Klöti, U. and Knoepfel, P. (Hrsg.), *Einführung in die Politikevaluation*. Basel: Helbing & Lichtenhahn. pp. 214–255.

Widmer, T. and Troeger, V.E. (2004) 'Event data based network analysis (EDNA)'. Paper prepared for presentation at the 45th Annual Convention of the International Studies Association, Montréal, Québec, Canada, March 17–20, 2004.

Widmer, T. and Troeger, V.E. (2005) 'Ereignisdatenbasierte Netzwerkanalyse', in Serdült, U. (Hrsg.), *Anwendungen Sozialer Netzwerkanalyse. Zürcher Politik- und Evaluationsstudien Nr. 3.* Zürich: Institut für Politikwissenschaft. pp. 161–181.

Yin, R. (2003a) *Applications of Case Study Research*, 2nd ed. Thousand Oaks: Sage.

Yin, R. (2003b) *Case Study Research: Design and Methods*, 3rd ed. Thousand Oaks: Sage.

11

Multi-perspective Exploration as a Tool for Mixed Methods Research

Katrin Niglas, Mauri Kaipainen and Jaagup Kippar

Introduction

During past decades mixed methods research tradition has undergone a rapid evolution and there is a body of excellent research which demonstrates various possibilities to combine qualitative and quantitative aspects into coherent research designs. However, several meta-analyses undertaken by different inquirers indicate that more extensive integration of qualitative and quantitative sub-designs as well as various types of data have been and continue to be a challenge for mixed methods studies (e.g. Bryman, 2007; Caracelli and Greene, 1993; Niglas, 2004). Thus, the question of how to combine statistical tools with more interpretive approaches to get the best understanding of the phenomena under study is still in focus today and waits for further innovative solutions.

As one way to meet this challenge it is possible to utilize new tools for multi-perspective exploration and knowledge construction, which are based on interactive media made possible by contemporary digital technology, in the framework of mixed methods research. In this chapter we will concentrate on the *exploratory soft ontology (ESO) approach* which has been used creatively to form 'ontologies' enabling, for example, the exploration of a single corpus of textual material or to achieve flexibility in interpretation of a class of phenomena by simulating different perspectives (Aviles Collao et al., 2003). As such, soft ontologies appear to encourage emergence of mixed research styles similar, for example, to Bourdieu's (1984) combination of ethnography with statistical correspondence theory.

In the following we first introduce the concept of ESO and related software as introduced by Kaipainen et al. (2008) for the context of knowledge environments. Thereafter, drawing on the argument that the research process can be seen as a specific form of knowledge building and the conceptualization of metadata in the context of knowledge environments resembles in many ways the more traditional ways of data handling in the framework of empirical studies, we demonstrate that the concept of soft ontology and related software can be fruitfully utilized within the context of academic research. As in the case of ESO the conceptualization of (meta)data brings together a structured way of thinking and a non-deterministic flexible approach to data, and the resulting research designs will combine features of quantitative and qualitative traditions. To illustrate this we propose several examples about the possibilities to use ESO in the framework of research studies.

Origins of an explorative soft ontology approach

The ESO approach is based on domain conceptualizations, such that allow themselves to be continuously and iteratively redefined through the process of defining multiple equally legitimate perspectives to a domain. The approach was originally created for experts, such as cultural heritage curators and analysts (Aviles et al., 2003) to describe, study and negotiate the nature of cultural artifacts with no or poor a priori definition.

The ESO approach has recently been elaborated and generalized for all knowledge environments, i.e. socio-technological applications of interactive media that are designed to facilitate individual and joint knowledge and meaning building (Kaipainen et al., 2008). The latter include learning environments, in which knowledge construction is facilitated for the purposes of education, knowledge management systems designed to support joint innovation and productivity of members of an organization, and communities that share and jointly produce knowledge, such as open source communities. In that context ESO has been shown to be particularly promising for structuring different people-driven media, such as the content-sharing virtual communities or the blogosphere that are constantly being redefined by their members by means of tags of folksonomies.

Exploration as knowledge building

A spectrum of recent thinking can be summarized to the idea that through the human life, environment is made sense of in terms of *exploration*, which is the foundation for increasingly more abstract levels of thought. The widely recognized principle of *constructivism* generally refers to the active process of constructing knowledge, instead of assuming a priori knowledge that is directly transferable in terms of instruction. Furthermore, construction of knowledge is seen as a self-directed exploration of the phenomenon 'beyond the information given' (Bruner, 1973) and the learner should be free to select and transform information autonomously in ways that are not dominantly pre-structured by some authority (Bruner, 1966).

Although useful starting points, these views remain too constrained to account for a full explanation of the ways in which the knowledge is constructed. Individualistic nature of experiences, interpretations and ways of sense-making do not imply the impossibility of shared understanding, which is regularly created through the process of social negotiation of meaning (Vygotsky, 1978). Jonassen et al. (1993) lay the ground for constructivist approach to design of learning environments that support personal knowledge construction without imposing a prescribed knowledge structure to a learner. Quite in line with Jonassen's thinking, Collins (1991) suggests the cognitive apprenticeship model for situated learning, where the learners are engaged in sense-making of the world or domain through modeling the processes they observe or experience (e.g. expert performance). The most important characteristics of cognitive apprenticeship are articulation (making tacit knowledge explicit) and exploration (forming and testing hypotheses). The ESO approach aims to concretize these views by means of a dynamic model of structuring domain conceptualizations.

Soft ontologies and multi-perspective explorability

Soft ontologies

Soft ontologies (SO) are flexible sets of metadata that describe a domain of information by means of spatially conceptualized properties, *ontodimensions*, that jointly define the *ontological space* (ontospace) in which an information domain "is" or exists. We, thus, interpret SOs as explicit specifications of conceptualizations of information domains.

Individual items of a domain are characterized by values representing the degree of salience of each ontodimension (Aviles et al. 2003). SOs are *open-ended* in the sense that they allow the creation of new ontodimensions, as well as the deletion of existing ones. Further, they are *flat*, that is, not structured a priori by multi-level hierarchies. Instead, such a specification of an information domain can be interpreted as a priority order of organizing criteria, which in this sense corresponds to a hierarchical conceptualization of a conventional ontology. The difference is that the implied hierarchy is malleable and interactively explorable instead of being rigidly fixed a priori.

Formally, a SO is an open-ended coordinate system $O = [x_1, x_2,..., x_m]$ that defines shared m-dimensional ontospace A, i.e., the shared and expanding vocabulary of describing a domain D. Each item i of domain D can be represented by an m-tuple $A_i = [a_{i1}, a_{i2},..., a_{im}]$, were a_{ij} stands for the salience of property x_j with respect to item i, spatially interpreted as the position of item i with respect to ontodimension x_j. Salience coefficient a_{ij} allows a range of reading options depending on the nature of that property, for example, presence, proximity, probability, strength-of-relation or agreement of item i with x_j. Ontological space A can be, thus, conceived as a framework of metadata that is associated and gives structure to some primary data.

Even though the idea behind the 'softness' is to allow the dimensionality of the ontological space to be continuously increased or decreased in the process of exploration at any given moment, the space A consists of a finite set of properties and items, and can thereby be represented by a matrix where ontological dimensions define columns and ith row represents positions of the item i in regard to every ontological dimension. As such the ontological space A does not differ technically from the data table commonly constructed for ordinary statistical analysis of data. The ontological dimensions can be seen as analogues to variables and items as analogues to cases commonly referred to in connection with statistical data. This intrinsic similarity gives us the possibility to apply the concept of soft ontologies and related software tools in the context of research settings.

However, the fact that ontologies here are conceived as being 'soft' or malleable rather than absolute allows us to go beyond simple statistical analyses and make ontologies i.e. data explorable in terms of perspectives as will be described in the following section. In the research context it means that the implementation of the soft ontology concept assumes the framework where structured and open approaches are to be intertwined calling thereby for mixed methods research designs.

Perspectives to a domain of information and dimensionality reduction

Several fields of research suggest quite consensually that organizing items to spatially laid-out clusters by their mutual similarity relations is the most natural strategy for making sense of environment's complexity. Based on the above, our approach relies on the general assumption that a representation of complex information on a low-dimensional space can be considered a rather universal model of sense-making, to be referred to as the assumption of *dimensionality reduction* (Kaipainen et al. 2008). Various algorithms exist for the purpose of revealing the structure of a multi-dimensional data set by producing approximating similarity preserving representations of lower dimensionality. The most generic and well-known algorithms of these fall into the family of multi-dimensional scaling (MDS), (e.g. Kruskal & Wish 1978; Kotz & Johnson 1985). In our treatment we generally refer to the MDS even though other algorithms can also be accommodated with this formalization.

In order to satisfy the conceptualization of soft ontology it is necessary to intro-duce first the means that allow each property to be taken into account to the degree chosen by the user. For that purpose we define weights $\mathbf{P} = [p_1, p_2, ..., p_m]$, $0 \leq p_j \leq 1$, for corresponding ontological dimensions x_j of A. P is conceived of as an *ontological perspective*, defining transformation $\mathbf{P}$ of $\mathbf{A}$ as $\mathbf{P}[x_1, x_2, ..., x_m] = [p_1 x_1, p_2 x_2, ..., p_m x_m]$.

Thus, a spatial representation $\mathbf{R_{P\sigma}}$ of a finite set of items $\sigma = \{i_1, i_2, ..., i_n\}$ of a domain D consists of the transformation $\mathbf{P}: \mathbf{A} \rightarrow \mathbf{A}$ followed by application of an algorithm that preserves similarity patterns from an m-dimensional domain $\mathbf{A}$ to some q-dimensional domain $\mathbf{B}$, $q \leq m$. In our application, $\mathbf{P}$ is used as the means of determining the desired degree to which each ontological dimension should be prioritized by a spatial representation. For the user-chosen values $0 \leq p_j \leq 1$, the extremes can be interpreted as follows:

$P_j = 1$ reflects the desire to maximize the preservation of the variance along dimension x_j and thereby prioritize the dimension over dimensions with lower values of p, while $p_j = 0$ reflects the decision to totally ignore the variance along dimension.

In interactive applications designed for exploring multiple perspectives, it is P that can be used as the means of determining the desired degree to which each ontolog-ical dimension should be taken into account in representation $\mathbf{R} : \mathbf{A} \rightarrow \mathbf{B}$. However, we do not assume that single representation with one perspective can make sense of the information domain but reflects a static, momentary meaning. While building a more encompassing understanding of it, that is knowledge, many subsequent representations with various perspectives are required.

Iterative exploration

In terms of the soft ontology approach, a single representation $\mathbf{R}: \mathbf{A} \rightarrow \mathbf{B}$ is only a step in the process of building a rich multi-perspective understanding of the domain. Such is constructed by means of a series of representations moving from perspec-tive to another, resulting a series of $\mathbf{R_1}: \mathbf{A} \rightarrow \mathbf{B_1}$, $\mathbf{R_2}: \mathbf{A} \rightarrow \mathbf{B_2}$, ... , $\mathbf{R_w}: \mathbf{A} \rightarrow \mathbf{B_w}$, with w growing until a satisfactory understanding has been achieved or the need for incorporating new dimensions perceived.

In order to clarify the idea of iterative exploration, it may be instrumental to compare a single perspective with a single saccadic fixation in vision. One fixation alone does not yet amount to a complete perception, but such emerges only as the result of iterative saccadic movements. As another analogy, it does not suffice for a complete idea of a physical object to emerge by seeing it as a two-dimensional picture taken from one side only. For any better understanding it is necessary to see the object from different perspectives. Consider for example a design for a piece of furniture or a building. Many CAD, VR and 3D visualization software tools facilitate this with respect to three-dimensional, real-world objects. Our approach aims at equal ease in exploring multi-dimensional information domains.

Exploratory soft ontology and ontological realism

In the research methods literature the term 'ontology' is often used in the meaning common to philosophical discourse reflecting beliefs about what exists and defini-tion of the ways or senses of being. From that point of view the question might be raised about the suitability of the concept of soft ontology approach, which is based on the constructivist principles, to the frameworks assuming realism or critical real-ism as an underlying ontological position. We will argue in the following that ESO approach as defined above can be used both within relativist as well as within realist ontological frameworks.

First, we can see that the term 'ontology' is used in the context of ESO approach, not in its philosophical meaning, but in line with the technical meaning of the word refer-ring to 'specification of a conceptualization', as concisely defined by Gruber (1993) and used in the field of information technology. Thus, ontology is taken here as a framework which defines and describes the basic characteristics of a particular domain. In the case of the domain being some kind of system, an ontology may also define the relationships between its elements which enable the system to operate. Ontology in this context reflects an underlying assumption concerning the being or existence of the domain but does not refer to any particular notion of truth or reality.

While in the case of relativist ontology this kind of soft conceptualization of the phenomenon can be seen as an act of creating 'reality' or more precisely 'realities', it can also be applied in the framework where the 'real' reality is believed to exist 'out there' while not being directly accessible to the human mind or the 'knower'. In the latter case what is constructed in the course of ESO approach is the knowledge about the reality which is not believed to be a direct reflection of that reality, but understanding mediated by our (post hoc) conceptualization of the phenomenon. In that context ESO technically frames the possibilities of organizing the informa-tion about the phenomenon, and more importantly, determines the possible perspec-tives that can be taken on it. Taken this way, soft ontology can be seen as adjustable lenses to look at the reality and make sense of it, which leave the conceptualization of the phenomenon unfixed and allow for multiple interpretations. The latter clearly implies an assumption of relativist position on the epistemological level no matter if the ontological position is realist or relativist.

However, from here further skepticism towards our approach could be raised on the basis of paradigmatic view on research methods advocated mainly by American methodologists like Guba, Lincoln and Smith during the last decades of the past century, but widely adapted by other authors as well, which proposes that there is a limited number of competing paradigms – sets of basic beliefs (or metaphysics) – in social research which the researcher follows (or should follow) (Guba and Lincoln, 1989; 2005; Lincoln and Guba, 1985).[2]

The aspect of paradigmatic view which has had the most extensive implications in the context of 'mixed methods' approach is that very often these paradigms are taken

TABLE 11.1   *The evolution of the 'paradigm system' in the texts by Guba and Lincoln*

1989	1994	2000/2005
Conventional (positivist)	Positivism	Positivism
Constructivist	Post-positivism	Post-positivism
	Critical Theory	Critical Theory
	Constructivism	Constructivism
		Participatory

as tightly bound to specific (that means quantitative versus qualitative) ways of doing research. Today the incommensurability of quantitative and qualitative methods as such seems to be off the agenda in the mainstream methodological literature. However, the question of paradigms and (in)commensurability between them is the issue which needs to be further tackled and clarified in the context of present discussion.

Having seemingly moved from the concept of two paradigms to the flexible and evolving five-paradigm picture (see Table 11.1) Guba and Lincoln in 2005 still argue for two broad but incommensurable 'philosophies' from which one relies on realist and the other on relativist ontology:

> So, ..., *positivism* and *postpositivism* are clearly commensurable. In the same vein, elements of *inter-pretivist/postmodern* critical theory, constructivist and participative inquiry, fit comfortably together. Commensurability is an issue only when researchers want to "pick and choose" among the axioms of positivist and interpretivist models, because the axioms are contradictory and mutually exclusive (op. cit.: 201; italics in original; see also Table 8.5: 198)

The paradigms, according to Guba and Lincoln, are then defined first and foremost by beliefs on the level of axiology, ontology, epistemology and methodology. According to their depiction of paradigms and incommensurability thesis between positivist-realist and nonpositivist-relativist paradigms there is no room for a worldview which would accommodate realist ontology with relativist epistemology nor for the possibility of valuing 'propositional knowing about the world' as such in parallel with seeing 'transactional' and 'practical' knowing as valuable means for social emancipation or improved wellbeing. (The latter is the predicable essence of the contradicting *axioms*.)

We do not agree with the basic ideas of paradigmatic view nor can we see any convincing argument on why one could not value the instrumental and practical role of knowing and believing at the same time that in some cases or situations also more descriptive or propositional knowledge about the world (if assumed to exist) is intrinsically valuable. We have argued elsewhere that the realm of different methodological approaches and underlying worldview positions is better depicted by the idea of continuum than by incommensurable paradigms (see Heikkinen et al., 2005; Niglas, 2001; 2004; 2007).

The roots of the problem seem to be embedded in the interpretation and usage of the terms ontology and epistemology in the context of research methodology by which the boundary between the two has blurred. Talking about the realist ontology assuming that there is a 'real' world 'out there' it is the physical or empirical world which is mostly referred to. As it comes to the relativist ontology and the claim that there are multiple locally constructed realities, people tend to talk about the social world or social reality, but leave the question of existence of a material world open as not important or relevant for their focus of interest. As such we do not see here an either-or question: if one believes the 'real' world to be out there (that means being an ontological realist) it does not impose intrinsically that she has to deny that different people or groups of people can interpret the existing world or reality in various ways and construct multiple and/or ambient social realities for themselves.

We argue, therefore, that soft ontology approach which enables one to explore the reality, both 'real' and constructed, from multiple perspectives can be seen as playing the mediating role between ontological and epistemological level and does not have to be seen as a manifestation of relativist ontology in the philosophical sense. This view on ESO approach enables us to accommodate soft or relativist epistemology and realist ontology within a single framework and ease the alleged ontological conflict between different research approaches and/or methods combined within mixed methods designs.

The use of exploratory soft ontology approach in the context of mixed methods research

We learned from previous sections that the ESO approach relies on the premises according to which knowledge is constructed in terms of active exploration, rather than being direct reflection of reality or something directly transferable or communicable from one person to another. This view implies that throughout the human life, including research settings, environment is made sense of in terms of exploration, which is the foundation of increasingly more abstract levels of thought. Drawing on this we argue that the concept of *multi-perspective exploration* is particularly applicable to complex information domains, often characteristic to mixed methods research projects to which there is no single 'right' perspective and which thereby call for multiple perspectives of interpretation.

In the context of knowledge environments, for which the ESO was originally developed, the notion of *environment* points to the idea of being immersed in information, and a sense-making community, which is essentially an interpretive endeavor characteristic of qualitative approaches like ethnography and narrative research, but also participatory approaches like action research and many others. On the other hand the ESO assumes the information about the domain to be systematized and scaled or categorized before the multi-perspective exploration can start and utilize statistical techniques to visualize various mappings of the structure emerging from the data. As such the approach supports and facilitates various types of mixed designs.

Thus, building on the ideas of ESO approach the ultimate aim would be to provide the user with the tools which would help to organize objects under exploration according to their mutual similarity or dissimilarity relations to spatially laid-out clusters. The software prototype we have developed on the basis of Kaipainen et al. (2001) is built to demonstrate this using the classical multi-dimensional scaling (MDS) algorithm, but in principle any MDS algorithm could be utilized and applied. The data suitable for this kind of exploration can be subjective similarity judgments given by people, 'objective' similarity measures like distance in kilometers or an index calculated by the program from multi-variate data by using some measure of distance.

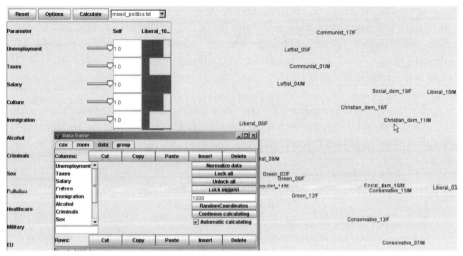

FIGURE 11.1 *Exploratory soft ontology tool – interface of the prototype*

Figure 11.1 depicts the simple interface of the soft ontology tool. All the existing ontological dimensions (or variables) are listed on the left hand side of the main window and followed by the sliders and input fields by which it is possible to change weights for single dimensions. On the right hand side there is a space for 2-dimensional projection of the original multi-dimensional ontological space where the items or cases are organized according to their similarity patterns. The rules for calculations and for visualization of the results can be set by clicking the Options button in the main window which opens the smaller window where one can change the settings (see Figure 11.1). It is possible to ask for immediate renewal of the projection as soon as the weight for any single dimension is changed or to set the weights for a group of dimensions and only then calculate the projection. The essential feature for the exploration and sense making is the possibility to rotate the projection so that new dimensions would allow clearer interpretations. On the projection space it is possible to point to any item with the mouse, and the bars in the middle of the window indicate the original values for this particular case. This feature allows very quick and easy interpretation of new dimensions.

In the following sections we will discuss several examples of the use of soft ontology concept and aim to demonstrate its applicability in the context of mixed methods studies.

Multi-perspective exploration – example 'Politics'

The simplest example to start with would be the case where the information domain is complex but data are collected by using a structured instrument as is the case for most surveys using questionnaires for data collection. As an example, let us introduce one case from the original knowledge environment context where the data are accessible and explorable not only for initiators of data collection (i.e. researchers) but also for the public via the web. Let us consider an information domain consisting of political agendas of candidates for a parliament.[3] The agenda of the candidate

c is expressed in terms of degrees of her agreement on the 5-point scale with political propositions, denotable as $\mathbf{A}_c = [a_{c1}, a_{c2},..., a_{c12}]$. The list of propositions given below corresponds to soft ontology $\mathbf{O}_{Polititics\ s_t}$, in this case a specification of a political 'climate' by what appear as its defining issues for initiator(s) of data collection s at time t.

1. The government has taken sufficient measures to fight unemployment.
2. Taxes should be lowered even if this would mean compromising the welfare society.
3. The increase of salary differences is acceptable.
4. The state should decrease its support to culture.
5. Tough immigration policies are justified.
6. Wine and strong beer should be sold in supermarkets.
7. Criminals are not punished with hard enough sanctions.
8. Buying sex should be criminalized.
9. Pollution of the environment should be controlled with an environmental harm tax.
10. Healthcare fees can be increased significantly if the savings can be used to increase the resources of the healthcare system.
11. The compulsory military service should be abandoned.
12. The country should leave the European Union.

After data collection the data table with 13 variables (including identifier) and 19 cases, called in this context ontological space $\mathbf{A}_{Politics}$ with $n = 19$, corresponding to the descriptions of candidates' political profiles, is composed and made explorable to both citizens and the candidates by means of an interface illustrated in Figure 11.1. With such an interface the explorers of information can visualize in real time various classifications and a multi-perspective structure of data computed using a real-time, MDS algorithm. Using sliders in the left block of the window and/or various options for calculation available through the dialog box it is also possible to get immediate visual feedback about the effects of the weights given by the user to the

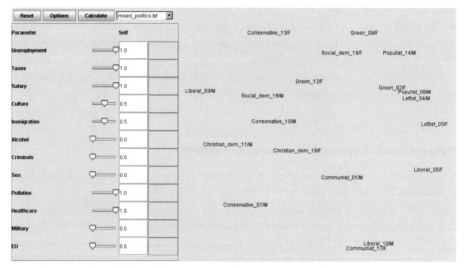

FIGURE 11.2 *Selected ontological perspective to the domain 'Politics'*

ontological perspectives/variables. Depending on the selected perspective, such as those relating for example to *social*, *criminal* or *immigration* issues, the resulting projections reveal different groupings of the candidates (Figure 11.2).

As a result, the user, in this case a citizen, may reveal similarity mappings that may or may not be consistent with a priori expectations, such as party lines or public image, or alternatively divide the domain into groups that are more relevant to the explorer's priorities. A candidate, in turn, may seek for a perspective from which her approach appears similar to or different from someone else's, to emphasize in her campaign. One purpose of exploration may be to try different what-if alternatives, say, those of a political opponent. This may facilitate finding compromises, or alternatively, work as a means formulating counterarguments.

Thus, there are several possible exploration strategies the user can practice depending on her aims and the relationship to the data. The first is the analytic approach in which the exploration begins with the simplest possible view that is, with one ontological dimension only, thereafter adding more ontological dimensions in order to make more refined distinctions. The opposite exploration strategy would be to start with a perspective in which all dimensions available are taken into account with maximum weights, and then continue by turning down dimensions which seem not to be relevant in order to find one or several classifications which could be well interpreted and give some new insights into the phenomenon under study.

Another method for an individual to explore the domain is *immersion*. In this case, the individual localizes herself with regard to each ontological dimension by adding an extra case to the dataset, and thereby determines her position in the projection domain. Within our example this kind of method can be used to find the closest matching candidate to your own views.

The demonstrated possibility to project the same dataset from multiple perspectives by changing weights to the variables (or ontological dimensions) in an interactive manner, is the feature which allows us to call the approach 'soft' and distinguish it from the mainstream exploratory quantitative analysis. Another example of how the ontologies (i.e. systems which define the phenomenon) can be unfixed would be the use of an environment where new possible dimensions could be invited from and negotiated within a community. Data to be added on the ontological dimension could be collected using a distributed community application that automatically forwards the proposition to all the candidates for opinion rating, perhaps via email or an SMS service. The updated ontological space with the expanded dataset will then be immediately at the disposal for further exploration.

It is also important to note that the individual explorer may also choose to ignore an ontological dimension totally by giving it the weight 0, or do so partially by choosing the weight between 1 and 0, as with all the other dimensions in the given ontological space.

Classification and interpretation – example 'Methodological Paradigms'

In our second example we use data from a small-scale study where 46 articles from the academic journal on educational research were analyzed with the aim to classify the studies according to the used methodological approach and to see if the emerged classification fits with the paradigmatic view which argues for two clearly divergent

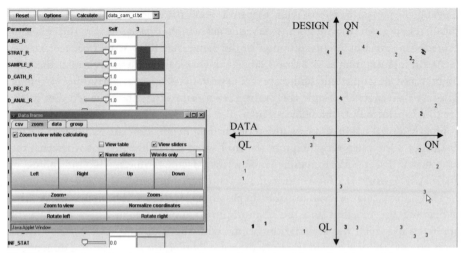

FIGURE 11.3 *Classification of 46 studies on the basis of 6 methodological features using exploratory soft ontology software*

and incommensurable methodological paradigms advocated for example in early texts by Guba and Lincoln (1989; 1994) in several influential books on research methodology (see Niglas, 1999). In this study the initial data was unstructured, but categorized by the researcher using content analysis. The whole article was used as a unit of coding and the following methodological aspects, categorized to the scale: 1 = quantitative, 2 = mixed/both_used and 3 = qualitative, were chosen to be the variables used for classification of studies:

1. Aims of the research (AIMS_R)
2. Strategy of the research (STRAT_R)
3. Type of the sample[4] (SAMPLE_R)
4. Data gathering methods (D_GATH_R)
5. Data recording and representation methods (DATA_REC_R)
6. Data analysis methods (D_ANAL_R)

In the original study the cluster analysis was used to clarify whether particular studies follow clearly only one of two broad methodological approaches or combine these approaches, mixing aspects from both of them in the framework of one study. Preliminary hierarchical cluster analysis on the basis of six methodological aspects suggested that there was one group of studies clearly different from others – these were studies using qualitative features consistently on all levels of inquiry. The k-means cluster analysis was also used and compared to the other possible solutions; the solution with 4 groups resulted in cluster patterns which were better interpretable and helped to define clusters as follows: 1. Qualitative studies, 2. Quantitative studies, 3. Mixed/quantitative case studies, 4. Mixed surveys and experiments.

To further explore the data and to see what kind of classification would be reached by other classification techniques we analyzed described data using explorative soft ontology software. The codes for cluster membership were used as labels for cases to see if there is a fit with previous analysis. From Figure 11.3 it can be seen that having used all the six dimensions with weight 1 and rotated the coordinates after the calculation of distances, we got the classification which broadly overlaps with the one gained in the original analysis. However, further exploration would be necessary, as the variable describing aims of the study is known not to be strongly correlated with other variables and could therefore cause some fuzziness in classification results. Thus, in the current example the further step to take would be to lessen the weight for the dimension/variable AIMS_R.

In this case the two-dimensional projection is easy to interpret as there are two broad perspectives: overall design of the study and data-related aspects, to which the six original dimensions converge. The coordinate axes can be set and interpreted as shown on Figure 11.3. However, to be able to find a reasonable position and interpretation for the coordinate axes of the projection it is necessary to access underlying data. In the ESO tool it is possible to move the mouse to any data point on the projection and see the bars indicating values of all original variables contained in the database for that case on the left side of the window right next to the projection. On the figure one can see that for the chosen case, which belongs to the third cluster by original classification, the data-related variables show values on the lower end of the scale (quantitative in this case) and design-related variables show values from the higher end of the scale (qualitative, respectively).

In combination with the possibility to give different weights to the variables, or to totally eliminate them, this feature which enables to see the original values of the cases in real time next to the visualized distances between cases makes further exploration of data and interpretation of the classification results interactive, as well as very quick and comfortable compared to traditional approaches.

Going beyond easier exploration and enhanced interpretation – facilitating integration of different types of data

Our current prototype of ESO tool uses the metric algorithm of MDS which sets several limitations to the type of data which can be used for exploration and classification. However, it is possible to build into the software other algorithms from the family of MDS and to allow the user to choose the best suitable one for the type of data they have. Some of these algorithms assume data to be quantitative (measured on the ratio or interval scale), while others can handle also categorical, that means, structured qualitative data (see, for example, Young and Hamer, 1987).

The latter is an important feature which allows seeing the use of soft ontology software as a second step in the process of integrating structured and initially unstructured data giving the ESO a great potential within the context of mixed methods studies. Before being able to explore data with the ESO tool, the data have to be converted to a simple table form, using for example some of the well-known spreadsheet software packages. In the case of ESO with a metric MDS algorithm, preparation of data means basically eliminating any possible string-type data from a database and handling missing data.

However, as in non-metric MDS algorithms it is possible to integrate categorical data into the process of exploration; the spreadsheet software can be used on the first step to record both pre-structured (i.e. quantitative) data from survey or structured coding sheets and unstructured textual notes (i.e. qualitative data) from open

	A	B	C	D	E	F	G	H	I	J	K	L	M	N	O	P	Q
	kood	qcl_8	explore	examine/ inve	test(hypothes	evaluate/valid	understand	determine/ dis	answer questi	develop/ impr	show/ provide	compare	aims	aimslong	who1	action1	what1
2	7		0	1	0	0	0	0	0	0	0	0	examine				
3	8	6	0	0	0	1	0	0	0	0	0	0	evaluate effectiveness	of intervention, reason for failure	progr		effect
4	9	2	0	0	0	1	0	0	0	0	0	0	evaluate	effectiveness of new approach, change in conceptions	approach		effect
5	10	2	1	0	1	1	0	0	1	0	0	1	explore,evaluate, answer,test hyp	compare classroom practices, efficacy of ...	classroo m pr		effect
6	11	3	1	0	0	0	0	0	0	0	0	0	explore	impact of methodology to councelling educ, q method and following feelings	progr	infl	educ
7	12	5	0	1	0	1	0	0	0	0	0	0	examine the value of methodology	monitor how, what effect of re-examining knowledge	method		value

FIGURE 11.4 *An example of a database where the unstructured data are post-categorized and can be used together with quantitative data*

questions, memos or interview transcripts at the same time in the same database. Spreadsheet packages have lots of features and tools which support this kind of open recording process and handling of resulting semi-structured data as well as making the initial integration of different types of data very flexible. These tools make it easy to learn from qualitative data in order to inform your decisions while analyzing and interpreting your quantitative data and vice versa. Furthermore, as it is rather easy to transport data from one program to another, it is entirely feasible to take (part of) your data from the spreadsheet to some software package like ESO which enables more complicated or flexible quantitative analysis (Niglas, 2007).

For the further exploration of data by ESO it is essential that the unstructured data is categorized. This process is well supported by sorting and filtering tools of spreadsheet packages. It is possible to use pre-structured categorical data or keyword variables to sort the data so that comments for various subgroups are brought together in the display, enabling one to see if there are common features in the comments or a trend for each subgroup. Thereafter one can add in a new column in order to post-categorize a variable that was initially recorded as text. For even better informed categorization, data transport between spreadsheet and software for qualitative analysis can be practiced, to benefit from possibilities for more substantial thematic analysis built into these programs.

We will take an example of this kind of post-categorization and integration of qualitative and quantitative data from another study focusing on the methodological aspects of mixed methods studies (see Niglas, 2004). In this study we used mainly a structured coding scheme for identifying various methodological aspects of the sample of 145 studies with combined research design printed in a number of academic journals on educational research. However, we also collected unstructured notes, memos and keywords about certain aspects of used methodology.

Figure 11.4 shows an excerpt from the database, where the notes about the aims as stated in the articles are first collected and entered in an unstructured format and thereafter categorized as binary variables (on the left) and as keywords (on the right). In the original database there are also a lot of pre-structured variables on the basis of which the cluster analysis was performed to filter out different types of combined designs used in the analyzed studies. Thus, we have in the same database original

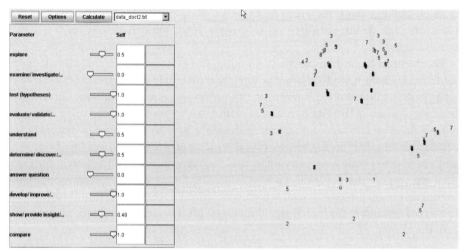

FIGURE 11.5 *One possible projection to explore the similarity patterns of a sample of studies on the basis of the aims set by the authors*

interval and ordinal variables and categorical variables calculated on the basis of this quantitative data as well as unstructured data which have been categorized to the form of binary variables in this case. To explore the similarity patterns of a sample of studies on the basis of the aims set by the authors the data can be taken to the ESO tool. Setting the cluster membership variable as the identifier, it is now also possible to explore the relationships between the aims of studies as set by the authors (initially qualitative data) and the type of methodological design (categorical variable emerged in the course of quantitative analysis) (see Figure 11.5).

After categorization it is possible then to use initially unstructured data independently or together with quantitative information as a basis for exploration by using the ESO tool. Indeed, there are several well-known MDS programs like ALCSCAL or PROXSCAL available which could also be used for the further analysis of categorized data, but as we have learned, the essential advantage the ESO has over traditional statistical tools is that it enables the user, e.g. a researcher, to set the weights for the dimensions/variables right in the user dialogue box and thus reveal and explore multiple similarity mappings or perspectives of the domain that may or may not be consistent with a priori expectations. The real-time exploration of the domain from multiple perspectives facilitates more informed interpretation and flexible knowledge construction.

Conclusions

In this chapter we aimed to introduce the concept of ESO and to demonstrate how it could be beneficially implemented within mixed methods research designs. Furthermore, we have argued that the concept intrinsically calls for the consolidation of structured and open ways of thinking in the course of organizing, exploring and interpreting data. Following our discussion above it can be concluded that the ESO approach potentially facilitates integration of different methods, methodologies and ways of thinking about the phenomena under study. As we have shown, this can take place on three levels: paradigm or worldview level, research design level and data processing level.

Having its roots in constructivist thinking, ESO denies the idea of knowledge as something which is ready-made and directly transferable and emphasizes the role of open and self-directed exploration as the means of personal and social knowledge building assuming thereby a relativist stance to epistemology. However, we have argued that the soft ontology approach does not have to be seen as a manifestation of relativist ontology in the philosophical sense: it enables one to explore both 'real' and constructed reality. In contrast to the paradigmatic view on research endeavor then we propose that ESO can be seen as playing the mediating role between onto-logical and epistemological level which enables us to accommodate soft or relativist epistemology and realist ontology within a single research framework and thereby ease the alleged paradigmatic conflict in mixed methods designs.

On the level of research design ESO brings together quantitative approach to initial data processing (i.e. structured data plus statistical techniques) and qualitative (i.e. open and flexible) ways of exploration, sense making and interpretation to get the best understanding of the phenomena under study. Thus it focuses on exploration of an ever-changeable framework for defining the phenomenon, which is essentially an interpretive endeavor characteristic of qualitative approaches like ethnography and narrative research, but also of participatory approaches like action research. On the other hand ESO assumes the information about the domain to be systematized and scaled or categorized at first, and utilizes statistical techniques to visualize vari-ous mappings of the structure emerging from the data. As such the approach sup-ports and facilitates various types of mixed model designs where quantitative and qualitative aspects are integrated into the design on different methodological stages of the study (see Niglas, 2004; Tashakkori and Teddlie, 1998). While designs where unstructured (qualitative) data are categorized and analyzed in a quantitative manner are rather common, the strategies supported by ESO, such as where initially struc-tured (quantitative) data are processed and interpreted according to principles common to qualitative approaches, have been quite rare so far.

Finally, it was demonstrated that ESO can support and facilitate the integration of different types of data in the framework of a single study, or help to bring together information (secondary data) from different studies. In this case ordinary spreadsheet software can be first used to bring the pre-structured (i.e. quantitative) data from a survey, structured coding sheets, unstructured textual notes (i.e. qualitative data) from open questions, memos or interview transcripts together into the same database. After the categorization it is possible to use initially unstructured data independently or together with quantitative information as a basis for exploration by using ESO tools. The latter allows seeing the use of soft ontology software as a second step in the process of integrating structured and initially unstructured data, giving the ESO a great potential within the context of mixed methods studies.

Drawing on the above we come to the conclusion that the ESO approach, which accrues from the concept of multi-perspective exploration of the environment with the aim of knowledge building, is particularly applicable to complex information domains, often characteristic to mixed methods research projects, to which there is no single 'right' perspective. Such domains thereby call for multiple perspectives of interpretation and the combination of structured ways of thinking with a non-deterministic flexible approach to data and data analysis.

Acknowledgements

We are grateful to Estonian Science Foundation who has supported our research by grant No 6148.

Notes

1 Due to limitations of the perceptual-cognitive apparatus, it is not usually reasonable to use projection spaces in which $q > 3$.
2 See, for example, Smith, 1983 and 1989; Smith and Heshusius, 1986; Lincoln and Guba, 1985; Guba and Lincoln 1989 and 1994.
3 See Kaipainen et al., 2008 for further details of this example. The data in this example are imaginary.
4 Here the term *sample* is used in its wider sense that means not only as a part of a population, but whatever set of objects/subjects are under study.

References

Aviles Collao, J., Diaz-Kommonen, L., Kaipainen, M. and Pietarila, J. (2003) *Soft Ontologies and Similarity Cluster Tools to Facilitate Exploration and Discovery of Cultural Heritage Resources.* IEEE Computer Society Digital Library. Proc. DEXA 2003. Prague Czech Republic, September 1–5, 2003.

Bourdieu, P. (Nice, R. tran.) (1984) *Distinction: A Social Critique of the Judgement of Taste.* Cambridge, MA: Harvard University Press; originally published in 1979 as *La distinction: Critique social de jugement.* Paris: Editions de Minuit.

Bruner, J. (1966) *Toward a Theory of Instruction.* Cambridge, MA: Harvard University Press.

Bruner, J. (1973) *Going Beyond the Information Given.* New York: Norton.

Bryman, A. (2007) 'Barriers to integrating quantitative and qualitative research', *Journal of Mixed Methods Research*, 1 (1): 8–22.

Caracelli, V.J. and Greene, J.C. (1993) 'Data analysis strategies for mixed-method evaluation designs', *Educational Evaluation and Policy Analysis*, 15 (2): 195–207.

Collins, A. (1991) 'Cognitive apprenticeship and instructional technology', in L. Idol and B.F. Jones (eds), *Educational Values and Cognitive Instruction: Implications for Reform.* Hillsdale, NJ: Erlbaum.

Gruber, T. (1993) 'A translation approach to portable ontologies', *Knowledge Acquisition*, 5 (2): 199–220.

Guba, E. and Lincoln, Y. (2005) 'Paradigmatic controversies, contradictions, and emerging confluences', in Denzin, N.K. and Lincoln, Y.S. (eds), *The SAGE Handbook of Qualitative Research*, 3rd ed. London: Sage.

Guba, E.G. and Lincoln, Y.S. (1989) *Fourth Generation Evaluation.* Newbury Park, London, New Delhi: Sage.

Guba, E.G. and Lincoln, Y.S. (1994) 'Competing paradigms in qualitative research', in Denzin, N.K. and Lincoln, Y.S. (eds), *Handbook of Qualitative Research.* London: Sage. pp. 105–117.

Heikkinen, H., Huttunen, R., Niglas, K. and Tynjälä, P. (2005) 'Kartta kasvatustieteen maastosta', *Kasvatus*, 36 (5): 340–354.

Jonassen, D.H., Mayes, T. and McAleese, R. (1993) 'A manifesto for a constructivist approach to technology in higher education', in T. Duffy, D. Jonassen and J. Lowyck (eds), *Designing Constructivist Learning Environments.* Heidelberg, FRG: Springer-Verlag.

Kaipainen, M., Koskenniemi, T., Kerminen, A., Raike, A. and Ellonen, A. (2001) Presenting data as similarity clusters instead of lists. Data from local politics as an example. Stephanidis, C. (2001).

Universal Access in HCI: Towards an Information Society for All. Proceedings of HCI International 2001. Mahwah, NJ, London: Lawrence Erlbaum Associates.

Kaipainen, M., Normak, P., Niglas, K., Kippar, J. and Laanpere, M. (2008) Soft ontologies, spatial representations and multi-perspective explorability, *Expert Systems* (forthcoming).

Lincoln, Y. and Guba, E. (1985) *Naturalistic Inquiry.* Beverly Hills, CA: Sage.

Niglas, K. (1999) 'Quantitative and qualitative inquiry in educational research: is there a paradigmatic difference between them?' Paper given at ECER 99. *Education Line.* Available at: http://www.leeds.ac.uk/educol/

Niglas, K. (2001) 'Paradigms and methodology in educational research'. Paper given at ECER 2001. *Education Line.* Available at: http://www.leeds.ac.uk/educol/

Niglas, K. (2004) 'The combined use of qualitative and quantitative methods in educational research', Dissertations on Social Sciences, Tallinn Pedagogical University. Tallinn: TPÜ Kirjastus. Available at: http://www.tlulib.ee/files/arts/24/nigalf737ff0eb699f90626303a2ef1fa930f.pdf

Niglas, K. (2007) 'Introducing the quantitative-qualitative continuum: an alternative view on teaching research methods courses', in Murtonen, M., Rautopuro, J. and Väisänen, P. (eds.) *Learning and teaching of research methods at university.* Research in Educational Sciences: 30. Turku: Finnish Educational Research Association. pp. 185–203. Available at: http://www.leeds.ac.uk/educol/.

Smith, J. (1983) 'Quantitative versus qualitative research: an attempt to clarify the issue', *Educational Researcher*, 12(3): 6–13.

Smith, J.K. (1989) *The Nature of Social and Educational Inquiry.* Norwood NJ: Ablex.

Smith, J.K. and Heshusius, L. (1986) 'Closing down the conversation: the end of the quantitative-qualitative debate among educational inquirers', *Educational Researcher*, 15 (1): 4–12.

Tashakkori, A. and Teddlie, C. (1998) *Mixed Methodology: Combining Qualitative and Quantitative Approaches.* Thousand Oaks, CA: Sage.

Vygotsky, L.S. (1978) *Mind in Society: The Development of Higher Psychological Processes.* Cambridge, MA: Harvard University Press.

Young, F.W. and Hamer, R.M. (1987) *Multidimensional Scaling: History, Theory and Applications.* New York: Erlbaum.

Index